THE COURTHOUSE AT INDIAN CREEK

The Courthouse at Indian Creek

The First Five Years of the Greenbelt, Maryland, Federal Courthouse

Frederick Quinn

Seven Locks Press
Santa Ana, California
Minneapolis, Minnesota
Washington, D.C.
Helena, Montana

Seven Locks Press,

P.O. Box 25689

Santa Ana, CA 92799

800-354-5348

Printed in the United States of America

ISBN 1-931643-11-3

Library of Congress Cataloging-in-Publication Data

Quinn, Frederick.

The courthouse at Indian Creek : the first five years of the Greenbelt Maryland Federal Courthouse / by Frederick Quinn. p. cm. Includes index.

ISBN 1-931643-11-3 (paperback) 1. Trials--Maryland--Greenbelt. 2. Justice, Administration of--Maryland--History. 3. United States. District Court (Maryland)--History. I. Title.

KF220 .Q56 2002

347.73'2--dc21

2002004734

Cover & interior design by Richard Cheverton/ Waypoint

For
Peter and Susan Messitte,
A.E. Dick and Mary Howard,
Herman and Mary Schwartz

Table of Contents

Preface

10 A.M. Three robed federal judges enter three different courtrooms on the fourth floor of the U.S. District Courthouse for the Southern Division of Maryland. Within an hour, their judgments will cause one person to be put behind bars, another to be freed. By day's end, a plaintiff will be awarded nearly a million dollars in damages, another will leave the building angry and with empty pockets. Bitterness, triumph, relief, frustration, fear, and numbness will be expressed by an increasingly widening number of participants. The court is a microcosm, a place where human emotions and motivations are distilled in their rawest forms, a constant theater with dramas of long and short duration. Judges and lawyers, the principals in the cases, all play roles in the unfolding drama, as do a chorus of court officials, each with a brief but distinctive role. It all comes together at the Greenbelt Courthouse, the Courthouse at Indian Creek.

I knew the exact moment when I wanted to write this book. Judge Peter Messitte was showing a group of Russian Federation judges around the recently opened federal courthouse in Greenbelt, Maryland, just outside of Washington, D.C. His judicial colleagues, Deborah Chasanow, a former magistrate judge with long experience in the Maryland state attorney general's office, and Alex Williams, once a state's attorney and a part-time law school professor, carefully answered the foreign visitors' questions on trial management, case settlement, and sentencing. A U.S. marshal, as authoritative as John Wayne in a 1960s film, showed the Russians the courthouse's holding cells and demonstrated why no prisoners had escaped from them. The clerk of court, looking like a respectable suburban lawyer, explained how motions are filed and cases docketed. The Russians inspected everything, asking questions of the judges. With the fall of Communism, they were turning to the West for assistance in building a new judicial system, and judges like Messitte, Chasanow, and Williams were receiving numerous visitors from the former Soviet Union and elsewhere. As we moved from office to office, I thought, "There's a book here—not only for foreigners, but also for Americans who would like to see their country's judicial system at work."

That was half of it. The other half of my interest was the human drama of the cases: prisoners arriving in chains, the wretched of the earth and plain folks down on their luck filing for bankruptcy, lawyers in thousand-dollar suits riding down the escalator like they owned the world, other lawyers in rumpled suits confidently huddling in corridors with clients, and defendants trying to impress the court by appearing in clean T-shirts and freshly laundered jeans.

Outside, on some days, TV reporters and journalists gathered like locusts, seeking a sound bite after a murder indictment in time for the six o'clock local news. I was witnessing a Balzacian human comedy (in old French, *comédie humaine* meant "the sum of human activities, a literary portrait of this"), the gathering of all manner of humanity displaying every guile and emotion, from aggressiveness to resignation, triumph to grief, a dry mock or genuine tears. As I talked with people in courtrooms and in the corridors over the next two years, I often wished I had been an artist, for the gestures and emotions were those of a Daumier etching. Whatever else the judicial process is, it is the raw theater of human emotion in conflict.

I thought of a book that would both explain how the courthouse works and illustrate some of its most representative cases. No such book exists. Studies of Supreme Court justices abound; law school texts, heavy as cannonballs, are stacked on bookstore floors; and technical works on federal courts and civil and criminal procedure are plentiful. I wanted something different, a book that would capture the human drama of the courts and the frank views of the judges and how they decided their cases and viewed their work.

For the most part, judges are notoriously tight-lipped. I had worked closely with Chief Justice Warren E. Burger for several years when he was leaving the U.S. Supreme Court to head the Commission on the Bicentennial of the U.S. Constitution. Burger was never comfortable with the press and, although I came to know several federal judges as friends, their tales told over bourbon and branch water were not for publication.

In two years of heading the rule of law programs of an international organization, the Organization for Security and Cooperation in Europe's Office of Democratic Institutions and Human Rights in Warsaw, Poland, I chaired constitutional and judicial reform consultations and seminars throughout the former Soviet Union and came to know several U.S. federal judges. We traveled from Riga to Dusanbe, Moscow to Almaty, holding seminars on the independence of the judiciary and separation of powers. Likewise, in two years at the Federal Judicial Center in Washington, D.C., I brokered contact between high-level jurists from abroad with U.S. counterparts in discussions ranging from ways to remove an incompetent or corrupt judge to how to keep order in the courtroom.

Would the Greenbelt judges be willing to frankly discuss their work? I put the question directly to Judge Messitte. After considering the outline of what I had in mind, Messitte, with a long career in public life before he went on the bench, agreed. So did his colleagues. The ground rules were, only closed cases would be discussed, not pending ones. During the next two years, we had frequent conversations, generally over lunch in various chambers. I told each person interviewed I would show him or her any quotes I used to verify their accuracy and to verify any citations on comments on the law and their interpretation, for federal civil and criminal procedure is labyrinthine in its complexity. Analysis and commentary would be mine. At first I thought the courthouse participants might be reticent to talk; but soon I had accumulated more cases and more views on jurisprudential issues than I could ever use. Lawyers wanted to retry cases in print, losers sought to make me their pen pal, legal scholars weighed in with their viewpoints like color commentators at a sporting event. I could have spent another year hearing everyone out, but I doubt that the book would have turned out differently.

This work begins with the opening of the Southern Division Courthouse of the U.S. District of Maryland (the full name of the Greenbelt Courthouse) on October 3, 1994, and concludes five years later on October 1, 1999, when several hundred leaders of the bench and bar, citizens and politicians, gathered to mark its fifth anniversary. The book is divided into five sections. The first part is devoted to explaining the history of the struggle in building the court. The main section chronicles thirteen of the most interesting civil and criminal cases to arrive in the Greenbelt Court during that time.

I knew some of the cases in advance from the wide media attention they received, and the judges and Lynne Battaglia, U.S. attorney, and now a judge on the Maryland Court of Appeals in Annapolis, and her Greenbelt office directors, Beth Gesner, now a magistrate judge in Baltimore, and Deborah A. Johnston, suggested others. In re-creating the cases, I tried to capture the drama and highlights of the contending legal positions without all of the procedural ballet of motion filing that adds ballast to legal files.

The next section gives a special insight into the lives of the Article III judges at Greenbelt, including biographical information and their views on some of the many issues related to jurisprudence and court management. The fourth part of the book discusses some of the "other players" at the Greenbelt Courthouse, both inside and outside the courthouse walls. Finally, the last part recognizes that justice is more than the work of judges. While the heart of the courthouse's operation takes place in the courtrooms, the judges are supported by or interact with more than 200 other employees located in such departments as the U.S. Marshals Service, the Pretrial Services Office, and the Probation Office, among others.

If I were to properly acknowledge each person who helped me bring this book to life, the list would extend to nearly 200 names. Two longtime colleagues provided valuable advice in the book's conceptual stage. Professor A. E. Dick Howard, White Burkett Miller Professor of Law and Public Affairs at the University of Virginia Law School, and Robert E. Peck of the American Association of Trial Lawyers. I am grateful to Judges Peter J. Messitte, Deborah K. Chasanow, and Alexander Williams Jr., and Magistrate Judges Charles B. Day, Jillyn K. Schulze and William Connelly, Richard J. Goodier, deputy-clerk-in-charge, and Arlene Johnson Hull of the clerk's office, for their generous assistance. Robin Shea, Marie Mooney, and Gloria Cherry, judicial assistants to the Article III judges, steered me through the arcanum of federal courts with dispatch and unfailing good humor. I thank them all.

Part I

The Courthouse

A Thirty-Year Battle

The wooded piece of land where today the Greenbelt Courthouse looms large just off the Washington beltway was once an important Indian hunting and trading ground. Nine thousand years ago the courthouse site was in a region traversed by Native Americans searching for stone to fashion spear points and arrowheads. Hundreds of such artifacts have been excavated in the wetlands around Indian Creek, but thousands more remain.

During the planning stage of the courthouse, the General Services Administration commissioned Washington, D.C. artist Jim Sanborn to design an environmental and sculptural setting for the courthouse that would reflect the region's historical Native American presence. Sanborn is an accomplished sculptor who studied art and archeology at Oxford University; his deep interest in mythology and the unseen forces of nature strongly influence his work. His design for the Greenbelt Courthouse includes an imposing bronze cylinder, colored by the elements to a pale blue-green, which contains the text of the Iroquois Book of the Great Law in perforated form, allowing spectators to look through the ancient words to the courthouse, the trees, or the suburban landscape.

Of the stream and nearby mounds, Sanborn said, "I basically wanted to re-create the Indian Run stream which ran across the site originally. It has since moved, but at the time, portions of it, the braided stream, ran directly across this site." He placed a stream with a small outcropping of stone to represent the original landscape and then had 10,000 arrowheads made in Mexico to seed across the site. The courthouse stands on a field of Indian arrowheads and pottery shards.

At night, a pinpoint of light from within the cylinder projects the Book of the Great Law over the entire courthouse site and the surrounding trees. "It is like a visual representation of an ongoing conversation that echoed through those trees," he explained. Written in the Onondaga language, the early legal text of the five Iroquois nations contained comprehensive injunctions on how a society should be governed; for example, "The firekeeper will take up the matter placed before him and consider it carefully. Then…he shall confirm the result of their deliberations. Thereafter, the decision becomes law."[1]

At various times over the next two years, I sat by Sanborn's sculpture while waiting for the blue-and-white connector bus to take me from the courthouse to the Metro station, trying to piece together a picture of the Southern Division, its Indian past, its expansive recent present, and its future. Shaping a coherent picture of the region is complicated by contrasts in the five-county region the court serves. Three of the southernmost counties, St. Mary's, Charles, and Calvert, are small; two, Montgomery and Prince George's, are the subjects of recent explosive growth.

It is easier to talk about law cases than what a courthouse should look like. In much of American history, it would be a building apart, like a church, school, library, or town hall, something immediately visually graspable as the place where justice was dispensed. In more recent times, courthouses are often indistinguishable from the buildings around them, which may be a regrettable way of saying that Americans no longer separate the functioning of the judiciary from the rest of civic life.

The $41 million Greenbelt Courthouse was one of fifty new federal courthouses and sixty others renovated in the 1990s in one of the largest public buildings programs since the New Deal. Justice was an expanding business, and new courthouses were needed all over the United States to accommodate a rise in the number of cases from 115,000 in 1945 to 1.2 million in 1995. Meanwhile, the number of federal judges of all kinds increased from 288 to 1,584. Court builders were sensitive to criticism from Congress and the public for building "Taj Mahal" courthouses. The Boston ($223 million) and New York City Foley Square (approximately $1 billion) courthouse buildings were frequently cited as examples of grandiose designs.

Hellmuth, Obata, and Kassabaum (HOK), a major international architectural firm, beat out eight competitors for the Greenbelt Courthouse project. The heavily wooded location was selected because the unused land, owned by the Department of Agriculture, was close to a major road and Metro transportation and near the border between Montgomery and Prince George's Counties, a central location between Baltimore and Washington, D.C. The land is flat, filled with thick clusters of poplars and maples, except in places where developers have carved it out to construct generic buildings that could be set almost anyplace in America. The courthouse's neighbors are an eight-story, gray, poured concrete and glass structure, a hotel catering to nearby high-tech and scientific companies, and an office building; probably more buildings will go up to hold law offices as court business expands.

Because the Greenbelt judges had not been appointed when construction plans started, it fell to a committee of Baltimore judges to preside over the design and construction of the new courthouse. The five Baltimore judges did not want a traditional redbrick and white-columned courthouse, and they asked that the judges' windows look out on greenery, since days in court are stressful. Another requirement was that the entrance not open on a parking lot. But the judges' caseloads were large, and visits to the construction site after the groundbreaking on October 15, 1991, were rare. After the designs were nearly completed, one Baltimore judge insisted on the addition of a second judicial elevator. (There was already one elevator for judges, a second one for prisoners, and a third for lawyers and the general public.) Eventually, construction costs for the

237,000-square-foot building rose from $32 million to $41 million ($48 million including the land) before it opened for business. "From a courthouse standpoint, it was a relatively good buy," Congressman Steny H. Hoyer (instrumental in quarterbacking the project) noted. "The irony of it now is the Maryland judges believe we've got to add on to it."

With Greenbelt in mind, Robert E. Barr, senior principal with HOK, said the courthouse should be "a very stately thing, a place of justice, reflecting the use of strong materials. A place where things will be fair. You are talking about harsh things happening here. It should be an important building that represents the public, a place where people will be helped, be served fairly."

As early as the 1960s, voices had been raised in support of building a federal courthouse in southern Maryland. They met with fierce resistance from the entrenched Baltimore legal community and the federal judges long ensconced there. This conflict was alluded to during the new courthouse's dedication on October 3, 1994. Some of the speakers joked about the "tepid" support from Baltimore. "It was tepid. I don't know if I would characterize it as support, but it was tepid," Congressman Hoyer remarked, adding, "We end twenty-eight years of delay. Today, federal justice moves closer to 1.7 million people in the southern region of our state. Like veterans of a war fought long ago, we gather as comrades to celebrate a new beginning."

Miller, Miller & Canby is a quintessential successful county seat law firm. Within walking distance of the Rockville court complex in quickly growing Montgomery County, it occupies a white-columned, spacious house. Inside, the subdued carpeting and English hunt prints lead to the downstairs corner office of James L. Thompson, a leading Maryland lawyer who worked hard from 1985 to 1988 to launch the Southern Division of the U.S. District Court.

It was an uphill battle, but if anyone could handle it, Jim Thompson was a likely candidate. A former Marine, president of the Montgomery County and the Maryland State Bars, tall, lanky

Thompson exudes quiet authority and certainty. A thick ringed binder behind his desk recalls the battle. In carefully chosen words, he described the situation in 1985. "It appeared to be a 'mission impossible.' We were trying to get a Southern Division for the United States District of Maryland, knowing that the ten active district judges in Baltimore opposed it, the Fourth Circuit Judicial Council opposed it, and that the council's consent was statutorily necessary. The Baltimore City Bar Association and the Baltimore Chapter of the Federal Bar Association opposed it, as well as many major Baltimore firms. The representatives in Congress outside our area had no interest in it, and historically our senators had taken guidance from the federal judges on matters of this nature. They opposed it. To make matters worse, Ben Cardin, the only Congress member on the House Judiciary Committee, which would take up the proposed bill, was from Baltimore.

"The financial power of the suburbs has grown," Thompson reflected. "If one-third of the population, one-third of the cases, and 40 percent of the state's wealth are from this area, why should we go to Baltimore to try a case?"

The reasons for opposition to the new court lay in Maryland's history. Since 1790, Baltimore had been the state's judicial capital; judges came almost exclusively from Baltimore, as did leading lawyers, and a clubby legal culture had been built up around the port city. The rest of the state was largely farms or shorefront, until recent decades. Montgomery County was mostly rocky farmland, run by individual farmers who laboriously worked their large tracts. Prince George's County contained the fertile Piedmont Plateau with its large tracts. The North-South divide during the Civil War ran between the two counties, but if the two counties were vastly different, all that blurred with the postwar expansion of the Washington suburbs. A look out Thompson's window leads to Rockville Pike, mile after mile of large malls, and behind them new communities and high-tech industries. Baltimore, the economic capital of Maryland until World War II, was losing out. Its population declined and welfare rolls shot up as its inner city deteriorated.

Meanwhile, the Washington suburbs grew exponentially. The Goddard Space Center, the National Institutes of Health, the expanding University of Maryland, and other sprawling government facilities helped spur the growth. In his statement before Congress supporting the new Southern Division, Thompson noted that "the business base of the five counties in the Southern Division is approximately equal to that of Baltimore City and the remaining eighteen counties combined." As the number and influence of lawyers in other counties rose, the Baltimore bar grudgingly agreed that every other year, a non-Baltimorian could be elected bar president, but it deflected arguments that, with the sharp rise in the number of cases and the considerable distance to downtown Baltimore, a more accessible federal court was needed. There were pocketbook issues as well. The "cozy monopoly for Baltimore's legal fraternity" would be broken, wrote Blair Lee, a Montgomery County lobbyist and scion of an old Maryland family, in a newspaper column. He observed, "Only Maryland has a single federal courthouse to serve 4-1/2 million people, while most states have multiple divisions to respond to community needs."

As early as 1968, the Montgomery and Prince George's Counties Bar Associations had argued for a new Southern Division. The Baltimore federal judges, however, remained unyielding, believing that a new courthouse would break the court's "collegiality," whatever that may be. Some of the judges asked Peter Axelrad, a prominent Baltimore litigator, to represent them in opposing the new court. But Thompson and his Prince George's County counterpart, George A. Brugger, were already in action. After preparing a comprehensive "Green Book" on the need for a new Southern District court, they built a broad constituency of twenty-three civic groups representing labor unions; chambers of commerce; women's groups; the handicapped; the Rainbow Coalition; the Gray Panthers; and the "Prince George's County 7" and the "Montgomery County 8," leaders in the General Assembly and the Maryland congressional delegation. It was like election day every day for several weeks in the tree-shaded Rockville law office as Thompson mustered support and Brugger hit the road in Prince George's County, where the imposing, affable, silver-haired attorney knew most everyone in positions of power.

George A. Brugger's name is the second one on the plaque in the Lawyer's Lounge of the Greenbelt Courthouse, along with Jim Thompson's, recognizing the two people who did most of the spadework to make the new court a possibility. Brugger is a name partner in a busy eight-person law office, which, like several other Prince George's firms, has moved into a new building not far from the courthouse. The elegantly tailored Brugger came to the county as a hungry young lawyer just out of Georgetown University Law School and stayed for the next three decades. He had worked as a law clerk to Robert F. Kennedy at the Department of Justice in the New Frontier's heady days but wanted to move out on his own. When a call came to the school's placement office, he headed to a sleepy rural town called Hyattsville and interviewed with a local firm with an expanding real estate practice. It was Brugger's good fortune to arrive just as federal prosecutors were indicting local attorneys and county officials on corruption charges; and the firm and he were clean. Also, the young lawyer, by working nights, learned the complexities of a new field-zone law and soon was an expert in this much-in-demand subject.

Prince George's County was one of America's fastest-growing regions. "As growth centered along rivers in earlier times, it gravitated to major roads and the beltway in our time," he noted. The county's racial profile changed rapidly as well. Originally a sleepy-time-down-South landscape of large tobacco plantations, the county is now 52 percent African American, with increasing numbers of two-income professional families flooding into the county.

"Nobody from Baltimore wanted to talk about it," Brugger recalled, speaking of the need for a Southern Division courthouse.

"The Baltimore white-shoe firms treated us like country cousins. When I came here in '67, there was already a movement for a courthouse. As pressure built and we rattled cages and knocked down doors, concessions were made. Some of the Baltimore judges were originally willing to come down here from time to time to try cases, but then they wouldn't come because we didn't have courthouses with high enough ceilings to convey the majesty of the judiciary."

Brugger remembered a meeting of the state bar in Ocean City where a leading figure, Chief Judge Frank A. Kaufman of Baltimore, had just waxed eloquently about why no new courthouse was needed (collegiality and efficiency) and new-kid-on-the-block Brugger stood up and refuted him point by point. Also, Brugger and the other Southern Division lawyers were both opposing the Baltimore judges and having to appear before them in cases the next week. "If you went into the ring, you could expect to get bloodied," he recalled.

At a key moment, Democratic Congressman Steny H. Hoyer, a self-styled "county seat lawyer" from Prince George's County, and a former president of the Maryland State Senate, guided the effort to completion. Thompson said of Hoyer, "He was the quarterback who took over and got it done." As a 1964 law student and intern with Maryland Congressman Daniel Brewster, Hoyer was handed a letter from the Prince George's Bar Association requesting legislation to build a federal courthouse in southern Maryland. Nothing came of the proposal, but thirty years later, by then a member of Congress himself, Hoyer spoke at the new courthouse's dedication.

Hoyer began work on the original project as a young congressional aide who made some inquiries and encountered unanimous opposition to the idea from the Baltimore judges, so the request went nowhere. But it kept coming back. "I got elected to Congress in 1981 and in 1986 introduced the initial legislation that was the genesis for the 1988 bill that was passed," he recalled. The proposed law was circulated to the judges of the Fourth Circuit, who initially opposed it. Recalling the fray, Hoyer remarked, "I have never experienced anything like this before. The Fourth District held a hearing where you got two judges from each state on the panel. The Maryland judge very much opposed the idea and wanted his colleagues to write to their congressional representatives to oppose the bill. Jim Thompson prepared the brief, I argued it, but the bottom line was we got extraordinary help from Sam J. Ervin III, the judge from North Carolina who heard our argument about this expanding region of the state." Ervin, son of Senator Sam J. Ervin II of Watergate hearings fame, was chief judge of the U.S. Court of Appeals for the Fourth Circuit. "He looked at every other state in the Fourth Circuit and saw that they had at least two divisions or more, and [he] was one of the keys in reversing the opposition."

While the Baltimore judges continued opposing the bill, the region's congressional delegation backed it. Democrat Ben Cardin, lawyer, descendant of a family of Baltimore judges and lawyers, and first-term congressman from Baltimore, supported the proposal on its merits, to the chagrin of the Baltimore City Bar Association. Republican Congressman Helen Bentley of Baltimore and Democratic Senator Barbara Mikulski were critical allies, as was Democratic Senator Paul S. Sarbanes, once a partner in a large Baltimore law firm. By late 1987, it looked like there might be a courthouse.

Thus, to a casual bystander, the dedication of the Greenbelt Courthouse appeared to be a cordial civic gathering, with the region's political and judicial leadership mixing politely. But, in reality, the courthouse at Indian Creek was the product of a three-decade battle.

Does the Greenbelt building succeed? Opinions vary. Drive along the busy highway just outside the courthouse and you could mistake it for a corporate headquarters, one of the many new computer or high-tech companies springing up along the beltway. The first vista, on approaching the building by road, is of the curved surface attached to a rectangular box, the new building set within easy walking distance of the old Indian trade route a few yards from the monuments to the Iroquois Book of the Great Law. Outside, four lights set on pedestals flank the entryway, like watchtowers guarding the entrance to an ancient Mediterranean harbor. In addition to the circular, black marble and gold, floor-high seal on the exterior wall, three additional seals appear over the three stainless steel and glass doors. It is as if the designers realized the building needed something more to make its purpose clear and tried to do so by adding more seals.

The building's central external feature is a four-story glass atrium. (Court architects refer to the "pre-" and "post-Oklahoma City" April 1995 explosion era in courthouse design. Greenbelt, with its immense number of glass panels, is definitely pre-Oklahoma City.) The impression on entering the building is contradictory. A granite terrazzo floor creates a sunray effect emanating from a center point, but proportions are thrown off because just inside the door is the marshal's security space, airport-style magnetometers, X-ray machines, and conveyer belts; thus, the effect on entering the building is a set of contradictory images, contributing to the lack of a consistent vision of the place.

Three floors of courtrooms and offices connected by an escalator and balconies open from the atrium. On the top floor is the large Ceremonial Court, which the senior local judge uses as a regular courtroom; this room is also used for those infrequent occasions when the entire bench from Greenbelt, Baltimore, and sometimes the Fourth Circuit assembles, such as at the swearing in or retirement of a judge; and for ceremonies when attorneys are admitted to practice before the federal bar or for naturalization ceremonies. In addition to three courtrooms on the top floor, the third floor has four courtrooms, with room for an additional one or two on the second floor, since a new bankruptcy judge has been requested for Greenbelt.

A design problem affects the courtrooms. All are wedge-shaped, with the judge's bench planted midpoint of the perimeter, from which the space narrows like a slice of pie, limiting seating, especially in the smaller bankruptcy courts. The unusual designs were a result of site constraints, an architect explained, noting, "You don't put a rectangle on a curve. You have to respect the curve." Frequent courtroom users complain of the distances between the witness stand and the jury box, between the clerk's space and the rest of the courtroom, and of the general difficulty in hearing.

A post-occupancy building evaluation, conducted by a team of California architects and planners, gave the courtrooms a "good" but not "excellent" rating, noting "courtroom shape and geometry impacts on the efficient use of space."[2] Dim lighting, marginally acceptable acoustics, inadequate sight lines, and no accommodation for advanced audiovisual and computer-generated display technologies within the courtroom were the main problems. In addition, "the excessive width at the bench end tended to separate the components to the extent that they were experienced as being 'too far apart.'" Each courtroom has a different color scheme; each has recessed ceiling lighting, oak paneling stained a mahogany color, and fabric panels on the walls for sound control. The effect is of a high-class hotel lobby or convention center rearranged for another function. "Not a Cadillac, but not a Chevrolet either; more like a Toyota," Judge Peter Messitte observed of the building, after spending four years in it.

As the courthouse was nearing completion, Judge Messitte, an avid art collector, noticed that the walls were bare. Wouldn't it be a good idea to showcase local artists? The vast empty spaces were soon filled with tastefully hung Amish and African American quilts, oil paintings, watercolors, and photographs from artists of the five counties served by the court. A rotating exhibit changes every three months, arranged by the Prince George's Arts Council. One exhibit featured the introspective graphics works of Tadeusz Lapinski, a Polish artist, now professor of fine arts at the University of Maryland; and works by Sy Mohr, from Bowie, Maryland, a big-brush mural painter in the folk tradition. Traveling shows are hung as well, and when a group of Brazilian judges came to Greenbelt, the works of prominent Brazilian artists were featured.

Was the thirty-year battle justified? What do the numbers show? Within a few years after opening, there was a clamor to add additional judges as the Greenbelt caseload expanded. The court accepted 132 criminal and 1,213 civil cases during its first year of operation. The numbers increased gradually after that, from slightly under 150 criminal cases in 1995 to slightly over that number two years later, and to 1,450 civil cases in 1997—about a third of the total Maryland federal criminal and civil cases. The numbers more than justified those who argued there was business enough to sustain the new courthouse.[3]

There are three federal judges in Greenbelt and ten in Baltimore (including three senior or partially retired judges). Active judges carry about 250 to 275 civil cases at any time, closing between twenty-five to forty each month, mostly by the parties' agreeing to settle. Active judges also carry approximately forty criminal cases at any given moment, opening or closing about three or four each month. (Most of the criminal closings come through a defendant's pleading guilty or plea-bargaining for a reduced sentence.)

In a May 1998 speech to the Montgomery County Bar Association Judge Messitte explained the court's division of cases and also the number of Greenbelt cases in relation to Baltimore: "Over the last six months, Greenbelt has had 797 civil filings as opposed to 1,313 from Baltimore, ours representing 37.8 percent of the total. The percentage has been steadily rising, and 40 percent of the civil total is about where we expect to be for at least the near term." Of the 3,334 civil cases, 76.7 percent were private cases (civil rights, 24 percent; torts, 20 percent; contracts, 15 percent; prisoner cases, 16 percent), and the remaining 25 percent were cases with the United States as a party. Greenbelt also drew approximately one-third of the state's federal criminal cases.

Three categories of criminal cases predominated: weapons and firearms (20 percent), fraud (16.7 percent), and drug (16.5 percent) cases. The rest were traffic, larceny, robbery, and even traffic cases that entered federal court because they took place on federal installations or were the result of arrests by federal officers, such as the National Park Service Police. Many petty offense cases grow out of traffic cases on the Baltimore-Washington Parkway, Andrews Air Force Base, the National Institutes of Health, and the national parks. During one six-month period in 1998, the Southern Division handled 3,318, or 64.8 percent, of the state's petty offense cases.

Most misdemeanor and petty offenses, as well as preliminary proceedings on felony matters, go before magistrate judges, who, in addition to Greenbelt, sit periodically at the Patuxent Naval Air Station, Andrews Air Force Base, Annapolis (the state capital), and Hyattsville, a nearby town where a courtroom is rented in the state courthouse for weekly hearings by a magistrate judge from Greenbelt. Many of the misdemeanors are minor traffic law or trespassing violations, about half of which are dismissed or are deferred, which means the case is left open for six months and, if the subject commits no further violation, is dropped. The Greenbelt Courthouse, even the most disinterested visitor would conclude, has become a very busy place.

Part II

A Sampler of Cases

SABOTAGING "THE PROJECT"

THE CASE OF THE DESTROYED ALPHA CELLS

> *"Why did you do it?"*
> *—Dr. Phil Skolnick to Dr. Prince Kumar Arora*
> *"To teach Yoshi [Dr. Sei] and Abah [Ms. Saini] a lesson."*
> *—Dr. Arora's purported answer*

The huge buildings of the National Institutes of Health (NIH) cover several acres of rolling landscape in Montgomery County, Maryland, just north of Washington, D.C. Some of the world's most advanced scientific research originates here, and the institutes are a Mecca for Nobel laureates and brilliant young scientists from all over the world. While much of NIH's activity is high profile, contributing to breakthrough scientific discoveries, sometimes a classic melodrama creeps onto the scene, a tale of good and evil in conflict, as in the 1992 case of *USA v Prince Kumar Arora*, which worked its way through the Greenbelt federal court. Its ingredients could be lifted from a soap opera: personal jealousy and professional rivalry, shifting female-male allegiances, and the massive sabotaging of a highly promising scientific experiment, the results of which might eventually aid in combating several diseases. Reputations in the scientific community were at stake, and for the judge who heard the case, there were significant questions of evaluating conflicting scientific testimony and assessing damages over the loss of experimental data whose worth remained uncertain.

"The Project," as it was called, "Expression and Functional Properties of Type I GABA Receptor in a Stably Transfected Cell Line," was launched in late 1990 as a high-risk, new-frontier effort to create a living cell line to treat alcoholism, Alzheimer's disease, neurotoxicity, and diseases in which regulation of brain cells is important.[4] DNA segments would be inserted in a host human kidney cell, which would then affect a specific brain receptor, GABA (gamma-aminobutyric acid). A distinguished senior scientist, Dr. Phil Skolnick,[5] headed The Project, assisted by two young scientists, Dr. Garry Wong, a postdoctoral fellow and molecular neurobiologist, and Dr. Yoshitatsu Sei, a Japanese postdoctoral fellow. Sei also worked on projects under the direction of Dr. Prince (a first name, not a title) Kumar Arora, a senior scientist who held a temporary appointment in Skolnick's lab and who would become a major player in the unfolding drama of the sabotaged experiment.[6]

The Project's purpose was to put some proteins that were normally found in brains into cells in a flask and to grow them. "Putting brains in a bottle" is how an associate of Skolnick's described the experiment. A leading researcher on the pathology of depression and the pharmacotherapy for stroke disorders, Skolnick recalled, "That is done fairly routinely now, but it was a pretty big deal back when we were doing it. It allowed you to do experiments with GABA receptors of a known type. It was much cleaner than doing that kind of experimentation in the brain. It allowed us, for example, to look at the way drugs worked in a very precise way."

Initially, Drs. Arora and Sei got along well, and during 1991 and 1992 collaborated on nine published research reports. During a February 1992 meeting of the laboratory staff, Dr. Wong announced good news; at long last the research team had succeeded in creating a new cell line, called Alpha 1–4. The next step was follow-on experiments allowing scientists to document Alpha 1–4's precise characteristics. To do this, scientists would undertake a month's worth of tests, using twenty to fifty flasks of Alpha 1–4. Each flask would contain millions of cells, and Sei, an expert in cell culturing, was tasked with preparing them. The ready cells were brought to Room 104 of the laboratory, where they were stored in an incubator.

Something went terribly wrong. When Sei routinely stopped by the laboratory to check on the cells on Sunday, March 1, 1992, he noticed massive cell death in the Alpha 1–4 cell line and in the host kidney cells and other project-related cells kept there. A look at the cells under a microscope confirmed they were dying quickly. Undaunted, Sei prepared a new batch of cells, thoroughly cleaned the incubator and flasks used to hold the cells, and settled back to watch the experiment's results.

On Monday, March 9, brought more bad news. All the cultures had suffered massive cell death. This time, Sei traced the source of contamination. New flasks were set out, and the cell mixture was fed into one flask, to which supernatant from the damaged cells was added. Flasks two and three were fed with the March 1 cell preparation; the final flask contained a brand-new mixture. Sei returned the next day and discovered that the cells in the second and third flask had died.

On March 17, Sei finally discussed the problem with Arora, who suggested the cause might be bacterial contamination. More bad news. Later that night, Sei and Wong discovered all the Alpha 1–4 flasks had been heavily contaminated with bacteria, despite their coming from a variety of sources. They were stymied. Sei later testified that a bacterial contamination was "very, very unusual" and that it was "absolutely impossible" for all culture flasks to be contaminated.

By now, Sei and Wong suspected someone had tampered with the experiment. After marking the caps on the experimental flasks, they returned to the laboratory the following day and found them moved. The lab director was brought into the discussions. "Garry and Yoshi came to me and said, 'Someone is fooling with our cells,'" Skolnick recalled. "I said, 'Boys, don't blame anyone else for your sloppiness.'" They claimed they had carefully followed scientific procedures, and Skolnick suggested placing a number of flasks in the incubator with caps set in different ways. After three days, the researchers returned. "The cells are dead and the flasks are turned," they reported.

"At that time, I was working the late shift," Skolnick recalled, "and I went to the NIH police and asked for a printout of who entered Building 8, because the doors are closed at 6:30 P.M. A card key system, with an identifying number for each employee, is used to access the building outside of normal business hours. Prince Arora had entered the building at 11:30 at night—that's not unusual. The same thing happened three days later—there was an entry at 3:30 in the morning. I went back to the NIH police and explained what happened, and they proceeded from there."

Skolnick told his two associates to again mark the caps. By Friday, March 27, the cell lines were dead or heavily damaged. The card key system was checked again, and Arora was the only person to have entered the laboratory after hours. Skolnick reported the sabotage incidents to the police and arranged for Sei to use a cell culture laboratory on another floor, where no cell deaths were experienced.

NIH police checked the card key entry records. Arora's card key record listed several entries after 10:00 P.M. during the weeks the cell death had occurred. Next, Detective Harold Miller of the NIH police devised a plan to set up a "fake" experiment in the incubator. On April 1, with assistance from Sei, new cell flasks were prepared and placed in the incubator in Room 104. Wearing gloves, Miller wiped the flasks clean of all prints and placed them in the incubator. He and Sei then left, after asking the police desk to alert them if anyone entered the building that night.

At 9:44 P.M., Detective Miller received a call from the night guard. The computer showed Arora entering the building. Miller and Sei then hurried to Building 8 where they "ran into" Arora in the hallway. After Arora left, they entered the laboratory. Heading for the incubator, the detective observed latent fingerprints on several flasks. Also, caps on the cell flasks were replaced in different positions. The police officer bagged the cell flasks and sent them to the Federal Bureau of Investigation laboratory for fingerprint analysis. The FBI report linked four identifiable prints on the flasks with those of Dr. Arora.

Detective Miller also removed some other flasks from the incubator for mass spectrometry analysis, which would identify any unknown chemical substances. The result: an infection with 2 mercaptoethanol, a powerful, commonly used chemical that, even in minute quantities, will destroy human cells such as those used in the research project. "Smells like sewer gas to me," Detective Miller observed of the unmistakable, powerful, and unpleasant odor.

The circle closed on Arora. With the fingerprint and flask content evidence in hand, Detective Miller invited him in for a lengthy interview on April 13. Accounts of the encounter differ. Arora disputed Detective Miller's account of his admission to contaminating the experiment, and his attorneys later argued that Arora didn't understand English well and that Detective Miller didn't know how scientific experiments work. But Miller said Arora, when confronted with the evidence, admitted his guilt but would not sign a written document. Following NIH police practice when a witness refuses to give a written statement, Detective Miller called in his supervisor, Captain Pickett, to witness the verbal confession. "Captain Pickett, an eighteen-year veteran of the NIH police department, gave clear testimony that Dr. Arora admitted he had 'adulterated' the flasks using 2 mercaptoethanol," the government later argued in court.

Skolnick met the following day with Arora, after having spoken with Detective Miller. According to the plaintiff's account, "Dr. Arora came into the room and apologized, telling Dr. Skolnick that he was ashamed and embarrassed. Dr. Skolnick asked him, 'Why did you do it?' Dr. Arora replied that Yoshi (Dr. Sei) and Abah (Abah Saini) were conspiring against him and that he had done it to teach them a lesson. Informed that he was being fired, Dr. Arora acknowledged that he knew he couldn't work at the laboratory any longer. Dr. Skolnick, who had worked closely with Dr. Arora for years, testified that there was no possibility of misunderstanding that he acknowledged responsibility for the massive cell death which had endangered the living Alpha 1–4 cell line and brought the research project to a halt."

"He kept destroying the cells, and we were down to one flask," the project supervisor recalled later, adding, "The irony of it is that if he had destroyed one batch of cells he probably would have never been caught, because laboratory conditions are such that sometimes that happens. But it happened quite a number of times." Speculating on the motive for Arora's destructive behavior, Skolnick later concluded, "I think it was scientific jealousy. The way we had the lab configured, Prince Arora was a fairly senior person…it was a very open environment, and when Yoshi Sei and Garry Wong made this really significant breakthrough and it was clear Prince would not be involved in it, I think he really resented that."

The government, in its civil case against Arora, raised several additional reasons. First, he had been denied tenure, something he believed had been promised him. (Skolnick had tried to obtain tenure for Arora, but "letters solicited on his behalf were not consistently favorable and tenure was denied.") Second, "In the fall of 1991, a young female graduate student named Abah Saini accused Dr. Arora of sexual harassment, an incident which came to the attention of Dr. Sei, Dr. Skolnick, and the personnel officer for NIH.… Dr. Arora freely admitted making inappropriate, personal remarks to Miss Saini, including directing her attention one afternoon to a pornographic image displayed on a computer screen. Finally, in October 1991, as a result of what she felt were highly inappropriate overtures from Dr. Arora, Miss Saini asked her graduate committee to transfer her supervision at NIH from Dr. Arora to Dr. Sei."

This, in turn, sparked tension between Sei and Arora. The former described the feeling of "losing trust" in his mentor. Later they sparred over credit for a research paper, and then Dr. Arora intercepted a conference invitation for Dr. Sei, who only learned about it accidentally a few days before the conference was held. Played out in a scientific laboratory, the elements of personal and professional jealousy were growing.

For the cells, things turned out better. Once the March–April 1992 disruptions were over, the project was successfully concluded, the results were published, and the laboratory donated the Alpha 1–4 cell line, now called WSS–1, to the American Type Culture Collection, where it became available to the scientific community for research.

Interestingly, the government chose not to prosecute Arora under criminal statutes, where it would have to prove guilt beyond a reasonable doubt, the heaviest burden of proof in the law. Instead, it chose to sue the defendant for civil damages, where the burden of proof was less demanding, "by a preponderance of the evidence." Thus, the government could make its point that scientific sabotage would not be tolerated, but by taking the civil damages route, it would have an easier time in doing it. NIH was originally reluctant to press charges. Its own legal staff was small, the damage inflicted was an open question, and actual prosecution of the case would fall to the U.S. Attorney's Office. Here the case would have to reach a minimum level of criminality before the office would commit resources to it. There were larger fish to fry, like drug dealers and bank robbers, but one of the NIH lawyers knew an assistant U.S. attorney, called her, and made the case. The U.S. Attorney's Office took the case, but as a civil rather than a criminal complaint.

Reflecting on the case several years later, Skolnick, retired now from NIH, said, "We recruited Prince Arora; he was a fairly well known scientist. And I put a lot of trust in him. It was a horrible betrayal. It was a very difficult time for everyone. I've never had that happen before, and it's never happened since. It was a difficult time for me. I think it was jealousy. The last thing he said, it was in the newspapers, was, 'Yoshi and Abah were plotting against me.' He said that to me. At the trial, his lawyer tried to make me imply that he was referring to something else, but I was quite adamant that in the context of our discussion that was the only thing he could be referring to. I asked him, 'Why did you do it?' One of his lawyers tried to isolate the remark and say that maybe Prince Arora didn't understand English well, but he went to Michigan State University and his English is as good as yours and mine, and the judge didn't buy that either.

"Prince Arora was not a government employee, and after we had that conversation, I just fired him on the spot because he couldn't work at the lab anymore," Skolnick, his former supervisor, recalled. "I went to the NIH legal counsel and I wanted him prosecuted, because he destroyed government property; but the government lawyers said, 'Walk away. You can kill somebody in this country and not go to jail.' In my estimation, this was a horribly serious thing. I let it go. About three months later, Yoshi comes in the lab white as a sheet. He has a piece of paper. Prince Arora sues him for slander in Maryland state court for a quarter of a million dollars or something like that, and he had no idea what to do. I was just furious, so I went to the NIH legal counsel and I said, 'You have to handle this for him, because he was employed by us. He couldn't afford legal fees, and the incident took place while he was working for us.' The legal counsel handled it, and it was thrown out of court. Two months later, he was sued for a half-million dollars in federal court for slander. At that point, I exploded and went over to the legal counsel and demanded that something be done about it. So she called a friend of hers who was an AUSA, Donna C. Sanger. She looked at it and said, 'It's clear he is guilty of the tort of conversion.' So he would not have been prosecuted if he had just walked away and let things go." (Even at the federal level, the suit was prosecuted as a civil, not a criminal, action.)

The original civil complaint, charging Arora with "willful and egregious destruction of property belonging to the United States located at the National Institutes of Health" and seeking monetary damages of $200,000, was filed on May 3, 1993, and was assigned to Judge Messitte on November 15, 1993. A bench trial, a trial without jury, was held from May 31, 1994, to June 7, 1994, after which Trial Briefs were filed by the parties, summarizing the facts and the law as they saw them. The narrative that follows is drawn largely from the Trial Briefs filed by both sides. (In addition to questions of guilt or innocence, the case presented a novel legal issue: How does a judge assess damages for a destroyed scientific experiment? For the lost potential of income and scientific benefits that would have been gained if it had proceeded on schedule, or for the dollars-and-cents value of the equipment?)

Arora was ably represented by two resourceful lawyers, Curtis S. Renner and Tom Watson, of the Washington firm Crowell & Moring, whose strategy was to poke as many holes as possible in what the prosecution pictured as a crime. First, they established Arora as "a successful and respected scientist who worked for more than thirteen years at the National Institutes of Health."[7] After receiving a Ph.D. in microbiology from Michigan State University, he joined NIH in 1978 as a visiting fellow in the Laboratory of Immunodiagnosis at the National Cancer Institute, then moved to another prestigious post with the Laboratory of Developmental and Molecular Immunology at the National Institute of Child Health and Development before joining Skolnick's project in 1987. He was so respected that at times he replaced his boss as acting laboratory chief.

It was Arora who hired Sei in 1989 from the Mt. Sinai Medical Center in New York, wrote an enthusiastic letter on his behalf for a teaching position in Japan, coauthored many research papers with him, and steered prestigious review work his way.

As for the purported sexual or romantic jealousy between Sei and Arora over Ms. Saini, the strikingly attractive graduate student who was working in Arora's lab, the defense argued, "The evidence has shown that neither Dr. Arora nor Dr. Sei were sexually or romantically involved with Ms. Saini and had no reason to be jealous of each other over Ms. Saini in March 1992.... Ms. Saini testified that she never had a sexual or nonsexual romantic relationship with anyone in the lab. While there may have been a few isolated comments from Dr. Arora to Ms. Saini that could be construed as inappropriate, the existence of these comments does not provide an explanation for the actions alleged to have occurred in this case." It was a clever strategy, for it broadened the Saini-Arora duo into a Saini-Arora-Sei trio, a professional relationship unimpeded by either sex or jealousy.

As for the dead cells and the fingerprints, they could be explained as well. Dr. Arora was just being a thoughtful supervisor, the defense contended. When Arora learned about the problems of cell growth, he suggested Sei check "certain elements that could influence the cell growth process, such as problems with the cell media, the incubator, or the ventilation." As for the fingerprints, "For Dr. Arora's fingerprints to be on three cell culture flasks used by Dr. Sei that were in Dr. Arora's own incubator is evidence of nothing more than the fact that a scientist with supervisory responsibility over a laboratory may have touched three of the many flasks in an incubator that he was responsible for and that he himself used for his own research."

The defense continued, "It is not unusual for a dedicated mentor to check on the experiments of one of his students." Dr. Arora "was a caring and responsible mentor" who had been alerted by Sei that he was having cell death problems with the cultures in Room 104. "Dr. Arora is himself an expert in cell culturing. Under the circumstances, it would be perfectly natural for him in his role as Dr. Sei's mentor, to examine the cell flasks to see if there was evidence of a continued cell death problem."

In addition to a scientific card, the defense also played a linguistic card—that Arora didn't understand English and Detective Miller didn't understand Indians, or how scientific experiments worked, for that matter. The defense devoted a major section of its brief to the encounter with Detective Miller and Captain Pickett.

"The disagreement about what was or was not said appears to be the result of ambiguities and misunderstandings caused by cultural and linguistic differences and expectations that confessions would be made." According to the defense, "This was the first investigation of this sort for Detective Miller," and the police officer was motivated to turn it against the foreigner, who was going to be fired anyhow and who had been the sole object of the laboratory investigation. "Under these circumstances, it is not particularly surprising that Detective Miller eventually heard what he believed was a confession.

"Detective Miller admitted that his interpretation of Dr. Arora's responses involved evaluations of Dr. Arora's body language. Prior to conducting the interrogation, Detective Miller had never met Dr. Arora. He could not have known Dr. Arora's mannerisms and whether these mannerisms reflected the differences between Indian and American cultures. Furthermore, Detective Miller had never before interrogated any scientist, much less a scientist born and raised in India."

Gestures, mannerisms, and verb tenses contributed to one giant misunderstanding, in the defense version. "Given Detective Miller's rapid speech...and that Dr. Arora is a non-native English speaker, the potential for misunderstanding was considerable. Furthermore, it is not difficult to understand that a non-native English speaker who is being confronted by a police officer speaking rapidly and accusing him of a serious act could misinterpret a question about what do or did you use as being what could you use.... It is also not difficult to understand that a police officer who needs and is anticipating a confession could believe he heard a confession when the only person he has investigated mentions the very substance he believes has killed cells, particularly if the police officer believes he has asked the suspect what he did use. In short, Detective Miller heard what he wanted and expected to hear."

Dr. Skolnick also came across as a stubborn man who had already made up his mind. In the defense version, on April 14, 1992, Skolnick told Arora that the evidence was solidly against him and that he could not continue working in the laboratory. Arora tried to explain that he had not done anything, but his boss would not listen. The Indian scientist was then terminated without any hearing. On other points of evidence, the defense attorneys argued, "There is no consistent pattern of off-hour entries by Dr. Arora that coincide with dates when cell death allegedly occurred, and some of the alleged cell death occurred on dates when Dr. Arora was not working late in the laboratory."

In summary, Renner and Watson wrote in the Defendant's Trial Brief, "Finding that the government has proved its claims would make it highly unlikely that Dr. Arora would be able to find any future work as a scientist. The sum total of the government's evidence against Dr. Arora is four fingerprints on three flasks in an incubator that Dr. Arora used in his own laboratory and three disputed confessions for which there is no confirming videotape, audiotape, or contemporaneous written notes. This evidence is simply an unworthy basis for bringing Dr. Arora's scientific career to an end."[8]

In a final round of exchanges before Judge Messitte decided the case, Assistant U.S. Attorney Donna C. Sanger, who prosecuted the case for the United States, responded to the defense claim that a serious scientist could not possibly have committed the egregious acts attributed to him. "There are talented people in every profession who have violated the trust and respect placed in them for reasons which seem irrational to observers."[9]

She continued, "The targets of the sabotage were colleagues of Dr. Arora who held him in a position of esteem and trust. The acts posed a risk of destroying a living cell line, which took two highly skilled scientists over a year to develop, with no guarantee that the results of the project could ever be duplicated should the last flask of Alpha 1–4 cells be destroyed. And when Dr. Arora was finally unmasked and fired, he openly turned his malice on Dr. Sei, suing him in a million-dollar civil suit, writing his former employer asking for 'valuable' but derogatory information, and harming his reputation with scientists in the community who had previously held Dr. Sei in high esteem."

On the police interview, the plaintiff noted that "Captain Pickett, an eighteen-year police veteran, testified that he first asked Dr. Arora if he had been read his rights, and he replied that he had. Only after several other preliminary questions from Captain Pickett did Dr. Arora admit 'that he had adulterated two cell tissues with 2 Mercal something' and 'that it was the first time, and that he would never do it again.' The word 'adulterate' was Dr. Arora's word and leaves no doubt as to his liability."

In the interview with his supervisor, Arora allegedly said, "First it was Abah, now it is Yoshi conspiring against me," but later he emphatically denied mentioning either name to his superior. As for the cross-cultural misunderstanding argument, "Dr. Arora also contends that the admissions stem from cultural misunderstanding, an argument he attempted to raise for the first time during trial by use of a linguistic expert. His command of the English language was evident in the courtroom. Dr. Arora admitted at trial that he was fully fluent in English. He also attempted to understate his 'Americanization' by omitting from his résumé both a teaching position at the University of Wisconsin as well as his attendance at Temple University Graduate School. Dr. Skolnick, who has known Dr. Arora for many years, testified that there was no possibility he had misunderstood Dr. Arora."

For the plaintiff, the most compelling evidence of deliberate tampering was provided by the marked caps on the cell flasks. The government argued, "All three of the incidents of cap marking followed by cell death coincide with late night entry of the laboratory by Dr. Arora. On the night of the 'fake' experiment, Dr. Sei and Detective Miller left the deserted laboratory after 8:00 P.M.; at that time, the flasks had been wiped clean of any prints. When they returned after Dr. Arora's departure at 10:44 P.M., the caps had been moved and Dr. Arora's prints were on several flasks marked 'Alpha 1–4.'"

On August 26, 1994, two weeks after the final briefs were filed, Judge Messitte issued his opinion. Several difficult issues needed to be resolved. Who was telling the truth—the government (that is, NIH through its agents, Drs. Skolnick, Sei, and Wong) or Dr. Arora, a solid scientist with impeccable credentials? Who, if anyone, among the known players adulterated the samples? Was there a confession or not, or just a cross-cultural misunderstanding? And if Arora was guilty, how does one assess damages in a scientific case in which the tangible results were several flasks of dead cells and an experiment gone wrong?

The judge reached the following conclusion: "Dr. Arora did tamper with, destroy, and convert Alpha 1–4 cells;...he is liable for the cost of the flasks and materials associated with the creation of the cells as well as reasonable value of the time it took a laboratory assistant to re-create the cells; and that, while not liable in compensatory damages for the delay he caused in the completion of the research project, he must respond in punitive damages, as to which the effect his actions had on the research project is a relevant consideration.

"The Court will award the United States $450.20 in compensatory damages and $5,000 in punitive damages."[10]

After discussing the scientific aspects of The Project, Judge Messitte stepped back. "As often happens in life, human passion slowly began to overtake cool reason. Throughout the initial phase of Dr. Sei's involvement in the Alpha 1–4 project, his relationship was entirely cordial...but, not long after, relations between Dr. Arora and Dr. Sei began to sour. Dr. Sei became disturbed when he felt Dr. Arora was claiming senior authorship on a paper involving AIDS research that Dr. Sei felt Dr. Arora had not really participated in. His distress was increased when Dr. Arora and not Dr. Sei was invited to present the results of the research at an international conference on AIDS. When Dr. Sei confronted Dr. Arora about Dr. Arora's use of Dr. Sei's research materials without permission, Dr. Arora apologized, but relations failed to improve."

Next came the incident with Abah Saini, who, after she complained of sexual harassment by Arora, was transferred to Sei. In consequence of Ms. Saini's problem with Arora, Sei later testified, he "lost trust" in his mentor. Ms. Saini, meanwhile, departed NIH in early 1992.

As for the pivotal police interview, the judge concluded, "Although Dr. Arora testified that for most of the interrogation he was not informed why it was taking place, it is undisputed that, at an early point in the encounter, Detective Miller read him Miranda warnings, and, although Dr. Arora refused to sign a written waiver of rights, he did agree to be interviewed."

Here is the version (the plaintiff's) of the encounter between Drs. Arora and Skolnick accepted by the court:

> On the next day, Dr. Arora met with Dr. Skolnick, who asked:
>
> "Why did you do it?" to which Dr. Skolnick testified Dr. Arora replied: "To teach Yoshi (Dr. Sei) and Abah (Ms. Saini) a lesson," suggesting that the two of them were "conspiring against me."
>
> Dr. Skolnick then testified that he went on to say: "You know you can't work here anymore," to which Dr. Arora replied:
>
> "Yes, I know that."
>
> Dr. Arora's thirteen years at NIH ended that day.

The case was unique for two legal reasons. First, would destroyed scientific specimens fit under a classic tort of conversion or trespass category? ("Tort" in this sense means a breach of a duty imposed by law, which gives a right of action for damages. "Conversion" means altering the object, as opposed to intruding on it.) On the second point, the issue of assessing damages for a destroyed scientific experiment of difficult-to-ascertain monetary value, Judge Messitte began his analysis by posing four questions:

1. Did Dr. Arora, in fact, tamper with the Alpha 1–4 cells?
2. If so, did the tampering constitute either the tort of conversion or trespass?

3. If either such tort was committed, what compensatory damages, if any, should be assessed?

4. If either tort was committed, what punitive damages, if any, are appropriate?

On the first question, the judge concluded Arora had indeed tampered with the cells. His fingerprints were present on the flasks, he had a potential animus or motive toward Sei ("a professional rivalry as well as possible resentment over Ms. Saini's shift of allegiance"), and three witnesses had testified that, when confronted with the alleged wrongdoing, he admitted culpability. "The burden of proof as to liability in this non-jury civil case is a simple preponderance of the evidence," the judge wrote. "The issue of credibility is one for the Court."

Was there a conversion or trespass?

"The difference between the two torts is fundamentally one of degree, trespass constituting a lesser interference with another's chattel, conversion a more serious exercise of dominion or control over it.

"Assuming for the moment that a cell line is a chattel capable of being converted or trespassed upon, it is clear that the United States owned the Alpha 1–4 cell line, and that Dr. Arora's dominion or control of it, while brief, was total. He intended to act inconsistently with Dr. Sei's right to control the cells, he did not act in good faith, and he committed the ultimate harm-he destroyed the cells. While certain easily identifiable expense was caused by Dr. Arora's inappropriate acts, it is also apparent that he caused serious inconvenience to what was a critically important research project. By this analysis, if any tort was committed, it was unquestionably a conversion, not a mere trespass."

But did he convert, or damage, the cell line?

A Supreme Court decision, *Diamond v Chakrabarty*, 447 US 303 (1980), has recognized that a living cell line is a property capable of protection. Based on this case, and other related cases, the judge wrote, "The Court thus sees no reason why a cell line should not be considered a chattel capable of being converted....The Court is satisfied, therefore, under the circumstances of this case, that the Alpha 1–4 cell line was capable of being converted and that in fact Dr. Arora converted it. The more difficult question, perhaps, is how to assess damages, the next question before the Court."

Assessing the physical costs for destroyed flasks and the laboratory assistant's time to grow new cells was easy; the difficult question was assessing value to "property of limited extrinsic or uncertain market value...the product of creative effort as to which no original or replacement cost can fairly be assigned—for example, manuscripts or professional drawings," where a calculation of the number of hours the project took was used as a baseline.

As for the damages caused by the delay, Judge Messitte reasoned they were too speculative to be counted as an item of compensatory damages, but the question of punitive damages remained. (Compensatory damages compensate someone for a monetary loss; punitive damages punish someone for a wrongful act.) At the punitive damage stage, the court is not held to a standard of precise quantification or to a rule of proportionality vis-à-vis the underlying compensatory award.

"The Court is satisfied...that Dr. Arora did act with an evil and rancorous intent against Dr. Sei. His intentional actions, moreover, not only delayed a vitally important research project; they were obviously calculated to diminish the reputation of the entire laboratory involved with the project. Beyond that, Dr. Arora had to know that his actions might deprive the scientific community of the benefits of the research involving the Alpha 1–4 cell line for some period of time, possibly forever. Finally—and here perhaps the deterrent effect of a punitive award comes most into play—his actions undermined the honor system which is ultimately based on truthfulness, both as a moral imperative and as a fundamental operational principle in the scientific research process. Taking all these considerations into account, the Court has determined that a punitive damage award in the amount of $5,000 would be fair and just."

Judge Messitte then entered a judgment in support of the plaintiff on August 8, 1994, awarding $450.20 compensatory damages for the loss of laboratory supplies and $5,000 punitive damages for the loss of time and effort on The Project. Finally, Arora was assessed with an additional $3,986.27 in court costs. His appeal to the Fourth Circuit was denied, and his Maryland state slander suit and million-dollar lawsuit against Sei were dismissed as well. A dictionary definition of jealousy is "Resentment or envy of another person or of his or her possible or actual success, advantage, or superiority; rivalry." It aptly fits the driving force in this case.

Dr. Sei moved on to the anesthesiology department of the Uniform Services University in Bethesda, Maryland; Dr. Wong became a professor in Finland. Dr. Skolnick retired after twenty-five years at NIH and joined Eli Lilly as a research fellow. Captain Pickett retired, and Detective Miller moved to another government agency. Dr. Arora still lives in a tranquil, middle-class housing development a short distance from NIH, but he declined to answer questions about the case, offering instead a series of strung-out letters to members of Congress seeking a refund of his fine and court costs and presenting his case as being one big, vindictive misunderstanding.

Limiting Police Ride-Alongs

From Greenbelt to the Supreme Court

> *"The poorest man may, in his cottage, bid defiance of all the forces of the crown. It may be frail; its roof may shake; the wind may blow through it; the storm may enter; the rain may enter; but the King of England may not enter; all his forces dare not cross the threshold of the ruined tenement."*[11]
>
> *—William Pitt arguing in Parliament (1776) against allowing discretionary searches of individual dwellings*

Not every district judge has a case that makes its way to the U.S. Supreme Court. Rarer still that the Supreme Court will, by a 9-0 decision, modify a decision made by an appeals court. Rarer still that the case will have national implications, as was true of *Wilson v Layne*, a case with serious free speech, privacy, and due process implications. When it was over, the Supreme Court ruled that henceforth the police could be sued for allowing reporters and photographers to accompany them on raids of private homes. That put a crimp in the style of media ride-along shows, with their shaky, handheld cameras and snap crackle and pop police band radio narratives, bouncing along mean streets in pursuit of surly-looking criminals in T-shirts and jeans. From then on, if the media entered a suspect's house, the entry was at their legal peril.

Wilson v Layne was an unusual case. In some court cases, the basic facts are in dispute and must be sorted out; in others, the facts are agreed upon, but there are prolonged disputes about what the law means and how courts should apply it. In the latter category was *Wilson v Layne*, which began in Judge Messitte's court, but which was argued before the Supreme Court on March 24, 1999, and decided two months later. The basic encounter from which the case sprang took less than fifteen minutes, and there was not much of a dispute about what happened; but it took three different courts seven years to sort out the meaning of the brief, heated encounter.

At 6:45 A.M. on the morning of April 16, 1992, five federal and state law enforcement officers, accompanied by a *Washington Post* photographer and reporter, banged hard on the door of Charles and Geraldine Wilson's home in an unassuming Rockville, Maryland, lower-middle-class suburb. Police were into the second week of "Operation Gunsmoke," chasing down potentially armed, violent criminals on whom there were outstanding arrest warrants. One such person was Dominic Jerome Wilson, Charles Wilson's son. Police believed he would be at the 909 North Stone Street address. He had given it to probation officers for years, and it appeared on other court documents.

A small child answered the door, Charles Wilson's granddaughter Valencia (Dominic's daughter, it turned out, but she did not say so). She was already awake, waiting for her early-morning school bus ride. Mrs. Wilson described the encounter:

"We were startled by loud banging at the front door. Charlie called to Valencia to see who was at the door. We heard her open the door but she did not say anything, and the banging continued but seemed even louder. By this time my husband (Charlie) got out of bed saying, 'What in the hell is going on?'" Charlie lumbered into the living room clad only in his underwear and met three armed, pumped-up representatives of the U.S. Marshals Service and the Montgomery County, Maryland, Sheriff's Department, who, within seconds, had him on the floor with a gun pointed at his head. Meanwhile, the *Washington Post* photographer shot away (though the *Post* never printed the pictures).

The police thought Charlie was Dominic (who had spent the night nearby with a girlfriend). Charlie said the police told him "to get the fuck on the floor now."

"You need to tell me what's going on," he replied.

"Get the fuck on the floor. Get on the goddamn floor now."[12]

Mrs. Wilson hurried to the living room. At this point, Charlie was laid out on the floor with his arms stretched out in front of him, still yelling. One of the armed police officers said, "Are you Dominic?" Charlie yelled, "Hell, no, I'm not Dominic. This is my house and Dominic is not here, he does not live here."

"I am standing here in my nightgown in front of all these men," Mrs. Wilson told the court, adding, "My husband is lying on the floor in his jockey shorts; how could we be making a threat to anyone? I asked to see the search warrant. I did not see any paper that read search warrant, or any order giving anyone the right to search our property. I saw four pictures of Dominic and some other papers, but as I began to read them they were taken from my hands.

"Charlie was finally allowed to get up off the floor. And there was still this one man yelling 'If he is here your ass is going to jail.' We were being treated like criminals and called liars.... There were pictures being taken of us. What had we done to deserve this kind of treatment? Most of them left out of the house, leaving just the one man in the brown jacket who began to apologize for the way some of the others were behaving.

"At this time, I called for Valencia, who came back upstairs from the basement. We sat on the couch, she crying and trembling with fear. She said the men had guns pointed at her when she opened the door and had pushed her out the door and were asking her where Dominic was and to stop lying. This has been one of the most horrifying experiences of my life. Every time I think of it I start shaking all over again myself, and the tears come. I try to put it out of my mind, but I can't, I just can't."[13]

Charlie's deposition differed little from Geraldine's, except it contained more expletives.

The Wilsons filed a lawsuit in the Greenbelt Courthouse against the federal and state officers who entered their home, charging them with (1) using excessive force, (2) lacking probable cause to believe the fugitive would be at the Wilsons' home, and (3) permitting media representatives to enter the Wilson home to photograph and report on the execution of the arrest warrant, thus violating the Wilsons' Fourth Amendment rights against an unreasonable search and seizure.

The case was heard as a civil action requesting damages and "declaratory relief," meaning the court was asked to declare what portion of the rights in dispute the Wilsons could seek to redress as violations of their civil rights.[14] On December 4, 1995, Judge Messitte issued several rulings from the bench in response to preliminary motions made by both sides. On the probable cause issue, he dismissed the Wilsons' complaint: "There's no question there was a reasonable basis and probable cause to believe Dominic Wilson resided at the indicated address. The fact that it was the address given by him during his active probation in the Court's view would suffice, but certainly there was more. He had used it on arrest records in the past....The Court finds as a matter of law objectively that it was reasonable to believe that the suspect, Dominic Wilson, was at the address. And that alone would make it reasonable for the officers to do what they did."

On the question of excessive force, the ruling also went against the Wilsons. The judge concluded that however harsh the words and actions might have been viewed by the Wilsons, they were reasonable and permissible in the search and seizure context.

The case turned on the final charge, by far the most contentious issue of all. Was this an unreasonable search and seizure under the Fourth Amendment, and, if so, could the officers be sued, or did they have qualified immunity as law enforcement agents acting in an official capacity? Was it a free ride for the *Washington Post*, or was the paper violating the Wilsons' constitutional rights by photographing them in a 6:45 A.M. police raid?

Addressing the Wilsons' charge that the presence of the officers violated their Fourth Amendment rights and constituted an invasion of privacy, Messitte said, "That's the essence of what we're talking about. And that particularly insofar as the home is involved, it is a particularly protected location." The judge concluded that no objective reason justified the media being present: "And whether you add the invasion of privacy or trespass element to it, the fact is there was a constitutional right to be free from unreasonable searches and seizures, and the presence of a media officer or media individual is not serving any legitimate law enforcement question." But then what? To be successful, a federal civil rights action requires more than a constitutional violation. The right must be "clearly established" at the time the violation occurs. If not, the officials are protected by what is known as "qualified immunity."

On this issue—was the right to be free of a media invasion clearly established as of April 1992—Messitte's ruling triggered an appeal that ended four years later in the Supreme Court. He said, "The right was clearly established. And any reasonable officer should have known that what was going on was a violation of a clearly established right." This sentence sent the chickens flying. Messitte predicated it on a description of what the journalists were doing—"snooping around, looking around, participating in one fashion or another with both the search of the premises for the individual, who was not found, and the seizure of the Wilsons, who were detained and actually photographed." On two of the three issues, he granted summary judgment in favor of the officers (the search was reasonable, the use of force was not excessive), but he denied it on the key media presence issue. The judge ruled the right existed and was clearly established in 1992. Thus, the officers were not entitled to immunity from suit. The issue of whether the officers violated the Fourth Amendment in permitting the media presence would have to go to trial.

The police defendants' response was straightforward. If a right had been violated, that right had not been clearly enunciated when the police stormed into the Wilsons' living room in April 1992. They appealed the decision to the U.S. Court of Appeals for the Fourth Circuit, where it turned out to be one of the court's most closely followed cases. Because they had been denied qualified immunity, the defendants could take an immediate appeal—without going to trial.

A bit of background: The Fourth Circuit was split between liberals and conservatives. Major cases, those with high-profile constitutional or political import, were usually heard en banc by the eleven active judges. Such cases were often decided by a 6–5 conservative majority, as was *Wilson v Layne* in 1997. A three-judge panel of Fourth Circuit judges reversed the district court, but later the entire court voted to rehear the appeal. *Wilson v Layne* was then argued in Richmond on March 3, 1998, and decided on April 3. Circuit Judge William W. Wilkins Jr. wrote the majority opinion; Judge Francis D. Murnaghan Jr. wrote a dissenting opinion. Generous displays of legal fireworks were evident in both the majority and minority opinions. The basic question the court considered was privacy versus media presence, and whether in April 1992 this right was clearly established and whether a reasonable officer would have understood that the conduct at issue violated it. The majority reversed Messitte, holding that the officers had the right to qualified immunity for their actions. Following the legal logic of the majority opinion is like following trail markers in the Shenandoah National Forest, where the desired outcome is clear but the way of reaching it is not.

The Court wrote: "We stress that we do not address whether the officers' conduct was constitutional or appropriate, or whether the legal landscape when these events occurred was sufficiently developed that it would have been obvious to reasonable officers that the actions were violative of the Fourth Amendment." The kicker was delivered at the close of a fifty–word sentence: "Because in April 1992 it was not clearly established that permitting media representatives to accompany law enforcement officers into a private residence to observe and photograph their attempt to execute an arrest warrant would violate the homeowner's constitutional rights, we hold that these officers are entitled to qualified immunity. Consequently, we reverse the decision of the district court refusing to grant summary judgment in favor of the officers." Score: Police 3, Wilsons 0, if the opinion holds.

Judge Murnaghan, in a "vigorous dissent," wrote: "No reporter's presence was mentioned in the warrants, and there were no exigent circumstances justifying warrantless action. Because no reasonable police officer could have believed that inviting the reporters into the home or allowing the photographer to take pictures either was authorized by the warrant or was reasonably necessary to accomplish its legitimate law enforcement purposes, the police officers' actions amounted to unreasonable searches and seizures in violation of clearly established Fourth Amendment law."

Murnaghan then ratcheted up the argument to the highest plane of constitutional jurisprudence: "We must not, when arguing whether some specific incarnation of Fourth Amendment rights was or was not clearly established, lose sight of the core values that the Fourth Amendment was designed to protect," the jurist cautioned. Then he cited William Blackstone (Chief Justice William Rehnquist would later use the same quotation from Blackstone's *Commentaries* in agreeing with Murnaghan and Messitte that the Constitution had been violated): "And the law of England has so particular and tender a regard to the immunity of a man's house, that it stiles it his castle, and will never suffer it to be violated with impunity.... For this reason no doors can in general be broken open to execute any civil process; though, in criminal cases, the public safety supersedes the private."[15]

Was the law unclear in 1992 on whether or not a media presence at an arrest in someone's home violated the ancient pillar of Anglo-American common law that "a person's home is his castle"? The Supreme Court would decide.

The thousands of tourists who visit Washington each day maintain a reverent silence when entering two buildings: the National Cathedral and the U.S. Supreme Court; one is fourteenth-century English Gothic in style, the other imperial Rome. And while visitors often swear the latter building dates to colonial times, in fact it went up in 1936, the work of the American architect Cass Gilbert, for whom Italian design was formative.

In this temple-like setting, Judge Messitte and his staff gathered on March 24, 1999. Occupying a box provided by General William Suter, clerk of the court, were Chan Park and Robyn Ryan, the judge's clerks; Helen-Louise Hunter, previously a permanent clerk; the judge's wife, Susan; and judicial assistant Barbara Barry. The Greenbelt delegation was excited, for rarely does a district judge have a case work its way to the highest court in the land. "Don't do the wave if it looks like it is going your way," Suter quipped.

Wilson v Layne was paired with another case, *Harlon v Berger*, which was argued first. In *Harlon v Berger*, CNN had sent a reporter and camera crew along with agents of the U.S. Fish and Wildlife Service to shoot pictures of a ranch whose owner was suspected of poisoning and shooting eagles. Justice Antonin Scalia came out swinging at counsel representing the officers and the prosecutor in the *Harlon* case, and other justices soon piled on, using expressions like "sounds like fluff" and "an amazing invasion of privacy."[16]

Then came *Wilson v Layne*. Arguing for the police defendants, Assistant Maryland State Attorney General Lawrence P. Fletcher-Hill opened his arguments directly with the immunity issue. No cases clearly prohibited such conduct in 1992, he argued. Justice Stephen Breyer asked: Would it not be obvious to an officer that a dwelling's privacy was protected by the Fourth Amendment, and that a journalist was infringing on that privacy? No, the officer had a valid arrest warrant, Fletcher-Hill responded. Justice David H. Souter then added the warrant was directed at the peace officers, so how could it allow journalists to enter the house? Because they were operating under the aegis of the U.S. Marshals Service, Fletcher-Hill replied.

The Wilsons were represented by Richard K. Willard, a Washington, D.C., lawyer, former Supreme Court law clerk, and head of the Civil Division of the Department of Justice during the Reagan administration. Speaking extemporaneously over twenty minutes, Willard forthrightly stuck to his main point—the centuries' old Anglo-American legal principle that the home is a sanctuary from prying eyes. If there are any recognized exceptions, Willard continued, they do not include police bringing the media inside anybody's house. Several members of the Court, led by Chief Justice Rehnquist, were skeptical of Willard's position. For Rehnquist, the question boiled down to interpretation of a single word. If you "serve" the warrant, does that limit the number of persons who may be present? For the chief justice, and others, the answer was not clear. The immunity issue was murky, the Court seemed to be saying.

Two months later, on May 24, 1999, in a 9–0 opinion the Court held that the media entering a home with the police clearly violated the Fourth Amendment. But the police officers were entitled to qualified immunity, the Court continued, because the state of the law was not sufficiently established at the time the entry took place. The Supreme Court elaborated: "It violates the Fourth Amendment for police to bring members of the media or other third parties into their home during the execution of a warrant when the presence of the third parties in the home was not in aid of the warrant's execution.... It does not necessarily follow from the fact that the officers were entitled to bring a reporter and a photographer with them." The Supreme Court dismissed arguments that publicizing the government's efforts to combat crime justified the intrusion. Such arguments, the Court said, "fall short of justifying media ride-alongs. Although the presence of third parties during the execution of a warrant may in some circumstances be constitutionally permissible, the presence of these third parties was not."[17]

But the next question was this: Was the right clearly established at the time of the search? Here the Court held that the law was undeveloped, that different federal circuits had reached different conclusions, and, "if judges thus disagree on a constitutional question, it is unfair to subject police to money damages for picking the losing side of the controversy."

Justice John Paul Stevens argued the principle of limiting police action in the execution of a warrant was clearly established and the police should have been held liable. The principle, like the broader protections afforded by the Fourth Amendment, he wrote, "represents the confluence of two important sources: our English forefathers' traditional respect for the sanctity of the private home and the American colonist's hatred of the general warrant."[18]

Stevens next excoriated a "document apparently prepared by an employee in the public relations office of the United States Marshals Service," the text of which "makes it quite clear that its author was not a lawyer, but rather a person concerned with developing the proper image of the Service." An example of the publication's unctuous, honey-coated language was cited by the justice:

> "Waving the Flag"
>
> One action of special consequence is 'waving the flag' of the Marshals Service. This is accomplished when Deputies can easily be recognized as USMS Deputies because they are wearing raid jackets, prominently displaying their badges, or exhibiting other easily identifiable marks of the Service. We want the public to know who you are and what kind of job

> you do. That is one of the goals of the ride-along.... You might 'grease the skids'... by offering the reporter, camera person, or other media representatives involved a memento of the Marshals Service (such as a T-shirt or cap).

Wilson v Layne had come a long way in seven years, albeit by a circuitous path. When it was over, a district court's decision was affirmed by the Supreme Court on the unconstitutionality of the media search. The sequence was as follows:

1. 1992—The police raid on the Wilsons' home took place, accompanied by the media.
2. 1995—The district court found the raid legal and the use of force not excessive, but the media ride-along was held to be illegal and the officers who approved it were found not to have qualified immunity from being sued for their action violating the Fourth Amendment.
3. 1998—The court of appeals reversed the district court and found the ride-along was legal, but it declined to decide the Fourth Amendment issue and said the officers were entitled to qualified immunity because no court had held at the time of the search that a media presence during a police entry into a residence constituted such a violation.
4. 1999—The Supreme Court upheld the appeals court in result but declared that a media ride-along in a home violated the Fourth Amendment. However, because the state of the law was not clearly established at the time the entry in this case took place, the officers were accorded qualified immunity from a lawsuit.

How should a law enforcement officer, journalist, or citizen act since *Wilson v Layne* was handed down? Basically, they know that participation in police raids by non-police personnel cannot include an invasion of a private dwelling without the occupants' permission. The *Washington Post*'s deputy managing editor, Milton Coleman, got the point immediately. "An individual house is a threshold that you don't cross" in such raids, he said. Somewhat relieved, Sheriff Raymond M. Kight of Montgomery County, one of the defendants, said, "It will give law enforcement throughout the country new guidelines where we didn't have any before, but I think it will definitely have a chilling effect on press coverage."[19]

So the journey to the high court ended. As often happens with appeals, even those to the Supreme Court, the case eventually returned to the judge with whom it originated, in this case Judge Messitte in Greenbelt, to enter an order consistent with the Court's ruling and dismiss the case. Charles and Geraldine Wilson had lost their chance for compensation, but, in the eyes of civil libertarians everywhere, the nation had won. The sanctity of the home had been resoundingly affirmed by the highest court in the land.

Mixing Up the Batch

Suhas V Sardesai and the Adulterated Drug Case

"He looked terrible during the second trial."
—Lawrence McDade, Prosecutor

In western Montgomery County, an hour's drive from the Greenbelt Courthouse, is headquarters of one of the federal government's largest regulatory agencies, the Food and Drug Administration (FDA). The FDA experienced a burst of regulatory activity following a 1984 amendment to the Food, Drug, and Cosmetic Act. It was the heady world of deregulation and privatization of the Reagan era, and, as the generic drug industry grew, many companies cut corners in racing their products to the market. Before long, approximately fifteen companies and more than 100 individuals faced criminal prosecutions for selling adulterated drugs. One of the most visible of such cases was *USA v Suhas V. Sardesai*, Criminal No. PJM-94–167, the first major case held in the large ceremonial courtroom.[20]

The central figure in the case, Suhas V. Sardesai, a handsome and brilliant scientist, was charged with altering the composition of numerous generic drugs produced at Mutual Pharmaceutical, Inc., a Philadelphia chemical plant where he worked beginning in 1984. A pharmacist from Goa, a Portuguese-speaking enclave on the west coast of India, Sardesai had done graduate work in the United

States and occupied a mid-level position with a Danbury, Connecticut, pharmaceutical company. Attractive, suave, and moving with gravitas, he came in on the new company's ground floor. If things went well for him at Mutual, it would be success like he never dreamed of. Sardesai was given responsibilities an immigrant scientist could only wish for. He created Mutual's manufacturing facility and supervised new product development, drug manufacture, and what some would consider a humdrum task, compliance with FDA reporting requirements. Sardesai did well with the firm and soon was promoted to senior vice president of operations. In December 1985, the firm hired Edmund J. Striefsky as a chemist in the quality control laboratory, responsible for quality control and regulatory compliance. Within a decade, Striefsky became vice president of the quality control unit. By then, Mutual was making a name for itself in the highly competitive generic drug market.

But all was not well. In May 1992, a confidential informant contacted the U.S. Attorney's Office with allegations of unlawful activity at Mutual. A disgruntled former employee, the informant had recently been terminated from a responsible managerial position at Mutual and left with revenge in mind and a bundle of documents detailing the illegal mixing of batch after batch of drugs at the company, a spin-off from an established pharmaceutical house, United Research Laboratories (URL). Most of the plant's approximately 100 production workers, few of whom spoke English, were from the Gujarat region of western India, north and west of Bombay, and were hired personally by Sardesai. During the 1970s and 1980s, the recently deregulated pharmaceutical industry was expanding and facing shortages of skilled workers; and graduates from recognized Indian pharmaceutical schools had no trouble finding jobs and green cards. Many of the Indians were part of a tightly knit ethnic community, living in Philadelphia, attending the same temples, frequenting the same schools and grocery stores. One of them had it in for Sardesai, who had fired him.

The informant, a line manager later identified as Nagesh Shirsat, was a controversial witness but a thorough record keeper who produced extensive photocopies of internal Mutual records and contemporaneous notes, later allowing agents to compare the charges with company records. Shirsat had confronted Sardesai and Striefsky over the Marx Brothers Chemical Company practices widely prevalent at Mutual. He was terminated three weeks later, caught on videotape illegally handing a prescription antihistamine capsule to another employee who complained of congestion. Shirsat was then hauled in to the company conference room, shown a videotape of his handing the drug to the employee, and told that if he made trouble with the FDA, Mutual would turn the tape over to the police because Shirsat was dispensing prescription drugs without a license. Shirsat was then led to the door by an armed guard. Sardesai later said he was ridding the company of a bad egg; Shirsat claimed it was a frame-up. (When the case came to trial, Shirsat faced numerous credibility questions for substantial résumé enhancement over many years, but stuck to his guns on the batch-alteration data.) Barred from future employment in the pharmaceutical industry for dispensing drugs illegally, Shirsat, who now runs a New Jersey grocery store, reportedly received a substantial payment to settle a wrongful dismissal civil suit against Mutual.

Meanwhile, in an effort to build a case, agents began interviewing other highly placed Mutual employees and awarded immunity letters to eight current or former employees who swore Sardesai had instructed production employees to regrind or remix batches using processes significantly deviating from FDA-approved master formulas, and had told them to fill out fraudulent production records.[21]

It was more than a little of this and a little of that being mixed in here and there, according to Bryan E. Foreman, an assistant U.S. attorney who helped prosecute the case. "Our argument was that changes in the manufacturing process can profoundly affect the dissolution of drugs in your body as well as the stability of the drug or its shelf life. Some of the drugs we were dealing with had a very short shelf life, often eighteen months. What they were doing was directing people to regrind tablets. Some of the formulas they put together didn't work. Possibly it's because they bought new equipment after doing the experimental work on older machines. You end up with products that are going to dissolve in different parts of the body. It was our contention at trial that some of these products would dissolve and be absorbed in the upper stomach, as opposed to the intestinal tract, where they were supposed to, or vice versa; it wouldn't be absorbed into the body at the time it was supposed to. So you have an issue of a product that may not be safe and effective for human consumption, because it is not digesting in the proper area, and a product whose pharmacological effectiveness is unknown."

Catherine M. Recker, a lead counsel for the defense, disagreed. "None of the alterations resulted in any injuries nor any recall." Later she argued, "The irregular results in the various tests resulted from employees wanting to make their jobs easier and not performing the steps appropriately. For example, you have to pour the water into the powder mixture at a very slow rate. That is tedious and difficult; it's a lot easier if you dump all the water in at the same time. But that resulted in problems if you are pressing the mixture into tablets."

It is a chilling experience to read investigators' reports, less for their legal content than for the range of human emotions they uncover. Beneath the dry, formal, restricted vocabulary of the police officer, there is a cat-and-mouse game between hunter and hunted. How much do they know? How much should I tell them?

"On September 1, 1993, Suhas V. Sardesai, Vice President Operations, Mutual Pharmaceuticals, Inc., Philadelphia, Pa., was interviewed by the below signed at his residence...during the hours 7:00 P.M.–8:15 P.M." The forty-six-year-old scientist lived with his family in Cherry Hills, New Jersey, an upscale Philadelphia suburb. You can imagine Sardesai opening the door and two strangers entering. "Credentials were presented and Sardesai was informed of the purpose of the interview, that the interview was voluntary and part of a Grand Jury investigation." You can imagine Sardesai, or Sunil (Sony) Shah, another Mutual employee, who was also interviewed at his home at the same time, one of five persons interviewed prior to the corporation being served with a subpoena. In Shah's case, agents asked "if we could talk to him privately since his wife, mother and his three daughters were present with us in the living room. Shah then asked them to leave."

Both men appeared eager to cooperate and said they would be truthful in their answers. But the agents were well prepared for the interviews, let both proclaim their innocence, and then systematically led them through most of the accusations for which they would soon be indicted. Of Sardesai's proclamation of innocence, the investigator wrote: "He knows nothing of these matters, nobody has told him anything about these things. He trusted everybody. If anyone did any of the (improper/illegal) things questioned by interviewing agents, he has no knowledge of such. He has great trust in everyone but acknowledged that things could be done without his knowledge.

"He knows nothing about the use of a blend from a failed batch being used to make up...a passed batch of Amitripyline (used to treat depression and neurological pain). He says our information on this is wrong...There has never been a rework of a lot to his knowledge...He knows nothing about sticking problems in the compression of tablets...He knows nothing about the writing of untrue information into batch records...He has no knowledge of nor ever told anyone to falsify batch records or log books....He has no knowledge of anyone switching samples; that is taking samples from passing lots and identifying them as samples from lots which had in fact failed testing....He denies taking any formulae from Danbury Pharmaceuticals upon leaving that firm."

The sequence Sardesai denied would be the foundation of the government's case—batches being altered, reports being falsified, and employees being told to commit illegal acts. The accusation that he stole drug formulas at his previous job would be used in an effort to discredit him.

Two former employees were mentioned in the initial interview reports. (Both would loom large in the investigation.) Sammy Baig had been dismissed just after returning from a trip home, and Nagesh Shirsat, who would also testify for the government, had been "fired for stealing drugs, unapproved drugs, and for giving them to outsiders." Sardesai could name no disgruntled employee at the firm now. He stated that this investigation stems from information originating with a disgruntled employee and that "there is no truth to the allegations."[22]

The Sunil Shah interview, conducted by different agents at the same time, was similar in content. Shah admitted problems of drugs sticking, cracking, splitting, and chipping—deficiencies that would be part of the government's case—plus the reworking of various lots of drugs, adding compounds, and falsifying records.

Shah said that after the FDA inspection in early 1992, Mutual's CEO, Richard Roberts, M.D. and Ph.D., who had a daily noon meeting with senior employees, "said no more deviations and everything will be done correctly, including accurate batch records. He added that no problems with production have occurred and if a lot now fails, it is destroyed and not reworked or mixed in with future batches." (Roberts, despite being head of URL and Mutual and day-to-day supervisor of the two companies, was never a subject of the investigation, which focused on Sardesai and those around him. None of the Indian employees reported to Roberts, nor did he sign any of the production documents.)

Early in the interview, "Agent Szymanski told Shah not to lie; he was not a target of our investigation; and we needed his cooperation to answer our questions truthfully." At the end, "Shah expressed repeated concern that his conversation with us will be found out by the firm. He said that he did not want to lose his job. Agent Szymanski said that everything is secretive and the firm will not find out....We said that at time of trial the company would find out what he said, but the targeted individuals would be indicted and hopefully fired or suspended from supervisory roles at Mutual."[23] In fact, Shah was indicted seven months later. Investigators said that, despite his assurances to do so, he never cooperated with the government in the case and was active in disseminating instructions to line employees about remixing the botched batches.

The grand jury indictment of the four Mutual employees was filed on April 28, 1994.[24] It named Sardesai and Striefsky, and two mid-level employees, Shah and Kurit R. Patel, in the quality assurance and production units.

The indictment charged for the period covered by the investigation, from about 1987 to September 10, 1992, the defendants "did lawfully, willfully, and knowingly combine, conspire, confederate, and agree together...to defraud the United States by impeding, impairing, obstructing, and defeating the lawful government functions of the FDA" through (1) false, fictitious, and fraudulent statements; (2) concealing and covering up their actions "by trick, scheme, and device"; (3) failing, with intent to defraud, to establish and maintain proper records; and (4) introducing adulterated and unapproved generic drug products into interstate commerce.

The specific charges were that when the conspirators encountered problems in manufacturing drug products, they ordered employees to use ingredients, processes, and equipment that deviated from FDA-approved master formulas, rather than conducting research and development and submitting the results to the FDA for review. Also, rejected portions of some batches were added to other batches of the same product, and, "when Mutual production batches failed quality testing, members of the conspiracy directed Mutual employees to disregard those failing results."

Next, the indictment turned to numerous overt acts in which drugs were altered. Numerous batch numbers were listed in which additions, regrindings, and recompressions were made, all unrecorded in company records. The drugs included acetazolamide, a generic drug used in the treatment of swelling due to congestive heart failure and in the treatment of glaucoma; ibuprofen, a product used for the treatment of pain and inflammation; imipramine, used to treat the symptoms of depression; sulfamethoxazole/trimethoprim, an antibiotic; and sulfasalazine, another antibiotic.

For one of the drugs, the indictment quoted from a letter Sardesai submitted to the FDA that said: "We acknowledge that in fact only after FDA approval of supplemental application may we rework a batch of this drug product. We do recognize we need to get approval to revise or rework formula. We, Mutual Pharmaceutical, Inc., do not intend to rework or revise the formula without approval from the Food and Drug Administration."

Later, during an August 1992 FDA Inspection, Striefsky, responding to an investigator's question on Mutual's policy on rework procedures, stated, "We don't do reworks."

On June 2, 1994, the defense asked for more time to prepare the case. Robert E. Welsh Jr., lead lawyer for the defense, said he would contest the admissibility of the government's contention, if offered, that Sardesai improperly misappropriated formulas of pharmaceutical products from his prior employer. He would need ample time to conduct his own research and to carefully review the other side's scientific data.[25] Judge Peter Messitte granted the motion to waive the Speedy Trial Act, which is designed to bring most cases to court within seventy days.

Another substantial pretrial exchange took place between the court and the defense counsel asking that the trial be held in Philadelphia because the company was located there, where most of the principals lived. Judge Messitte denied the motions, accepting the argument that the FDA was located in nearby Rockville, Maryland, and the FDA was bringing the case to trial.

The seven-week jury trial, the first such lengthy trial in the new courthouse, extended from February 14 to April 4, 1995. Lawrence McDade, who had spent twenty years with the Department of Justice's Consumer Litigation Division, was the lead prosecutor, along with Raymond A. Bonner, a seasoned assistant U.S. attorney, and, later, Bryan E. Foreman, an assistant U.S. attorney from the Greenbelt office. For the defense, Welsh, a former assistant U.S. attorney in the Eastern District of Pennsylvania, was assisted by Catherine M. Recker, hired for the complex case, but soon to become a partner in Welsh and Recker, a small but well-known Philadelphia criminal defense firm. It was an all-star cast.

Because most of the witnesses were from India, translators who spoke Gujarati and English were required. Eventually, two American speakers of the language were found, but neither was a professional interpreter. Witnesses kept drifting in and out of both languages. Part of the problem is Gujarati has only two tenses, present and non-present. The court stenographer, attempting to create a trial transcript, would signal the translator to backtrack and repeat the exchange in English for the record. McDade recalled, "You would ask a question, and then there would be this debate back and forth. At one point Judge Messitte was totally exasperated, so he went to the translator and said, 'Sir, in the last fifteen minutes Mr. McDade has told you five times "Just repeat what the witness has said. If it doesn't make sense we will ask follow-up questions. You should not get into a discussion with the witness." Do you understand that?' The interpreter replied, 'Your honor, you have to understand, in Gujarati there are only two tenses, the present and the non-present, so you can mistake yesterday and tomorrow. You have to tell from context if it is past or future.' He told us the witness did not understand the context, so he had to explain it to him. We were all there looking at each other, thinking, The past and the future are the same in this language, there is only the present and the non-present, but this is a case where the charges go back several years."

The courthouse was new and the courtroom thermostat was located in the jury box, so when the juror nearest it leaned back, his head registered a high body temperature on the thermostat and shut off heat in the courtroom. It was a cold February, and during the morning session, the temperature would drop twenty degrees. Jurors began arriving in sweaters and coats. During the luncheon break no one was near the thermostat, so the temperature rose again to a normal seventy-five degrees. Warmly clad jurors returned for the afternoon session, but the temperature was back up by now.

"I think it took about three weeks before everyone figured out what was going on," one of the lawyers recalled. "At one time, they moved the jurors out of the jury box into chairs on the floor just to get them away from the thermostat."

A key issue early in the trial was admission of the formulas stolen from Danbury. The prosecution had introduced them in an effort to prove continuity of Sardesai's criminal actions between Danbury and Philadelphia. The defense objected, arguing they were extraneous to the case and represented a backdoor way of discrediting Sardesai. The court admitted the Danbury information.

The government later argued, "Sardesai took these formulas surreptitiously from Danbury to Mutual. Sardesai, having these stolen formulas in hand, used them without ever conducting the proper research and development—the absence of which eventually led to the regular manufacturing problems Mutual encountered with numerous products."[26]

On the issue of the Danbury formulas, Recker disagreed. "First of all, it couldn't be proven that he stole them; second, it had no bearing on this case. What we wanted to do, if the government was allowed to let it come in, was to show that the formulas were significantly and substantially different."

The defense argued that Sardesai was actively involved in creating the drug formulas at Danbury, but that "any similarity in certain drugs is due to the fact that the defendant formulated them first at Danbury and then at Mutual; that there are substantial differences in the manufacturing procedures" in the two plants.

A chief government trial witness was an FDA scientist, Dr. Henry J. Malinowski, who provided important testimony linking the fact that many of Mutual's formulas were virtually identical to Danbury's formulas, including some of the formulas for the reworked drugs. "We wanted to show that the reason they were having problems in production is that they had just stolen the formula, pasted it into a different facility, with different equipment, and it didn't work. What they were doing is tinkering in the way you would do before you got approval, but they were doing it afterwards," McDade recalled.

Welsh vigorously contested the Malinowski testimony, saying, "There is no accepted scientific basis for his similarity rating.... Dr. Malinowski is not qualified to render an opinion on the matter of the design of formulations....[27] What Dr. Malinowski has done is to assign an arbitrary similarity rating based upon his examination of, in many cases, simply the contents of the ultimate product manufactured by Danbury and Mutual.... Dr. Malinowski has been an employee of the FDA for many years and therefore has no recent experience whatsoever in the actual design of formulations."

Shah, through counsel Stephen Robert La Cheen, argued a "just a good soldier" defense; specifically, "he personally acted in good faith in reliance upon the orders of his superiors at Mutual Pharmaceutical. Shah maintained he was no different from other blending and tableting production line employees" (none of whom were prosecuted by the government), since he had no reason to question his superiors' justification for the orders he followed.[28] Shah was found not guilty at the trial's end. For Patel, it was a hung jury, and the government decided against a retrial. "We got the two people most responsible," McDade said later. "We had our chance at Kurit Patel and we didn't make it."

The alert defense team moved for a new trial shortly after a jury verdict of guilty was returned against Sardesai and Striefsky, a request granted by Judge Messitte on February 5, 1996. Such motions are frequent but are rarely granted. (Messitte recalled only two other such requests he had granted in fourteen years on the bench.) In this case, Welsh and Recker cited a recent Supreme Court decision, *United States v Gaudin*, 115 S. Ct. 2310 (1995), which held that the "materiality" of false statements was for the jury, not the judge, to decide. Materiality meant the relevance or significance of information presented. Following established Fourth Circuit practice, Judge Messitte had interpreted it as the judge's role to make these determinations, but the Supreme Court decree had now established that this role belonged to the jury. Recker said, "The case was at the Supreme Court at the time we were submitting our case to the jury. It was a very important case for the criminal defense bar because the whole materiality issue is so important." She added, "It was a pretty exciting victory, and I have to credit Judge Messitte with having the courage to grant a new trial. A lot of judges wouldn't have done it."

Messitte explained, "For some reason, there was at that time in the Fourth Circuit no requirement as to instructing the jury about materiality, but the issue was bubbling up to the Supreme Court, and the defense attorneys, knowing that, objected to my use of the Fourth Circuit definition on materiality. So when the Supreme Court decision came down after the trial, they filed a motion for a new trial, and on the basis of that, I thought they were right. They had a good argument, and my problem was, as I looked through the entire case, I thought that issue affected all the possible charges on which the defendants could be convicted. The jury could arguably be confused as to how material the different charges could be, so I granted a new trial."

The prosecution tried to dismiss the lack of implicit instructions to the jury on materiality as a "harmless error," an often-used legal phrase meaning that any judge was allowed to make a slight procedural error that would not otherwise affect the case. The prosecution argued, "The harmless error doctrine serves a very useful purpose insofar as it blocks the setting aside of a conviction for errors or defects that have little, if any, likelihood of changing the result of the trial." But Judge Messitte saw it differently.

Once Judge Messitte had granted a retrial, the government appealed the case to the Fourth Circuit, where it was argued on November 1, 1996, and decided by a three-judge panel about a year later on October 10, 1997. The lower court was affirmed, and the unpublished brief opinion contained no surprises. The Fourth

Circuit judges wrote: "Although we might not, ourselves, reach the same conclusion as the district court regarding whether a new trial is required on each count for which Sardesai and Striefsky were convicted, we do not find that the district court abused its discretion in being cautious and preventing a clear *Gaudin* error from irrevocably affecting the rights of criminal defendants."[29] The heart of the *Gaudin* issue was summarized by the appeals court: "In *Gaudin*, the Supreme Court held that when materiality is an essential element of a crime, it must be decided by the jury and not reserved as a question of law to be decided by the judge."

On October 6, 1998, the new trial of Sardesai and Striefsky began, and, after jury selection, opening statements were made on October 13. On October 28, both defendants entered plea agreements, and on January 29, 1999, both were sentenced. Sardesai pleaded guilty to a count of introducing adulterated drugs into interstate commerce; the remaining counts were dropped. He was sentenced to eight months in jail, fined $20,000, and voluntarily surrendered at the Allenwood Federal Prison in Montgomery, Pennsylvania, on February 26, 1999. Striefsky entered a similar plea and received a four-month sentence and a $20,000 fine. As convicted felons, both were barred from further employment in the pharmaceutical industry. "The ultimate sentence was one that we thought was very fair," Recker said, adding, "In the first trial, the government was looking for a ten-year sentence, which we thought was patently unfair."

In arguing for a lesser sentence for Sardesai, Welsh had petitioned the court: "This defendant has been thoroughly ruined in a professional sense. He has been out of work and virtually unemployable for approximately five years and, upon the imposition of sentence, faces debarment from the pharmaceutical industry for the practical duration of his career.... He has seen the destruction of his health and finds himself, at age 51, having to virtually start all over. Moreover, he faces the prospect of deportation, or at least a substantial risk of that happening. Mr.

Sardesai, perhaps, ill advisedly, maintained his Indian citizenship for ease of passage upon visiting his family in India."[30] As part of the plea-bargaining process, it was agreed that the government would not seek Sardesai's deportation, since his offense level fell below that which would trigger automatic deportation proceedings.

"Sardesai was a strange guy," McDade reflected after the case was over. "Whatever vices he had, sloth wasn't one of them. When he moved to Mutual, it was a big step up. This was a new company, and he was in on the ground floor. He had a chance to make a name for himself in the pharmaceutical industry as Mutual grew. It was a zero-product company when he went there. Money and reputation are what drove him. Sardesai's income may have been $250,000 to $300,000 annually at the top of his game." Now barred from the pharmaceutical industry, he was employed at a homeless shelter shortly before entering prison.

Following the trial, Foreman, who was a prosecutor only in the second trial, was asked if he felt sorry for Sardesai. He thought for a moment, then replied, "Sorry in the sense that even at the end he did not recognize his criminality. This was an individual who was well educated, who had a tremendous understanding of what the pharmaceutical industry was about. But he got caught up in the drive to produce the product rather than understanding what the end result of that product would be if you didn't follow proper formulas."

The same question was asked of McDade. He paused a moment. "Weird as it sounds, yes. Here is this guy. He worked extremely hard. During the first trial, if you went down to central casting looking for the image of the international businessman, there he was. He looked like a young, prosperous, well-dressed, fashion-conscious Omar Sharif. In the second trial, he looked like he had lost forty pounds. We had been told by some people he had been drinking heavily. He had diabetes. His health gave every impression of deteriorating. He looked terrible during the second trial."

Dismantling Desegregation

> *"Twenty-five years ago a bunch of us embarked on a scary journey that changed our lives forever. And now that a judge has agreed this experiment should cease, I have to say the trip was worth taking."*
>
> —*Kevin Mireda,* Washington Post *Staff Writer*

The atmosphere in the ceremonial courtroom was festive, more like a high school graduation than a much-publicized courtroom hearing. African American and white attorneys shook hands, community activists hit each other with high fives, and politicians flooded outside for radio and television interviews.

It would not have been like that twenty-six years ago when the Prince George's County school desegregation suit was first filed, resulting in one of the country's largest busing desegregation orders. The county was "Old South" then, with almost 80 percent of its schools filled with white students, and local and state white politicians, good old boys in Arrow shirts and wide-brimmed hats, stealthily trying to keep it that way. Blacks, and whites sympathetic to their cause, demonstrated and went to court. Huge counterdemonstrations were the response. "It was the most wrenching political experience that I have gone through," Congressman Steny H. Hoyer, then a young state politician, recalled a quarter-century later. "But in point of fact, it did work. There was incredible anger, but not one child or one administrator or parent was injured during the implementation of the busing order." Racial hatred was in the air, sharp words were exchanged, and the papers contained their share of the taunting-white-crowd-jeers-at-silent-black-children photos.

But it was a quarter-century later, August 25, 1998, when Judge Peter Messitte strode into the courtroom and invited the first of seventeen listed community speakers to present their views on a proposed settlement to end the long-lasting suit. First to speak were attorneys for the three contending parties, Sean D. Wallace (county), Andrew W. Nussbaum (school board), and Patricia A. Brannan (NAACP). All said the same thing: The court should now lift its mandatory busing order and get out of the active business of running the county's schools. Also, African Americans had shifted from being a minority to becoming the county's majority population group. The problem now was less one of integration and more one of improving the abysmal quality of the county's schools, ranked twenty-third out of twenty-four school districts in Maryland, one step ahead of the City of Baltimore, which was rock bottom on everyone's list.

One of the presenters was John J. Williams, a retired teacher who spoke with the authority of someone who had lived with the case much of his professional life. Thin, elderly now, but impeccable in a carefully pressed suit and neatly aligned pocket square, Williams had recruited six of the nine original plaintiffs in the 1972 class action desegregation suit known as *Vaughns v Board of Education of Prince George's County*. "We thought Nixon would be elected," he explained. "We knew he opposed busing. This would be our last chance."

The goal was never busing alone, Williams said. "Our purpose was not to integrate—that takes a lifetime—but to break down the legal barriers that kept our children from educational opportunities. We had hand-me-downs. We had three microscopes for the whole school. When the white kids came, we got a whole laboratory. I taught French with one tape recorder. When the whites came, we got a language laboratory."

Speaking with the clarity of a teacher with a thirty-five-year career who had been through the refiner's fire, Williams told the court, "The magnet school program, however unique and beneficial in educational opportunities, failed to achieve the elimination of the vestiges of segregation.... It is not difficult to understand what has happened to the Prince George's County student population since 1972, when enrollment was more than 85 percent white and less than 15 percent African American. With a loss of more than five thousand white students per year because of white flight and massive transfers, we now have the reverse, or about a 77 percent African American student population to 15 percent white. Thus, the demographics dictate change in student assignment, or busing arrangements."[31]

Six days after the hearing, Messitte issued a two-page court order followed by a longer opinion, effectively ending the case. The brief order, suggesting nothing of the case's contentious history, made binding the Memorandum of Understanding and the Comprehensive Plan that the parties had submitted, and moved the case to the court's inactive docket. The opinion expanded on the order, calling the agreement "a fitting denouement to one of the most serious dramas of modern America," but the document's dry legal language hardly reflected the raw human emotion of a generation battling over school desegregation.

Looking back on the intense negotiations and their resolution, Messitte said, "I inherited this case when I came to the federal bench in 1993. I was the only one of the three judges sitting in the Southern Division who wasn't from Prince George's County and that's why I got it. I thought the case was out of focus from the start. The school board was submitting annual reports to me showing the racial composition in each of the various county schools. The NAACP was concerned that the school board wasn't trying hard enough to find qualified non-African American students to fill slots for those races. It became a debate over whether the existing

Memorandum of Understanding of the parties was being breached—in effect, a contract dispute.

"I didn't see it that way. The demographics of the county had shifted radically; the county leadership including the school board was largely African American. You had to wonder, was it likely that these administrators were still doing anything to foster school segregation or not doing enough to mitigate its effects? In the community, parents were highly interested in the quality of education; there was very little enthusiasm on the part of anyone for continued busing. Courts were getting out of school desegregation cases all over the country.

"My thought was, take a comprehensive look at the issues. By then the litigants began to see that this was largely a problem probably resolved through the political process. They also realized that it was a case that couldn't go on forever. It was at that point that I decided to appoint a blue-ribbon panel, neutral and dispassionate, but containing national experts who could tell us what the future of Prince George's County schools might be. They did a road show throughout the county, held hearings, talked with anyone who wanted to meet with them, and made their findings available to the media and the public at libraries and schools, etc. We wanted the widest possibility for public comment.

"All along actually I thought, this is a case that could be resolved outside of a trial. The problem was to get the parties talking to one another. After the December 1997 trial, time was running out. The (Maryland) General Assembly would come into session in early 1998. If they had the expert report and the results of the court proceedings, they would have material to make a political judgment. At that point, it could become a legislative matter, and the court could reduce its role. I convened counsel and asked them if there was anything I could do to get them talking. They said yes. The issues were complex enough and the time demands such that a mediator might be in order. I appointed Larry A. Shulman. He got the parties moving. I waited, remembering what John Dewey once said: 'Keep the lights low, give the ghosts a chance.' Several months later, they had reached an understanding. It was clear we could see the end of the road of the court's involvement in schooling in the county."

A key player in the suit's resolution was the chair of the Prince George's County School Board, Dr. Alvin Thornton, also chair of Howard University's Political Science Department. A transplanted Southerner, Thornton had moved from Alabama to Prince George's County in 1971. The atmosphere at that time was one of massive institutional resistance to change, fed in part by real estate interests wanting to keep things the way they were.

Thornton decided now was the time to resolve the issue. As Williams had a generation earlier cast a cold eye on the Nixon administration's racial desegregation policies, Thornton believed the anti-busing decisions of the Rehnquist-Thomas court would prove equally restrictive.

Also, the older civil rights generation was giving way to newer, more affluent African Americans less interested in continuing the struggle with the same intensity. "We had to create a window of opportunity to give the political system a chance," Thornton reflected, adding, "The most important thing Judge Messitte did was to give local decision-makers a chance to come up with what was in their interests."

The magnet schools were not working. The magnet school concept initially caught hold when thousands of parents of all races tried to register their children in the newly designated schools, hoping for better educations. However, the schools were soon seen as Potemkin villages in a declining educational system. Prince George's County had undergone a tectonic shift in school populations across a quarter-century. Whereas the county of 660,000 persons was 85 percent white in 1970, by 1996 it was 100,000 more citizens, but only 26 percent of them were white. In twenty-six years, 350,000 whites left the county, and 430,000 African Americans moved into it or were born there.[32]

Broadly stated, a magnet school is a school in a predominantly black district expanded, enriched, and enhanced with attractive educational offerings it didn't have before. "Mirror" magnet schools are also designated in white districts to attract African American students. Students are then bused from their neighborhoods to magnet schools. That is the plan.

In Prince George's County, the magnet schools' tragic flaw was that, although a few participants in them received excellent educations, most students continued to slip on test scores. "There is no such thing as a good magnet program in an average school system," Thornton concluded.[33] Neither busing nor magnet schools achieved their desired goals, and the original lawsuit that produced both was dead in the water. More bad news: In 1978, Prince George's County passed a Proposition 13–type resolution, TRIM, freezing property taxes but also eliminating them as a source of additional school revenues.

After the case was reopened in July 1996, Messitte appointed a panel of independent education experts led by Dr. Robert E. Shoenberg, former dean for undergraduate studies at the University of Maryland, College Park, and a former member of the Board of Education of Montgomery County. After visits to more than fifty schools, the panel concluded: "Much remains to be done to improve educational outcomes for African American students and to raise this level of student performance generally. But those results are more likely to be achieved through the efforts of the schools and the community, with the support of state and county governments, not through the agency of the Court."[34]

The expert report was a prelude to the two-week trial Messitte scheduled for the first half of December 1997, at which the parties would made their last best pitch. Plaintiff NAACP argued for continued court supervision and for more extensive court-ordered remedies to address the inequities it believed resulted from past segregationist policies. The school board and the county said it was time for the court to end the suit, because as much as could be done to remedy the effects of segregation had been done through the courts. A new approach was needed.

Each side buried itself in statistics, charts, bar graphs, line graphs, and lengthy analytical commentary. Each side lined up its experts, veterans all of many other school desegregation lawsuits.

The trial went forward, with less fanfare than might have been expected. When Prince George's County Executive Wayne Curry testified near the trial's end, the seats were filled. Otherwise, only a handful of observers were on hand from day to day. When counsel concluded just before Christmas, Messitte announced he would take the matter under advisement and render a decision by May 1. The parties were given thirty days to file proposed findings of fact and law and reply briefs. Messitte closed the proceedings by urging the parties "as strongly as possible" to try and settle the case.

The timing—as the judge later admitted—was anything but coincidental, for in early January 1998, the Maryland General Assembly would convene. If a political deal was to be found that would put money into Prince George's schools and settle the long-standing court case once and for all, the time was now. Also, 1998 was an election year, and Governor Parris Glendening, a former Prince George's County executive who had lived with court-ordered school busing, was up for reelection.

The key period in resolving the suit was between December 1997 and June 1998. To consolidate issues, Messitte appointed a leading Montgomery County lawyer, Lawrence A. Shulman, a real estate attorney, former president of the Maryland State Board of Education, and Washingtonian of the Year. Of medium height and with wound-up energy, Shulman combined bulldog tenacity with unflappableness. If there is such a thing as reincarnation, the immensely successful commercial real estate attorney might emerge as an elementary school principal who is always gesturing, maintains lively eye contact with everyone in the room, is rarely far from a blackboard, and speaks of "the kids" as if they were the county's most important people.

A judicial settlement would have been meaningless without funding for new schools, and the issue of funding the settlement was a hot topic in the general assembly during the winter of 1998. Legislators were prepared to allocate some money for schools, but only with significant accountability measures attached. County

Executive Wayne Curry was especially combative in this regard and wanted all power to rest with the county. He was also highly critical of his predecessor, Governor Parris Glendening, who had worked hard to move the political solution of the complex problem toward resolution. Messitte recalled, "My appointment of Larry Shulman came at a point somewhere in the legislative session when it looked like the parties weren't going to get it together on their own. It was something like a peace treaty—you need an outside mediator.

"Shulman reported to me on a fairly regular basis during the negotiations not to tell me what the shifting positions of the parties were, just to let me know the parties were in fact talking and making progress, and to take back the message to them the judge had said, 'Keep at it.'"

Shulman's negotiating technique was simple. In complex commercial real estate deals, he observed, "you have to make it a win-win situation for all parties, otherwise someone will get even. This is a three-, five-, ten-, or twenty-year arrangement, and if one party is unhappy with it, it won't work. I always go over the agreement line-by-line, word by word, and I use a white board or a blackboard because they make people visually aware of what they are doing. You don't want unhappy participants in a negotiation."

In addition to heading his own sixty-seven-lawyer firm, Shulman had been the deal-maker in the construction of many shopping malls, hotels, apartments, warehouses, and commercial buildings around Washington during the past quarter-century. His grandmother was both a Jewish businesswoman and a civic activist; his father was a successful dentist who founded a Jewish dental association when the District of Columbia Dental Society denied him membership (he later became the latter's president after its policies changed). Shulman grew up believing improving society was just as important as making money, which led him to as many educational, artistic, and civic boards of directors as banks and chambers of commerce.

Though not a politician, Shulman knew the corridors of power well. The judge had known Shulman from the days when Messitte was a circuit court judge in Montgomery County and was a longtime admirer of Shulman's skills as a negotiator. Once he received the basic Memorandum of Understanding drawn up by the contending parties, Shulman spent a weekend reading it, then scheduled a session for February 4, 1998, with all participants in the spacious downtown Washington offices of Hogan & Hartson, a blue-chip firm representing the NAACP. Shulman kept the lawyers, the county executive, and the school board representatives there until midnight, narrowing the issues, shuttling between working groups, bringing them together for brief meetings on specific points, getting the agreement in writing, then moving to the next point.

"I had a chart, because if people can see things, they can hold the ideas better," Shulman recalled. "As they told me things, I broke them down: eight or ten 'typos,' not major points, but something someone didn't like; six to eight mid-level issues; and two monstrous issues. We got through the typos fairly quickly; people wanted 'plaintiff' changed to 'county,'" things like that. The middle-range issues took longer, and the parties moved to breakout rooms. Sometimes the issues were between two parties, sometimes between all three. "I walked between the rooms to get an idea of what their thoughts were. There was give and take, but they weren't big issues, but legitimate questions that bothered people. By late afternoon we were left with one mid-level and two massive issues."

The two big issues involved (1) Whether the case should be brought to an end and (2) school construction. The NAACP did not want to end the case because it didn't trust the politicians to deliver on their promises to build new and better schools. The county wanted to end the case because the reality of a court-supervised school system drove off potential businesses and affluent persons from settling there. Regarding the school construction issue, the county executive wanted to build the schools, arguing his office was better equipped to do so than the school board. The board argued they were the elected representatives of the people and this was their mandate, even if the money came from the county council.

By early evening, attorney Patricia Brannan and the NAACP suggested a compromise—if everything else could be agreed to, why not ask the judge to move the case to his inactive docket? Brannan, who heads Hogan & Hartson's national educational practice, which includes numerous school desegregation cases, recalled, "It occurred to me there must be a creative way to both keep the issue alive but end the present dispute. I suggested moving it to an 'inactive docket,' not knowing whether or not such a thing existed." That way, the court case was over but could be revived if the terms of the Memorandum of Understanding were not complied with.

Shulman crafted the needed language. "If you have momentum, use it," he recalled. "In one day, we resolved it all. I don't believe you give up. You don't let people out the door, you don't let them go to the bathroom. If you've got the momentum, go with it. That doesn't mean people were happy with me, but the judge said I was in charge, so I kept them there," along with the law firm's secretarial staff, which churned out clean draft language until late of night. Shulman wanted every word agreed to before ending the session.

By midnight, agreement had been reached; the twenty-six-year impasse was over, assuming funds for the new schools were forthcoming and the court approved the passage. "We were fortunate," Shulman recalled. "We all wanted the same thing, better schools for the kids, and a level of trust had been built up among the negotiating parties. Later, when they all had to face the governor, they did so in a united way."

"It was a pretty tough meeting," Brannan recalled, "but basically the people had a lot of respect for one another. We had been dealing on the up-and-up." Of Shulman's role she said, "He never gave people a chance to backslide. It got to be a joke among us. It was clear we weren't walking out of there until there was language on paper. It was a tough group working on tough issues. "

Two obstacles remained—obtaining agreement from the full county school board and the governor and legislature. School board approval was soon granted, but there remained the major hurdle of finding state funding for what the parties had agreed to—building sixteen new schools and upgrading others, plus increasing teacher salaries.

The Memorandum of Understanding called for a total of $300 million, part of it in matching state and county funds. Eventually, the legislature provided enough money to fund thirteen schools, with the prospect of additional funding. By July the legislature had approved the additional funds—it was an election year and the state had a budget surplus. After almost three decades of litigation, seven months of recent negotiation, and a breakthrough fifteen-hour marathon session, the issue was solved.

The heart of the Memorandum of Understanding focused on improving student achievement, particularly achievement by African American students. There was no sense in stopping the buses from moving horizontally across the county if student academic achievement didn't mount vertically. This would be realized through five specific actions: (1) continuing the magnet schools with modifications; (2) beefing up the educational programs in "racially isolated schools," sometimes called "racially non-diverse schools," essentially single-race schools; (3) phasing out current mandatory student assignments as new schools were built and old ones renovated; (4) accountability for the academic progress of African American students, aimed at improving academic performance, reducing drop-out rates, and increasing graduation rates, plus hiring more African American faculty and staff, and increasing the quality and developmental prospects of teachers in general; and (5) capital funding. The state would provide additional capital funding of $35 million each year for the next four years, and the county $32 million in each of those years for school construction and improvement. Without the additional funding, there would have been no settlement.

Assuming such goals could be realized, the parties agreed to jointly ask the court to remove the case from its active docket. Then the terms of the Memorandum of Understanding were translated into a Comprehensive Plan, as detailed as the order of battle for any military campaign, including a timeline with completion dates for each activity and plans for monitoring every step. Slowly but surely the issue was being moved from the courts to the political arena. "I never called this an end-of-busing decision; I always said it was about community development," Thornton remarked. "We asked the court to continue supervision of this case until 2002, allowing programs to be in place to improve the skills of the students and teachers and to build more and better schools."

It all came together on August 31, 1998, when Judge Messitte approved the proposed settlement. "The parties' disagreements have been strongly and fully expressed," the opinion stated. The settlement will "preserve the benefits of desegregation where practicable but phase out mandatory student assignments, most of which no longer promote desegregation, as additional classroom space becomes available closer to students' homes. This is a fair and reasonable resolution.... It will also, all things considered, serve the educational needs of Prince George's County as a whole as it enters the 21st Century." [35]

Kevin Merida, a *Washington Post* writer, was a student in Prince George's County the day the buses first rolled in January 1973. He was required to be ready each morning at 6:00 A.M. to travel twelve and a half miles from a predominantly African American to a predominately white school in the middle of basketball season. "Here I was in tenth grade, thriving as a student-athlete at Central High School, surrounded by familiar faces from my Seat Pleasant neighborhood, intoxicated by our rock-and-roll cheerleading squad, loving the vibe of a nearly all-black school (92 percent), even though Central—with its constant disruptions—often seemed hilariously chaotic. Some things you overlook at 15."[36]

Merida weighed the pluses and minuses of the busing experiment. "I readily admit to conflicted feelings about my own twenty-five-mile round trip to high school," he concluded, adding,

"Twenty-five years ago a bunch of us embarked on a scary journey that changed our lives forever. And now that a judge has agreed this experiment should cease, I have to say the trip was worth taking."

Williams, retired now but still working as a substitute language teacher, thinks so too. Now he lives in a predominantly African American county with much higher economic and educational levels, plus an influx of Africans, Asians, Europeans, and Latin Americans. One of his two sons married a Jewish girl and moved over to Montgomery County; the other took an Ethiopian name and gave his two children Ethiopian names. "It's the old people who see race. There is not a clash between blacks and whites like in the 1970s. Go to a prom or a social event at a school. You'll see what I'm talking about. The young people don't think about color."

Breakfast at Denny's

The $35,000 Meal That Never Arrived

> *"What we're trying to do through all the lessons we have learned—obviously difficult lessons—is to get people to talk about race."*
>
> *—Jim Anderson, new head of the corporation that bought Denny's*

The president was coming to the Naval Academy that morning to speak, and the uniformed Secret Service detail gathered at Andrews Air Force Base at 6:30 A.M. for roll call. It was April 1, 1993, and the twenty-one-officer unit needed to have the magnetometer sites operating by 9:30 A.M., which meant arriving at the academy an hour earlier. It would be a big crowd and a full morning of activity, so the seven African Americans, one Hispanic, and thirteen white officers stopped for a quick breakfast at Denny's, just outside of Annapolis, not far from the academy.

All twenty-one members of the detail, led by Lieutenant James E. Suber, an African American, arrived at Denny's dressed in full Secret Service uniforms—black shoes, black pants with wide gold stripes on the outside, white shirt with gold badge and presidential patch, black tie, gun belt and sidearms—looking and acting like an elite unit.

The Denny's Restaurant at 2095 West Street in Annapolis, one of 1,460 Denny's restaurants around the country, is a sit-down establishment, different from a fast-food chain, although the smells may be the same. Waitresses take food orders at the tables, send them to the kitchen, and deliver the prepared food. According to court documents, a Denny's hostess directed all twenty-one members of the detail to the same corner of the restaurant. The officers seated themselves at several tables and booths. Six African American officers sat together in a large booth, the remaining officers nearby. (Lieutenant Suter was at a table with some white officers.) A white waitress named Sherry and another waitress took orders from all twenty-one officers, progressing from table to table and taking the African American table's order last. By 7:40, they had finished writing the breakfast orders, the African American officers said in court documents.

The six officers selected breakfasts similar to those ordered by other members of the detail. Like their Secret Service colleagues, all six ordered juice, coffee, and/or other beverages, which were served by 7:45 A.M. And by 7:50 A.M., every member of the detail, except the six African American officers, was served the food they had ordered. At about 8:00 A.M., one of the African American officers got up from the booth to inquire about their order and was told it was on its way.

A few minutes later, between 8:05 and 8:10 A.M., they noticed that three or four white people who had come into the restaurant as a group at least twenty minutes after the Secret Service detail arrived had already been served their food. According to the Secret Service officer's deposition that arose from the incident, "Plaintiffs (the six African American officers) decided that they should speak with the waitress again, and Officer Robin D. Thompson got up and asked the waitress to come over to the booth. The waitress complied. When plaintiffs asked about their orders, the waitress stated that customers were being served in the order that their orders had been taken. The waitress then walked away from the booth.[37]

"As the waitress walked away from the plaintiffs' booth, she walked past Officer William Winans, a white member of the Secret Service detail who was seated at a nearby table. Officer Winans observed the waitress roll her eyes as she walked away from the plaintiffs' booth. When she reached the counter, the waitress made a comment to employees working in the kitchen area that mocked plaintiffs' request for service." Meanwhile, second orders from the all-you-can-eat breakfast special were served to other members of the detail.

At about 8:15, the six officers still had not been served any food. Officer Thompson told the waitress the officers would like to speak with the manager. The waitress headed toward the back of the restaurant and spoke with the manager. Meanwhile, the officers also advised Lieutenant Suber they were having difficulty being served. Suber told them to gather the information necessary to file a complaint.

At about 8:20, the waitress returned and told the six the manager was on the telephone. "The waitress promised that the manager would be right out and offered plaintiffs fruit and more juice while they waited. Plaintiffs declined the offer as an inadequate substitute for the hot food they had ordered.

"By approximately 8:25 A.M., all of the other members of the Secret Service detail had finished eating and were in the process of paying for their meals and leaving the restaurant. Even though the plaintiffs had not received their breakfast orders and had not been contacted by the manager, they knew that they were expected to leave along with the rest of the detail, and they started to get up from their seats. The detail's schedule required an imminent departure for the Naval Academy to begin setting up the magnetometer equipment."

As the six men began to leave, the waitress arrived with a single tray of food. They told her it was too late for them to sit back down and eat breakfast. After offering to pay for the juice they had been served earlier, they repeated an earlier request to speak with the manager. As the Secret Service detail waited for the manager in the front of the restaurant, near the cash register, one of the cooks told them their food had been ready, sitting under heat lamps on the restaurant counter, during the time they were waiting to be served.

According to the plaintiffs' court document, "Shortly thereafter, the manager, who identified himself to the plaintiffs as 'D.L. Nasser,' came out to speak with the plaintiffs. Plaintiffs asked the manager for the address of the regional office of Denny's. The manager gave plaintiffs a false address in an effort to deceive plaintiffs and hinder their efforts to seek redress for the discriminatory treatment they had suffered. The plaintiffs unwittingly wrote down the false address the manager gave them," which turned out to be the address of the restaurant, not the regional office.

All twenty-one members left the Denny's parking lot together at approximately 8:35 A.M. On the way to the Naval Academy, they stopped by a Roy Rogers restaurant where those who had not been served at Denny's grabbed some fast food to eat in their van en route to prepare for the presidential visit.

If an establishment was going to practice racial discrimination, it would be wiser to try it on something other than a unit of twenty-one uniformed Secret Service officers. The six African American agents filed a complaint, buttressed by corroborating individual declarations from other black and white members of the detail, written in the language of trained investigators.

On May 24, 1993, through the Washington Lawyers' Committee for Civil Rights and Urban Affairs, the six officers filed suit against Denny's, seeking a jury trial on the discrimination charges plus compensatory and punitive monetary damages. The Department of Justice's Civil Rights Division, after reviewing the complaints, joined the suit. The Washington Lawyers' Committee for Civil Rights and Urban Affairs, which had litigated many class action civil rights lawsuits, had earlier won what at the time was the largest class action settlement fund ever obtained in a public accommodations case, $6,320,000 in *Kernan v Holiday Universal, Inc.* (1990). They were joined by Hogan & Hartson, a major Washington firm. The plaintiffs were not lacking in legal firepower.

The lead lawyer in the case for the Washington Lawyers' Committee was John P. Relman, a Harvard and University of

Michigan Law School graduate and product of Philadelphia Quaker schools, with a deep commitment to civil rights law. The walls of his new law firm's offices were filled with reproductions of historic civil rights shots—lunch-counter sit-ins, Martin Luther King Jr. addressing a church gathering, Rosa Parks, students confronting white cracker cops—a photo tour of recent American history. Relman, with thirteen years of experience in housing and employment discrimination law, was struck by two aspects of the Denny's case: how close it was to the issues usually associated with a fair housing case, and how creditable the testimony of the Secret Service agents was. If there ever was a case of its kind worth trying, this would be it.

The charges were carefully crafted and comprehensive, stating that on April 1, 1993, the defendants, acting through their employees, agents, and/or representatives, refused to serve, or otherwise denied, the plaintiffs food because of their race, actions that were taken with racially discriminatory animus. The discriminatory practices were carried out at the direction of and with the consent, encouragement, knowledge, and ratification of the defendants, the charge continued, under the defendants' authority, control, and supervision.

The complaint also sought a permanent injunction against Denny's barring the corporation from engaging in illegally discriminatory conduct, and a permanent injunction directing Denny's to "take all affirmative steps necessary to remedy the effects of the illegally discriminatory conduct," "award compensatory damages in an amount that would fully compensate plaintiffs for the economic loss, humiliation, embarrassment, emotional distress, and mental anguish caused by defendants' violations of the law," and award punitive damages.

News of the incident mushroomed in the national media, and blacks from all over the United States began writing and calling the Lawyers' Committee, complaining of not being served at Denny's. This caused the plaintiffs to file an amended complaint, making it a class action suit rather than an individual suit. Investigators claimed to have turned up persuasive evidence of fifty incidents of racial discrimination against more than 160 African American customers at thirty-three Denny's restaurants in twelve states. The suit had moved far from 2095 West Street in Annapolis.

Denny's responded vigorously though its lawyers and press releases. First came a May 22, 1993, press release about the "alleged discriminatory incident": "Our company does not tolerate discrimination of any kind and we take any charge of discrimination seriously. A toll-free number is posted in every Denny's restaurant inviting guests to call our headquarters on any issue that is not satisfactorily resolved by our local management. We are disappointed it has taken over six weeks to learn of these serious allegations and we have not had the chance to investigate and respond prior to any further action."

Two days later Denny's dashed off another press release, saying the manager of the Annapolis restaurant was fired for failing to report the discrimination complaint, and the incident was "a problem of slow service and not racial bias."

Denny's counsel, the Washington law firm of Latham & Watkins, responded on June 30, 1993, to the Housing and Civil Enforcement Section of the Department of Justice's Civil Rights Division with a preliminary report stating the failure to provide prompt service "was a result of the large size of the party...the time at which the orders were taken from the six men as compared to the rest of the detail, and the large number of customers in the restaurant due to a new 'All You Can Eat' promotion the restaurant had begun two days earlier. We have not discovered any facts suggesting that any events at the Denny's Annapolis restaurant on April 1, 1993, were racially motivated."[38]

The report continued: "The orders were transmitted to the fry-line for preparation at 8:04:31 A.M. The kitchen was one cook short that morning and Sherry realized that the orders for the six men were delayed in comparison to the orders of the others in their party. She went to the table, apologized to the men, and gave them complimentary refills of juice, even though company policy requires that customers pay for extra juice." The men asked to see the manager, and the information was twice relayed to Tom Nasser, who was on the phone. "It was Tom's usual practice to place his weekly phone order every Thursday morning between 8:00 and 9:00 A.M." By Denny's estimates, the food was ready by 8:23 A.M., just as the detail was leaving.

As for the final exchange with the manager, Denny's offered the following version: "During our investigation, the manager stated that he then understood one of the officers to ask him for the address of the Annapolis restaurant, which he gave him, but the officer stated that he wanted the District Leader's address. Tom went to his office to retrieve the District Leader's address, but the officer replied that he would rather call the restaurant later for this information. Tom wrote the restaurant's phone number on the same piece of paper on which the officer had originally written the restaurant's address, and again apologized to the men, inviting them back to the restaurant for a free meal."

Denny's corporate headquarters was unaware of the April 1 events at the Annapolis restaurant until May 1993.

Denny's concluded: "All of the employees involved in the above-described series of events adamantly deny that they were in any manner racially motivated.... Sherry stated in the course of our investigation that she expected to earn a substantial tip from table 13/14 because of the size of the order and therefore had every motivation to provide attentive service."

The Denny's Annapolis suit, and the media attention it attracted, focused public and legal attention on the restaurant chain. Ironically, the same day the six black Secret Service agents sat foodless at Denny's was the day a federal court in California approved a class action settlement between the Department of

Justice and Denny's over widespread charges of racial discrimination at Denny's restaurants in that state. Meanwhile, in Washington, the Secret Service asked Denny's for an explanation, and at the White House, George Stephanopoulos, presidential communications director, said, "Discrimination against black Secret Service agents would be a very serious problem."[39] A TV news anchor weighed in: "These agents put their lives on the line every day, but they can't get served at Denny's." An article in *The New York Times Magazine* of November 6, 1994, chronicled Denny's poor racial relations, and elsewhere Denny's was listed among the Ten Worst Corporations of 1994. Denny's was on its way to becoming a household name.

On November 1, 1993, a year and a half after the Annapolis encounter, the case was assigned to Judge Deborah K. Chasanow, who was still in Baltimore before the Greenbelt Court opened. By then both sides were interested in reaching a settlement; January 13, 1994, was set as the date for a settlement conference before Magistrate Judge Catherine C. Blake. Magistrate judges assist district judges in doing much of the preliminary work on such cases and Judge Blake spent many hours with both parties over the next four months hammering out an agreement, leading to a settlement hearing before Judge Chasanow on August 5, 1994.

As part of the negotiations, a litigation moratorium took effect, shutting off additional lawsuits. By then, the plaintiffs had amassed allegations of discrimination against 1,200 victims at more than 170 Denny's restaurants in thirty-six states outside of California. Former employees said they were trained to discriminate against black customers; African American customers provided examples of discrimination; white customers claimed they had witnessed discriminatory practices. The California class action case, which Denny's settled through a $28 million consent decree, was originally brought by thirty-two African American customers, who complained of Denny's "blackout" policy—of managers telling employees to limit the number of black customers when they became disproportionate to whites.

The heart of the proposed consent decree was a $17,725,000 settlement fund, making this one of the largest monetary awards in a public accommodations discrimination lawsuit, and the most sweeping injunctive terms ever obtained by the Justice Department or private plaintiffs in a public accommodations discrimination case.

The decree covered all Denny's restaurants outside of California, imposing monitoring obligations that would stay in place for five to seven years, including training programs for all Denny's managers and employees. An independent civil rights monitor would oversee comprehensive compliance, record keeping and reporting, training and testing, and advertising provisions. The decree also provided for a forty-nine-state settlement class. Applicants, if certified eligible, would receive compensation from the $17,725,000 settlement fund. The six black officers who filed the case received $35,000 each, and twelve additional plaintiffs to the class action suit were awarded $15,000 each, the difference reflecting the amount of time and involvement in the suit invested by each.

A $2.1 million media plan targeted black audiences, telling them they were welcome at Denny's, and a nationwide notice campaign was launched, informing members of the affected class of procedures for filing claims. Finally, the decree provided for payment of $1.9 million in attorneys' fees and expenses for the plaintiffs, slightly less than 10 percent of the total settlement costs.

Although Judge Blake had done much of the preliminary work, the law required a district judge to approve the settlement. Judge Chasanow had several issues to examine, in particular to see if the negotiated agreement was fair and adequate.[40] Additionally, she would look at the "case at the time settlement is proposed, the extent of discovery that has been conducted, the circumstances surrounding the negotiations, and the experience of counsel," she recalled.

"Here, I don't think there is any question. There certainly has been no suggestion of any collusion. Quite to the contrary, I am aware from the proceedings that this was very definitely an arm's-length negotiation process. Judge Blake, as has been mentioned, was intimately involved in at least certain portions of the discussions. I know that they were lengthy and went on over a relatively long period of time as settlement negotiations go.

"The adequacy of the proposed settlement is the other aspect that I must look at," the judge concluded. "Settlement was far better than going forward with litigation, for a variety of reasons. The injunctive relief was also, obviously, a very important aspect of this litigation. It went a long way to making sure that the allegations of the plaintiffs in this case were not going to ever happen again at Denny's—and, we hope, by the publicity, anywhere."

Of the class action aspect of the suit, Judge Chasanow said, "It is to include within the action or the litigation all people who are similarly situated, because it is impractical for everyone to come forward initially and file his or her own lawsuit.... It is really of necessity that we give notice and we try to bring in to the settlement procedure here all of those who can legitimate a claim that they were discriminated against during the appropriate time period—in this case, in any Denny's restaurant, outside of California, in this country."

The basic period was set; claims would be considered for discrimination between July 1, 1987, and May 24, 1994, and all claims had to be filed by September 24, 1994. Not every claim would be accepted at face value, and obviously the scent of money would result in false claims. Procedures were put in place to evaluate claims, and a dispute mechanism established, including appeals to the court. "So, while we recognize that there is a danger that there may be people who try to take advantage of this situation, we expect that they will not be successful," Judge Chasanow noted.

In addition to monetary damages, Denny's agreed to train all of its employees on both the antidiscrimination requirements of federal civil rights laws and racial sensitivity and cultural diversity. The company also paid for an independent testing agency to conduct 450 anonymous tests at Denny's restaurants each year to determine whether the defendants were discriminating against African American customers. An internal disciplinary system was created and a civil rights monitor was hired to review Denny's performance of its obligations under the consent decree.

Each of the 136,014 persons included on the Final List of Qualified Applicants in the *Dyson v Denny's* case was awarded $132.28 in full payment of his or her share of the class settlement fund. The sum was arrived at by dividing the settlement figure by the number of claims, less attorneys' fees and case costs. (Seven thousand of the checks were returned as undeliverable, but 2,000 were re-mailed to addresses provided by the post office or claimants.) Approximately $900,000 remained unclaimed. Both sides petitioned the court to award $100,000 each to the National Association for the Advancement of Colored People, the National Urban League, the Leadership Conference on Civil Rights, and similar groups.

Four years later, both sides were satisfied the major issues in the suit had been resolved. On September 22, 1998, Judge Chasanow signed a decree, submitted by both sides, seeking to move the monitoring function from an independent Office of Civil Rights to Advantica, the new parent company of Denny's, since the company had made its commitment clear to incorporating numerous aspects of the monitoring functions contained in the decree as a regular part of their business operations.[41] Eight months later, in May 1999, both parties asked for termination of the Office of Civil Rights monitor and early dismissal of the court action. The May 4 decree, approved by the judge, came just before the fifth anniversary of the original court order. Both sides scheduled transfer of the training programs, spot testing, and customer complaint and investigative functions to Denny's.

■

Can a corporation change its spots? By all accounts, Denny's, a name once synonymous with racism for many people, became a model corporation for its radically different treatment of customers and employee training programs. A new generation of top management both turned its precipitous losses around and reengineered its racial performance. "What we're trying to do through all the lessons we have learned—obviously difficult lessons—is to get people to talk about race," said Jim Anderson, new head of the corporation that owns Denny's, five years after the settlement was reached.[42] Through ads, internal management changes, training programs for its 50,000 employees, and working closely with groups such as the National Association for the Advancement of Colored People, Denny's changed. In 1999, minorities comprised 48 percent of the corporation's workforce and 33 percent of its management. Although only one Denny's was owned by a black franchisee in 1993, when Officer Dyson and his companions walked into the Annapolis restaurant, in 1999 there were 123 black-owned franchises, and the numbers were increasing. Denny's created a program allowing qualified minority applicants who complete a rigorous training program to buy a franchise with a loan guaranteed by Denny's.[43]

Relman reflected on the case after its completion. "The thing that is amazing about this case is that Denny's has become a laboratory for race relations in America." A minimally paid workforce constantly exposed to a high-pressure, high-volume working environment has become, in the plaintiffs' attorney's phrase, "a crucible for race relations." And Denny's, once near the brink of financial disaster, under new management has been making money by the fistful, appealing to an interracial dining clientele.

One gray Saturday morning, six years after the Secret Service detail stopped there, I pulled into the parking lot at 2095 West Street in Annapolis. Next to a Big & Tall Casual Male shop and a detached truck body advertising "Mattress Warehouse—Sleep Happens" is

Denny's, a 1950s stainless steel and plastic panel building with huge plate glass windows and period middle-America light fixtures. In bulging his-and-her T-shirts, two chunky customers moved through the glass doors, his meaty hand resting comfortably on her shoulder. Attempting to blend into the crowd, I bought a paper yesterday's, it turned out. Susan, a white waitress past middle years, seated me, providing amiable banter. It was 7:30, the time the Secret Service detail entered the same restaurant starting the multi-state class action lawsuit that changed Denny's racial practices.

"Which is booth thirteen?" I asked casually.

"The one in the corner," Susan replied, her pale blue eyes now focusing on me. Change the subject, I thought.

"What is your most popular breakfast?"

"The Grand Slam." Susan was relaxed now. The Grand Slam was among the breakfasts the six African American officers of the U.S. Secret Service, Uniformed Division detail, tried to order on April 1, 1993, and never received. It was now 7:40. The place was crowded, but service took only ten minutes. Most of the customers and serving staff were white, but African Americans were not lacking. The fry-line was all black; so was James, the dishwasher, who joked easily with Susan, who chatted casually with her African American customers, neighborhood regulars.

A black waitress delivered my food, and a black threesome sat at the table opposite me, making easy conversation with the white couple next to them. Nearby, an interracial family tucked into a huge pile of eggs, breakfast meats, pancakes, and home fries. Denny's is not a place for tofu-and-sprouts enthusiasts. An inveterate menu reader, I leafed through the richly illustrated plastic-covered menu to the back page, with its racial disclaimer and the historic note showing the first Denny's—the architecture was unchanged—in Lakewood, California, in 1953. "People were taking to the road in record numbers—and bringing their appetites with them. They pulled over to Denny's." Then, modern times:

"Welcome back to Denny's.... Although you never really left, did you?" Yes, I did, and so did America, so did its racial attitudes, and now so have Denny's racial policies.

Joining the checkout line, I read the blue and white plastic sign screwed into the Formica panel near the cash register. "Denny's is committed to providing the best possible service to all customers regardless of race, creed, color, or national origin." A cheerful cashier with a tattoo on her right hand counted my change. At 8:35 A.M., the same time the Secret Service detail headed west for the Naval Academy and the presidential visit, I turned east toward Route 50 and pulled into traffic.

Linwood (Big Boy) Gray

From "Chicken Places" to Crack Cocaine

"Sure, I was a bad kid, but I'm not a bad man."
—Linwood Gray

Drug cases are a staple of the American court system, accounting for 16 percent of the Greenbelt criminal docket. Their numbers increase as Congress makes more and more drug crimes federal offenses without increasing the number of police, prosecutors, and judges to process what are often dangerous, complicated crimes.

Take the case of Linwood (Big Boy) Gray, fifty, sentenced by Judge Chasanow on December 21, 1995, to thirty-three and a half years in prison after a six-week drug trial in which he and three others were found guilty. Gray was charged with: (1) conspiracy to distribute heroin and cocaine, plus criminal forfeiture (loss of his "ill-gotten gains," estimated by the prosecution at $1,150,000 in drug revenues, and piles of expensive rings and watches); (2) witness retaliation (on which he was acquitted); (3) attempted murder in aid of racketeering (charge dropped on petition of the defense, and approved by the judge; basically, other charges were easier to prove than this one, which would require proof of a collaborative criminal enterprise beyond the drug enterprise); (4) distribution of heroin and cocaine; and (5) possession with intent to distribute heroin, plus aiding and abetting a criminal activity.

All bases in the drug count were covered in the indictment—conspiracy, possession, and distribution. On each count, the Sentencing Guidelines, which judges must adhere to, provided stiff penalties. For example, because at least one kilogram of heroin was involved, the minimum sentence would be ten years without parole, with a maximum of life.

Drugs and crime had been the fabric of Gray's life since childhood; so had bank robberies and armed robberies of "chicken places," his name for fast-food outlets. After robbing drugstores as a teenager, Gray's adult criminal record began in 1963 at age eighteen.[44] Growing up in the crime-ridden Garfield Heights section of Southeast Washington, he was a boxer and a bully with a mean stare and an arrogant manner. He liked baiting police, who called the six-foot-one, 250-pound muscular youth "Big Boy" or "Bruiser." If a neighborhood disturbance involved Gray, police sent several officers, never just one, an officer later recalled.

Arrests for petty larceny and possession of a pistol were followed by charges of robbery, forgery, and physical assault of a probation officer. Found not guilty by reason of insanity on the assault charges, Gray spent six years in St. Elizabeth's mental hospital before being given a conditional release in April 1974 to attend school, which he never did. Gray wrote to a friend from St. Elizabeth's that he feigned insanity, allowing him to beat the charges against him.

Bullying court officials was part of his repertoire, and his manner on the street was the same as the way he conducted himself in court. At a preliminary hearing on drug charges, he told the magistrate judge, Henry J. Kennedy Jr., an African American, "You claim you're a Kennedy; you're not a Kennedy.... You can be Governor Wallace or somebody but not a Kennedy."[45] In another instance, he struck a probation officer in court. Later he told a judge he was not a hostile person. "Sure, I was a bad kid, but I'm not a bad man." (When arrested, Gray's wallet contained pictures of his heroes—

not sport figures, but Al Capone, Lucky Luciano, Crazy Joe Gallo, and Vito Genovese.)

Gray's first citywide notoriety came in 1979, when he was charged with masterminding a $30 million international heroin-smuggling ring, the largest such operation ever prosecuted in the District of Columbia. The elaborate operation included regular trips (by others) to Amsterdam, where they picked up the drugs, sealed in fake Marlboro flip-top cigarette packages, then flew back first class to airports in Chicago, Boston, or other cities, thus avoiding New York or Washington airports, which were more prone to drug surveillance. At trial, Gray told the jury the $300,000 he had spent in recent years came not from drug sales but from money carefully saved from earlier bank robberies. Gray also bought three houses for a total cost of $200,000, although his only listed employment was a $14,000 job at the dumpy Club Camelot, a front for drug sales, at 3859 Alabama Avenue, S.E. (It burned to the ground during one of Gray's trials; police suspected arson.)[46]

During this drug trial, prosecutors wore flak vests. One was hit in front of the courthouse by a cyanide-drenched bullet in an assassination attempt.

Gray was convicted of only four of the original fifty-two offenses, two counts of attempting to evade taxes and two of willfully filing a false tax return, and received a twenty-month prison sentence, although prosecutors believed they had presented an ironclad case. This was a case of jury nullification, many observers believed. The judge would not allow the prosecution to introduce information about most of Gray's extensive criminal history, the assassination attempt on the prosecutor, or much of the violence surrounding Gray. Additionally, the prosecution had only ten jury challenges, the defense twenty, resulting in an all-black jury for the black defendants. District of Columbia juries have a much lower conviction rate of defendants than the national average. Some 60 percent of criminal cases in the District federal courts result in convictions, compared to more than 90 percent in Maryland and

Virginia federal district courts. Prosecutors will often try a case elsewhere than in the District, if they can.

At least three drug associates of Gray's were murdered and one was reported missing and has never been found. Testimony in related trials linked Gray to the murders of all four individuals and the shooting of the prosecutor.

To pay his attorney's fees, Gray signed over title to a $60,000 house to his lawyer, who then rented the property back to Gray's common-law wife, Darlene B. Fleming. Following a dispute over the nonpayment of rent, Gray repeatedly threatened the attorney's life and hinted to the lawyer that an assassin had been hired to eliminate him. "You say you'd put my babies out," Gray is quoted as saying. "You got a wife and babies.... You want your family hurt?"[47] Given the threats, the lawyer transferred title of the property to a close friend of Gray's.

In another trial, in February 1985, Gray was sentenced to twenty-five years in prison for extortion and conspiracy in a scheme to threaten his lawyer's life, but was paroled in December 1990 and began to put together the drug ring that would lead to his latest arrest. I asked Barbara Skalla, lead federal prosecutor in the latest case, to compare the profile of drug gangs from the time of Gray's heyday until his final arrest in 1994. "I don't see the same kind of drug organizations that we once saw, where the chairman of the board directed his minions from the top. Sometimes you see organizations like that, especially in cities, like Baltimore, and that was the trend probably up until four years ago. You see much more loosely organized groups now." This time the dollar value of Gray's operation was smaller than in his palmy days, the organization more rickety. There was Gray, a solo impresario, speeding about Washington in his Mercedes-Benz, meeting in fast-food joints and disinfectant-scented motels, reviving the old patterns, picking up old allies as they made it out of prison.

"I think Gray got a kick out of it," Skalla observed. She had been following him professionally for several years. "He didn't have to do this. One son was deeply involved in this with his best friend. Gray could have sat back and directed the show, but he chose not to. I think the thrill of it attracted him, and also that he could make money."

Gray's final skirmish with the law began on June 9, 1994, when he was indicted in the Greenbelt federal court as a result of a sting operation in a College Park, Maryland, apartment. Gray bought a kilogram of heroin for $180,000 from an undercover agent of the Drug Enforcement Administration (DEA). The heroin's street value would be something under a million dollars. Heroin prices vary enormously, following free market supply and demand principles. A kilogram might wholesale for $18,000 to $22,000, then be sold in $100-a-gram units, or $100,000 for the kilo. The profits were enormous.

In this case, the DEA and metropolitan police had tracked Gray since he left prison four years earlier, anticipating his return to his old role. After a long investigation, they arranged with a "cooperating individual," a drug trafficker who knew the suspect, to offer heroin to Gray. After phone calls and a session to test the heroin's quality, Gray arrived on June 9, 1994, ready to pick up the drugs at an apartment rented by the police in a nondescript College Park apartment building.

With audio- and videotape running, Gray and the "CI" (the Confidential Informant, as the person would henceforth be known in court documents) sat at a table while Gray diluted samples and packaged them for distribution to customers, rambling on about who his customers were and how he would apportion the entire kilogram. Skalla had a still from the surveillance videotape of Gray with the kilo of heroin, hovering over it like Santa Claus and the Christmas goose. (Prosecutors sometimes keep such souvenirs of high-profile cases on their office walls. A neighboring office contained a framed, rusted automobile gas tank with an indentation where a kilo of heroin had been stored, presented to the successful prosecutor by police who had worked on the case.)

As he left the apartment, Gray was arrested and the heroin retrieved. Next morning, a furious Gray was on the phone from jail to the CI's wife, leaving a message that the CI "needed to decide what he was going to do so that Gray could decide what he must do." This was thinly veiled code language saying Gray would retaliate if the CI continued to cooperate with police.

Gray's trial lasted six weeks, from January 10 to February 16, 1995, during which the prosecution presented repeated examples of Gray's drug-related crimes. Evidence came from wiretaps, camera surveillance, and the use of informants over four years. If some trials are characterized by dramatic moments, this one was more the steady unfolding of meticulously presented evidence about numerous crimes.

Some random examples:

December 1990: Linwood Gray was released from prison and started riding around with Linwood Gray II, his son. Opened L&L Communications.

December/January 1991: Gray began obtaining cocaine from Colombians in New York.

February 1991: Investigation began.

May 1991 (Memorial Day weekend): Linwood Gray II and girlfriend, Bernice Richardson, traveled to New York to pay more than $100,000 to Colombians for cocaine. Gray paid his son $1,000 for the trip but complained the cocaine was of poor quality.

Spring/Summer 1991: Gray found a new source of heroin and opened L&M Motors using his son's name on incorporation papers and Darlene Fleming's on the lease.

September 4, 1991: Another of Gray's sons, Troy Davis, was released from boot camp to a halfway house in D.C. Gray met with Davis at L&M and offered his son career counseling—he would help him get started in the heroin distribution trade. Gray's price per kilo ($21,700) was lower than others ($24,000 to $26,000).

March/April 1992: Four more heroin transactions between Gray and Troy Davis; Gray also obtained heroin from Nigerian drug dealer Roland "Beady" Cole.

December 4, 1992, to summer of 1993: Joyce Chambers, a jewel thief, now a police informant, went to L&M with five rings, four Rolex watches, and other jewelry, which she exchanged for cash and heroin. She attempted to pay for her car with stolen jewelry but Gray, ever the businessman, refused to mix the two accounts.

Summer 1993: Gray became suspicious of Joyce and planned to kill her outside her apartment building, where he and others waited for hours, not knowing Joyce was in jail in Virginia on a different matter.

February 1994: L&M Motors closed.

June 9, 1994: A police search at the residence of Ronald Humphries (another longtime Gray associate in Fort Washington, Maryland) resulted in the seizure of arms, ammunition, and plastic bags containing mannitol and quinine hydrochloride (cutting agents) with Humphries' fingerprints on them.

June 9, 1994: Gray was arrested in the sting operation.

And behind it all was Gray himself. In one case, Gray told the jury he only used heroin for "therapeutic" reasons. In another instance, he fleeced his sons for the costs of a trip to Amsterdam and the crack cocaine they paid for and brought back "to teach them a lesson not to get into the drug trade." Gray would deliver such comments earnestly, and without blinking.

(In the fall of 1991, Roland "Beady" Cole had complained to Gray that one of Gray's sons had ripped off drugs belonging to Cole. A police car with flashing lights arrived at Cole's house, and two men in police uniforms confiscated the drugs. One of the uniform-wearers was Gray's son, Cole told the father. Impossible, the indignant Gray replied, because his son was in jail. Gray took Cole to the D.C. jail and showed him the young man behind bars…but didn't tell him he was one of two identical sons—Gray called them "fractions"—only one of whom was presently in jail.)

To make their case against Gray airtight, prosecutors used his son and a friend as witnesses against him. Both entered the witness protection program, a device used frequently in criminal cases to protect important government witnesses from violent retaliation against them or their families. Local prosecutors can recommend who is accepted into the program, but the final determination is made by a special unit in the Department of Justice. Once a person enters the program, they and their family are moved to a different part of the country and are given new identities and jobs. Only the U.S. Marshal and the program's Washington office know their whereabouts. No one who has entered the program and stayed in it has been killed, but there are examples of persons in the program going back to their old haunts after several years and meeting a violent end.

"I don't think Gray knew his son was going to be testifying against him until the very last minute," Skalla observed. "We relocate witnesses regularly, but the full program is difficult to abide by. It is extraordinarily expensive and extraordinarily difficult on the witness. We often relocate a witness temporarily. Especially in a place like Washington, D.C., so many of these folks have never been out of Northern Virginia, Prince George's or Montgomery Counties, or the District of Columbia—that is their world. If we move them to a small town in a nearby county, often that is all that is necessary. Sometimes we move them to a hotel for the duration of the trial. It all depends on the nature of the threat."

At the trial, Judge Deborah Chasanow delivered a forty-six-page charge to the jury. Both sides were invited to contribute language to the jury charge, which the judge weighed and decided to use, modify, or discard. Judges develop their own language for various situations, and a volume called *Modern Federal Jury Instructions*, plus a companion volume on Maryland law, provides standard language. "From the beginning of the trial to the end, the government has the burden of establishing, beyond a reasonable doubt, every fact essential to the conviction of a defendant," the judge reminded the jury. "A defendant has no burden to sustain, and has no duty to prove that he did not commit the alleged crime.... A defendant is never required to prove that he is innocent."[48]

Three types of witnesses who would appear in the criminal case were also commented on. The first were law enforcement officials, whose testimony is not "necessarily deserving of more or less consideration or greater or lesser weight than that of an ordinary witness." Second were undercover agents and informants, of whom the judge said, "There is nothing improper or illegal with the government using these techniques, so long as the defendant's rights are not violated.... Certain types of evidence would be extremely difficult to detect without the use of undercover agents and informants." Finally, regarding witnesses who pled guilty to charges arising out of the case, "You are instructed that you are to draw no conclusions or inferences of any kind.... In exchange for the witnesses' agreements to plead guilty and testify at this trial, the government promised to bring the witnesses' cooperation to the attention of the sentencing court and to recommend that they receive reduced sentences. The government is permitted to enter this type of plea agreement."

A pillar of Gray's defense was that he was the victim of entrapment by Joyce Chambers. For entrapment to take place, Chasanow pointed out, three things must happen. First, the idea of entrapment must come from the government agents and not the person accused of the crime. Second, government agents must persuade Gray to commit the crime, not just give him the opportunity to do so. Third, Gray must not have been ready and willing to commit the crime before the government agents spoke with him about it.

Many criminal defendants argue they are being unjustly tried in Maryland when in reality the crime occurred over the line in the District of Columbia. Speaking to that issue, the judge told the jury. "The government need not prove that the crime itself was committed in this district or that each defendant was present here. It is sufficient to satisfy this element if an act in furtherance of each crime (such as a planning meeting) occurred within this district."

Defense lawyers then summarized their cases. Arcangelo Tuminelli, an experienced criminal defense attorney, was Gray's third and last lawyer. Tuminelli came out, guns blazing in every direction, painting a picture of two principal investigators, Special Agent David Crosby and Detective David Hayes, as driven cops who were out to get Gray at any cost. The other key witnesses, Gray's sons, Linwood Gray II and Troy Davis, plus two other drug dealers, Terrance Bailey and Sean Washington, became government cooperators to save their skins. The government's case was really entrapment, Tumenelli continued. As for Linwood Gray, he was a fence, not a drug dealer. "So the first thing is, Linwood Gray is someone who is unsavory, if you don't like fences. There are other problems with Linwood Gray. His conversation, his testimony, is peppered with profanity. That may not bother some of you, but it may bother others. You may not like him for that. That—that creates a problem for Linwood to defend himself, if you don't like him, then maybe it's easier to convict him."[49]

It remained for Skalla to make the prosecution's final arguments. She began: "There is an old expression about a defense attorney's job being to argue the law if the law is on your side. If the facts are on your side, you argue the facts. If both are against you...you distract the jury...and you demonize everyone associated with the other side." Calling the law and facts "devastating" to the defense, she reviewed the core of the prosecution's case, refuting the defense "distractions" that tried to water it down. For example, on the entrapment charge, "You can't be entrapped if you're predisposed to commit the crime. Well, what has Mr. Gray been doing since December or January 1991? He's been selling drugs." In rapid succession, she reviewed each of the defense arguments, relating them to key points in the law and facts testified to by the witnesses, leaving the jury with a vivid, condensed outline of the prosecution's case.

On February 21, 1995, the jury returned its verdicts. Gray was found guilty on count one (conspiracy to distribute and possess with intent to distribute heroin and cocaine from January 1991 through June 9, 1994), not guilty on count two (witness retaliation), and guilty on counts four, five, and six (distribution and possession with intent to distribute a controlled substance). The jury decided he should forfeit $1.5 million in cash assets, should they ever be recovered, plus his trophy collection of rings and watches. (The jewelry was never recovered.)

The defendant scored high on the Sentencing Guidelines. Gray was committed to the custody of the U.S. Bureau of Prisons on December 21, 1995, for a term of 405 months (thirty-three and a half years) on count one; 240 months concurrently on count four; 240 months concurrently on count five; and 405 months concurrently on count six. After release from prison in his early eighties, Gray will be on probation for five years.

Gray gave the courts one last try before heading off to prison for the long haul. He appealed his case before a three-judge panel of the U.S. Court of Appeals for the Fourth Circuit in Richmond, Virginia, on November 1, 1996. It was a tricky issue. The government had planned to call Joyce Chambers as a key witness early in the trial. But street-smart Joyce hid out for the duration of the trial, so the prosecution, in a private conversation with the judge, asked to introduce her grand jury testimony and subsequent written statements as evidence. Skalla argued that such privileged communication between judge and attorney, almost never allowed in a trial, was justifiable in this instance. If the defense was aware Chambers was missing and unprotected, Gray, who had once threatened to kill her, might do so again. Judge Chasanow admitted the grand jury testimony, since it was already a sworn deposition, but not Chambers' subsequent statements. "We find that the district court committed no error, and therefore affirm," the appeals court ruled a year later, on December 30, 1996, in a brief, unpublished opinion.

■

"Did you fear for your life during the trial?" The question was asked of Skalla, a diminutive blond, soft-spoken, but immensely self-assured person with a ready laugh, who frequently prosecutes some of Maryland's biggest drug cases. The Department of Justice installed an alarm system in her house and at the home of the other government attorney in the case. The marshals showed them how to follow alternative routes to and from the courthouse and take other precautions. Reflecting on the case, she remarked, "It is compelling that two of his sons testified against him and were fearful of him. In my view, that says what Linwood Gray was about.

"I never heard any stories of him being physically abusive. I could see how he could be charming to women, because he was very smooth. It was frustrating for me in cross-examination because I got nowhere with him. If he knew where you were going, he was fast enough to cover before you got there. He would come up with stories. He would sit there and explain something away very smoothly, and expect you simply to believe it.

"What makes the Gray case so interesting," the prosecutor reflected, "is not so much the drug activity, although extensive, but Gray. Clearly he enjoyed the money and everything he got, but I don't think that is what motivated him. I think clearly he loved the life of being a criminal. He liked being dangerous, he liked being feared, he liked being the notorious thug. I think that was his motivation."

The string ran out on Linwood Gray after four decades of active crime. Beady, Box, and Nighthawk, associates at various stages, were gone (Nighthawk, murdered possibly several years back). Homicide, Pow Wow, and other lesser characters had moved on. His two sons had turned against him. There are good bad guys, and bad guys, and Gray's life story falls into the later category, a case study in violence and greed, unredeemed by any evidence of human caring or constructive purpose. From the Petersburg, Virginia,

Federal Correctional Institute, Gray's post-conviction energies went into an endless chain of handwritten petitions to the court, scripted in ink on lined paper, with a careful hand that revealed both craftiness and a destructive energy that ruins everything around it. He asked for a new trial because his first, second, and third lawyers had provided ineffective counsel, and so on. Judges in criminal cases often receive continuing communications from prisoners, frequently extending for years. If legal errors were found, the case would be reopened. But that was not the case for Linwood Gray. The Big Boy who had fought his way up to enjoy the reputation as one of Washington's largest drug dealers was behind bars for years to come.

A Grade-B Bank Robbery

The Gang That Couldn't Plan Straight

"Robert, you'll be free long before I probably will..."
—April Montague, convicted bank robber,
to her jailed lover-accomplice, Robert English

It was rush hour, 5:30 P.M., Thursday, April 30, 1998, and police sharpshooters surrounded the College Park Credit Union in a neon and cinderblock suburban Maryland strip mall. Nearby, a main traffic artery, Route 1, would be blocked for the next four hours. Believing a robber and two frightened bank clerks were trapped inside the building, a SWAT team moved into place. From a command center in a Pizza Hut, police edged an armored vehicle into position, responding to the largest bank robbery in Maryland's recent history.

Moments earlier, an overweight man with a plastic bag over his face and wearing gloves was seen lugging a large duffel bag filled with money from the bank into a Ford Taurus and heading into traffic. The bank had closed at 3:00 P.M. It was Fat Thursday, and the credit union stored large amounts of cash in its two vaults in anticipation of Friday withdrawals and first-of-the-month paycheck cashing by state employees, retirees, and neighborhood Social Security annuitants. By 9:00 P.M., police had stormed into the building, once they were satisfied the robber had left, and freed the two tellers, a frightened April Montague, twenty-three, and a trainee teller.

Montague, who had worked her way up to a supervisory position after four and a half years with the bank, told a story of being surprised by a robber as she entered a vestibule near the bank's front door to deposit the day's receipts in a lockbox. Brandishing a silver handgun, the masked robber held the thin woman in a headlock and forced her back into the bank. Montague and the other clerk were forced to crawl, on hands and knees, to one of the two credit union vaults. The other clerk was ordered to kneel in a corner while Montague was forced to stuff the black duffel bag with cash and then remove the security videotape from a back room. Next, the robber locked the two women in the vault and took their driver's licenses, so he could track them if needed. "I'm going to kill you," he yelled at Montague. The masked man then ordered the women to remain in the vault for twenty minutes or he would shoot them.[50] The other clerk called police from a telephone inside the vault, telling them she thought the robber was still in the bank. This caused police to wait for several hours before entering the bank.

Meanwhile, during the robbery, several customers came by to use the automated teller machine. One heard a teller's voice from inside cry, "We're being robbed!" Out came a receipt with the words "Call the police" printed on it. Using a nearby pay phone, a woman did just that, as did several additional customers. An elderly neighborhood resident, Pamela Carbon, and her sister stopped by to withdraw twenty dollars for dinner money, and watched a man laboriously hauling the loot into the Ford Taurus. They copied the car's Maryland license plate, EJB821, and reported it to police. Within minutes sirens were screaming.

FBI Special Agent Louis P. Luciano Jr., a violent crimes and bank robbery specialist, was given the getaway car's license number shortly after the robbery. Because the local Enterprise Rent-A-Car office was closed for the night, Luciano called a friend with Enterprise on the West Coast who quickly traced the car rental to the name of Robert English, April Montague's boyfriend. English had listed Montague's Columbia, Maryland, address on the rental agreement. When questioned a few hours after the robbery, Montague was thus confronted with links of the getaway car to her boyfriend. After denying everything, Montague was released. Then she roamed the Baltimore beltway, talking endlessly to English on her cellular phone. The phone calls were recorded on her bill, information later used in evidence against her.

By 9:00 A.M. Friday, police recovered the getaway car near a Baltimore residence inhabited by Marques Boyer, twenty-four, a friend of English's and a fellow low-order drug dealer who, they soon learned, was robber-in-residence the previous day. English was questioned on May 1 by the FBI and confessed to his role in the crime. When he learned of English's defection, Boyer turned himself in and agreed to testify against Montague as part of a plea-bargaining arrangement. English, her lover, did not testify against Montague but later, as part of his guilty plea, admitted to renting the car and providing Boyer with a .38 caliber revolver and a cellular phone. It was late morning Friday and police were on their way to mopping up Thursday afternoon's robbery, finding everything but the missing $414,000, which was never recovered.

The bank robbery charge was a federal crime, and the case was scheduled for Judge Deborah Chasanow on July 22, 1998. In his opening statement, Assistant U.S. Attorney Maury S. Epner, a prosecutor who had handled many bank robbery cases, quickly linked the trio to the crime, telling the jury, "We're here because Marques Boyer would not, could not, and did not rob that bank by himself.... April Montague planned and helped carry out Marques Boyer's robbery." Boyer meanwhile provided information on planning meetings, a map Montague had made of the bank, a reconnaissance drive-by he and Montague had made of the bank, prearranged phone signals, and her leaving a side door open for his easy entry. [51]

Not much had gone right with the robbery, which the trio had decided on less than a week before it occurred. Boyer, who lived in

Baltimore and was car-less, had great difficulty finding his way to College Park unaided, and then couldn't find the credit union. Montague showed him its location in a drive-by the night before the robbery. And during the robbery, he waited for her to open the second vault, doubling the take but allowing more time for witnesses to observe the getaway car.

If prosecutors could establish Montague was the leader, her sentence would be higher. Of Boyer and English the prosecution said, "They are small-time Baltimore hustlers. This is a different crime and it is out of their neighborhood. They didn't do this without her help." As for Boyer, "He didn't even know how to get from Baltimore to College Park. The guy couldn't even tell you that 95 connects to 695 and 495."

Montague took the stand in her own defense, a tactic lawyers reserve for desperate or cocksure cases. "I know I'm being charged with bank robbery and that I didn't do it," she told the prosecutor, pointing a finger at Boyer, while denying that her boyfriend, English, was guilty, although by then he had entered a guilty plea.

Theirs was a star-crossed love story. A month earlier, on June 18, Montague from jail had written to her lover, also behind bars, "Robert, you'll be free long before I probably will" and asked him, "Will you promise me that if you go on with your life and it doesn't include me, will you promise to just tell me?" She testified that her former attorney and police investigators had intimidated her by urging her to enter a guilty plea. "I didn't think I had a chance," she told the jury. Law enforcement officials "told me I was going to prison for twenty to twenty-five years and I'd never have kids and see my family." [52]

As part of their case, prosecutors presented several bank employees who described Montague's unusual behavior the day of the robbery—that she failed to restock the bank's automated teller machine, leaving large amounts of cash in the vaults; that a door should not have been left unlocked; and that she appeared unduly nervous, pacing back and forth in front of the bank, looking from side to side. She also reminded a bank employee, Charles Clapsaddle, and his supervisor, that he should leave early for a course. During the trial, Randolph O. Gregory Sr., her attorney, tried to create an impression of a hard working, conscientious employee, the first to arrive and the last to leave, someone who had never been arrested. The prosecution, however, countered that prior to the robbery she had used a $1,000 ATM deposit slip error to add extra money to her boyfriend's account. (Actually, the $1,000 was lifted from the account of Bentley Kalu, himself a fraud artist who was ripping off credit card companies, and who understandably never complained to the credit union of his loss. Rod Rosenstein, one of the prosecutors in the Montague case, prosecuted Kalu's case several months later as well.)

The industrious Montague was also part of a counterfeiting scheme at the credit union. Customers complained of finding counterfeit twenty dollar bills in their ATM machine withdrawals in early to mid-April 1998. In such instances, it is almost always an inside job, because money placed in the ATM machines is carefully guarded and is usually counted at a main bank, transported in sealed containers by armed guards, and placed directly in the machines.

Montague would not answer prosecutors' questions about the incident, nor about counterfeiting charges, pleading a Fifth Amendment constitutional right not to testify against herself. (Defense and prosecution would later duel over the appropriateness of introducing this derogatory information into the bank robbery trial. The defense called it inadmissible, the prosecution legitimate. The judge ruled it was admissible information, and the defense would use this as a basis to appeal the case. Judge Chasanow said, "There is some mention in this case already about an investigation, the Secret Service, and counterfeit bills, and that is why I think the preliminary questions can and will be available to the cross-examiner without regard to the Fifth Amendment. They are clearly within the scope of what she has talked about; but when we get to allegations of her personal involvement in them, we cross the line. I think any questions to which she would invoke the Fifth Amendment are of necessity going to cause confusion and are too prejudicial in that respect to the defendant because they are so close to what we are dealing with here."

As for the improper crediting of money to English's account, "It again does bear on credibility because it is an act which, if it occurred, would bear on a person's character for truthfulness or lack thereof."

Assistant U.S. Attorney Rod Rosenstein, who had prosecuted public corruption cases nationwide for the Department of Justice, summarized the government's case: "The evidence shows from start to finish April Montague produced, directed, and choreographed the robbery of the College Park Credit Union. She produced the robbery when she came up with the plan and recruited the accomplices to commit it. She directed it when she told them what to do. Then, ladies and gentlemen, April Montague starred in the robbery by insuring that things went the way they were supposed to go by playing the role of the victim in the robbery."[53] Rosenstein quickly traced the linkages among the trio. Boyer had introduced Montague to English. English was Boyer's brother's roommate before the latter went to prison. The prosecution produced a picture from a wedding party twelve days before the robbery showing a happy Marques Boyer and April Montague together.

Later Rosenstein said, "There are differences in the testimony of April Montague and Marques Boyer. Those are pretty stark differences obviously. One of them is completely lying about the events of the crime. If you find that the defendant was lying about it, then you can use that as a fact to evaluate her credibility and to determine whether or not you think she was guilty of the crime."

Rosenstein quickly highlighted Boyer's shortcomings: "In contrast, Marques Boyer, who is a crook and who was prosecuted by the

United States, took the witness stand and answered every question that was put to him. When he was asked about drug use, he admitted it. He didn't take the Fifth Amendment. He admitted it.

"He testified that when he learned the game was up and he learned that the hoax was over, when he realized that Rob English was cooperating, he decided to just tell the truth. The evidence shows, ladies and gentlemen, that as much of a crook as he was, he told the truth. The reason I say that is because everything that Marques Boyer said that matters checks out."

In concluding, the prosecutor said with a flourish, "April Montague played her role very well and she deserves a reward for her performance. The reward that you should give her is a verdict of guilty on both counts because the evidence proves April Montague guilty of both counts beyond any reasonable doubt."

Defense attorney Randolph O. Gregory Sr. was a nimble lawyer, but he didn't have much to work with and had only been given the case a week earlier, after Montague had fired her two previous lawyers. He set out to prove that the government "has fallen woefully short of presenting credible, reliable evidence that April Montague was involved in the commission of these crimes." Finding a discrepancy between Boyer testifying he wore latex gloves and an FBI agent saying they were canvas gloves, Gregory attempted to poke holes in the government's case. Elsewhere, he cited the lack of any photos of the robbery and the failure of the prosecution to produce a 911 tape reporting the crime. "Excuses are not evidence. Excuses do not meet the burden of proof," he said.

Gregory made much of the fact that no fingerprints had been submitted in evidence linking Boyer to Montague's car. "If Marques Boyer's fingerprints are on some mirror or some smooth surface in her car, then they've got her. She has no way to explain that. But we don't have anything to corroborate that she came down here on the Tuesday before the robbery and cased the place out and rehearsed an escape plan with Marques Boyer. We have the word of Marques Boyer. That's all we have, is the word of Marques Boyer."

The attorney tried to establish his client's character as that of a diligent worker: "Everybody who has testified about Ms. Montague's work performance will tell you that she worked all day long, didn't take lunch. The best she would do is go out there and have a cigarette for a five- or ten-minute break. The woman worked all day long."

Gregory argued that other employees' career interests skewed staff testimony against Montague. "We've got a problem here, ladies and gentlemen, with the staff.... Some people have to cover their ass because Policy Number 12 states two employees are to exercise closing procedures.... Well, Mr. Clapsaddle had at least an explanation for him not being there. He had to go to school. Ms. White (the branch manager) never offered an explanation as to why she wasn't there. They're covering their ass. That's plain and simple."[54]

Rebutting the prosecution's argument that Boyer did not have a car or any reason to visit College Park, Gregory argued, "Well, I think Boyer made it clear that he is a big basketball fan. This credit union ain't located in the boondocks. This is in College Park, home of the Maryland Terrapins, a big basketball team."

In his peroration, Gregory referred to the June 18 love letter and concluded, "It ain't clear whether she admitted to this robbery in this letter, but it is clear in this letter her trust is with God, even though her passion is with Robert English. It is clear in this letter her trust is with God. Through God's hands she has placed her life in your hands. I only ask that you hold the government to the higher standard that exists in our judicial system. There is no standard any higher than beyond a reasonable doubt. There is nothing more sacred than the presumption of innocence."

In its final response, prosecutor Epner went carefully over the discrepancies in Montague's testimony and that of the other bank employees: "She disputes the testimony of virtually every witness in this case.... She alone, among the bank employees, has a motive to lie. You saw her lie. You heard her lie.... She lied because she is guilty and at this stage she has nothing to lose by lying. She doesn't have anything to lose at this point. Where is the downside risk of taking the stand and lying now?

"Boyer, on the other hand, has a lot to lose. So you know who is telling you the truth, not because he is a good guy. We don't think he is a good guy. We prosecuted him, for goodness sake. We think he is the scum that he is. He is a bank robber, an armed bank robber who put a gun in somebody's face."

In her charge to the jury, the judge noted the seriousness of the firearms charge, which carries with it a five-year consecutive sentence tacked on to whatever the sentence is for other crimes. "A dangerous weapon or device includes anything capable of being used to inflict serious bodily harm upon another person or anything capable of provoking a dangerous response from a person who perceives the device to be dangerous. Thus, a firearm constitutes a dangerous weapon or device.

"But to satisfy this element, the instrumentality need not be a firearm. In other words, even an imitation gun, or a metallic object which appears to an individual familiar with guns to be a firearm, qualifies as a dangerous weapon and device.... The law requires only that the robber display the weapon."[55]

The trial took five days; the jury took eight hours to find Montague guilty as charged. The ex-teller, thin and of medium height, was led away in handcuffs after looking furtively toward her mother and sister.

Judge Chasanow set sentencing for October 19 and sentenced Montague to eleven years and three months on count one, armed bank robbery, and five years on count two, use of a firearm during a crime of violence. Because the sentence was consecutive, the total time was sixteen years, three months. Judge Chasanow told her, "You are a relatively young individual and this is your first offense." Montague's jail time would be followed by a five-year term of supervised release on count one, and a concurrent three-year term on count two. Additionally, "I'm imposing a restitution judgment in the amount of $414,278 jointly and severally with the other two defendants in this case. There are no current assets from which to make that restitution, as far as I can tell. I'm going to make it a condition of supervised release that, assuming you are employed, that you pay at the rate of $200 per month towards that restitution obligation, should it still be outstanding at the time of your release.... I do impose a $200 special assessment. This is money that goes into a fund to help people who are victims of crimes, and for that reason have additional financial problems they didn't otherwise have. That is a requirement of law that I impose a hundred dollars on each count, and I do so."

Later, on March 18, 1999, April Montague also pleaded guilty to one count of possession of counterfeit currency; she was sentenced on April 5, 1999, to ten months in prison, running concurrently with her earlier sentence.

English was sentenced to ten and a half years in prison and was ordered to repay the missing $414,278. (If he earns credit for good behavior, English could be out after a little more than nine years.) Public Defender John Chamble was English's attorney. He told Judge Chasanow his client was immature and got the idea for the bank robbery from watching the film *Set It Off*, in which a group of inner-city women, bored in dead-end jobs, found thrills in robbing banks. During the sentencing hearing, prosecutors said they found English's fingerprints on counterfeit bills in the credit union's ATM around the time of the robbery.[56]

Boyer, who cooperated with police, drew a reduced sentence of eight years and seven months in prison. All three defendants were ordered to pay $200 per month while on "supervised release," the new term for probation, for five years after release from prison. Like Montague and English, Boyer was ordered to pay restitution for the $414,278 stolen from the credit union.

(Epner, who had left the U.S. Attorney's Office for private practice, wore a special tie at sentencing hearings—a shimmering blue, green, and orange Boston Trader number. He passed it on to Rosenstein, a starched-and-tailored product of Harvard Law School, who hung it on the wall behind his office door, a memorial to a departed colleague.)

The resourceful Gregory filed a motion for a new trial for his client on October 19, 1998, arguing it was improper for the government to question Montague in front of the jury about the prior transfer of $1,000 into Robert English's account. Gregory said introducing information of this nature by the prosecution was a backdoor way of attacking Montague's credibility. This was, Gregory argued, a way of "getting the extrinsic evidence in by including certain facts within questions posed to Ms. Montague that are not in the record," which could "inflame the jury." The prosecution's answer was simple and direct: "There is no such valid objection in cross-examination. The cross-examination questions do not need to be predicated on evidence that is in the record, particularly when you are dealing with credibility issues."

The judge called it "one of the many difficult evidentiary rulings I was called upon to make during the trial. My major concern during trial was with the knowledge that the defendant would exercise her right under the Fifth Amendment, and how that should be dealt with, and I became convinced that it was not necessary or appropriate to preclude the inquiry simply because she would exercise that right. But instead, I needed to work into the equation as I determined the probative value and the prejudice from that process.

"I gave the jury the cautionary instruction or limiting instruction as to how the invocation of the Fifth on that issue could be used, and I guess it will remain for another court to determine whether I properly balanced those concerns. But I am not persuaded that it justifies the granting of a new trial and, therefore, I deny the defendant's motion in that regard."

Gregory appealed Montague's case to the Fourth U.S. Circuit Court of Appeals, which upheld Judge Chasanow's verdict. Montague, English, and Boyer are behind bars; the money is still missing.

An Age and Sex Discrimination Case

"Judy wanted to be a K-9 officer.... Judy loved dogs."
—Plaintiffs' attorney

The rise of civil rights to the forefront of American political life has resulted in a dramatic increase in the number of lawsuits based on allegations of age, sex, or gender discrimination. Congress has decreed that such suits go directly into the federal courts, instead of into state courts, which means that considerable time must be devoted to the preliminary work of hearing what are often nuts-and-bolts cases. A question frequently asked in these cases is: Did the person lose out because of discrimination, or because his or her performance was mediocre or noncompetitive?

On August 13, 1993, Judith L. McClosky and her husband, Shawn R. McClosky, filed a civil suit against Prince George's County, Maryland; its county executive; its police chief; and two officers, Captain Gerald Speck and Lieutenant Colonel John Moss, the equal employment opportunity officer of the police department. The charges were age and sex discrimination, both violations of the Civil Rights Act of 1964 and the Civil Rights Act of 1991. The McCloskys asked for $21 million in damages.

Judith McClosky, who had been a police officer since 1980, working as a patrol officer and youth services investigator, triggered the suit when her application to join the elite Canine Unit was turned down. This was a sought-after job in the prestigious Special

Operations Division (SOD), which in 1992 had 100 male officers and only one female. (About 10 percent of the county police force was female.)[57] Forty-six persons applied for the opening. One of the questions asked by Captain Speck, chair of the hiring board, was, "Why should we consider you? You are forty years of age, compared to the twenty-three-, twenty-four-, twenty-five-year-olds that want to be considered." Captain Speck was later sued for asking that question. (The board contained a woman, an African American, and two other county police officers.) McClosky's answer, according to her deposition, was, "Because I am mature. I am a seasoned veteran officer of twelve years, which gave me more experience than those who were younger. I felt that some of the younger officers would be too aggressive and eager to have a dog commit an attack. Quite frankly, I told them, my job would be to protect the citizens, myself, and, of course, the county police of the liability factor of being a canine handler. I further said I am in better physical shape now than when I first came on this department twelve years ago."

McClosky, age forty, was rejected. Four officers, all males, all under thirty years of age, were selected for the SOD Canine Unit. She sued for age and sex discrimination, arguing, "There is no business or professional necessity requiring questioning as to age during an oral examination." On the sex discrimination charge, McClosky's deposition painted Speck as someone insensitive to women colleagues, given to making offensive remarks and hanging pictures of nude women on the wall above his desk. "Defendant Speck commented at least once (but in another setting) that women should stay at home having babies, and not serve as police officers" and asked during the oral board review "why she would want to give up straight day work to go on shift work when she had a family."

McClosky also argued that the denial resulted in an intentional infliction of emotional distress; she claimed to have suffered severe stress, depression, and "a loss of interest in intimate marital relations, society and companionship with her husband" and asked for compensation of $150,000 for medical expenses, $15 million in punitive damages, plus legal fees. Additionally, her husband sought $1 million, plus legal fees on the loss of consortium count.

Just before trial, a flurry of activity occurred. All charges were dropped but the single count of sex discrimination. Such last-minute dropping of charges is common. It is the plaintiffs' way of saying, these charges are difficult to prove, so we will concentrate where we have the best chances of prevailing. Also, by casting a wide net in the original charges, plaintiffs have more maneuverability in the discovery process, seeking to uncover documents and individuals that might aid their case. When it becomes evident the prospects are thin, the charges are dropped.

The case came to trial in September 1995. Both sides had carefully staked out their positions in pretrial documents. The Question (Speck's asking McClosky why she should be considered, instead of a younger person) was a tricky piece of evidence to build a case on. It could be seen as discriminatory, on one hand, or an ill-phrased but legitimate inquiry, meaning, "What skills do you bring to this position that a younger officer might not possess?" If there were other hostile questions during the interview, or a pattern of discriminatory questioning, it would be a stronger case. In fact, the panel, beyond reviewing officers' profiles and saying a bit about working with dogs, conducted a pointless, meandering interview. So, if the evidence coming from the interview was not strong, there were two other ways the plaintiff could make the case: (1) demonstrate a statistical pattern of discrimination department-wide and/or within the Canine Unit, and (2) demonstrate a convincing pattern of discrimination against the individual officer throughout her career. Both approaches would require careful documentation, both would exert an emotional toll on the plaintiff and would likely trigger hostility from the defendants. Both would be hard to prove, because in such cases the lingering question is always, discrimination or competence?

McClosky's lawyers argued that female police officers were severely underrepresented in the Special Operations Division compared with the police department as a whole. Basically, during 1992 and 1993 female officers comprised 10 percent of the department's sworn personnel, but only slightly more than 1 percent of the SOD's total officer corps.

The plaintiffs painted a picture of a unit hostile to women, designed to keep out "undesirable" candidates and support "traditional" male officers. They offered the following example of the hostile working environment in trial documents: "Captain Speck's opinion of female police sergeants, as articulated to another officer, was that they needed to have more 'testosterone.'" Sergeant Herl, another panel member, "prominently displayed posters of naked women on the walls of his business office." Speck, commander of the Special Operations Division, prominently displayed a Frederick's of Hollywood photo calendar, later submitted in evidence, depicting various "women clad in lingerie and panties on the bulletin board of his business office at the Riverdale station."

The plaintiffs concluded: "The attitudes of the supervisors in SOD, the manner in which the July 1992 Oral Board was conducted, and the statistical evidence in this case is conclusive. Corporal McClosky, because of her sex, was denied a transfer to SOD before she ever walked into the interview room before the Oral Board."

In his summation before the jury on September 13, 1995, James D. Milko, one of Ms. McClosky's attorneys, said how much life on the police force had meant to her since she joined it in October 1980. It had become the family she never had, the new starting point in her life. Now all that was shattered by her being rejected for the K-9 Corps because of her age and sex. "No one in this case disputes that Judith McClosky had, at best, a tumultuous home life when she was a youngster, and worse, a horrible one. There is no dispute about the terrible things that happened in her family background, the problems she had growing up and the kind of difficulties she faced in life.

"However, she reached a turning point in her life in the 1980s, and that turning point was she found something that began to play an anchor in her life that she had always lacked until that point, and that anchor was her role as a police officer in the Prince George's County Police Department."

Milko painted Speck as the ringleader in the discrimination suit, as much for his attitude as for his actions: "And finally there is the comment that Captain Speck made regarding the Frederick's of Hollywood calendar during testimony." When asked if this depiction in his office in a public place could be offensive to a female officer, "his answer was flat out no. What does that say about Captain Speck's mentality?" Ditto Sergeant Herl's "full frontal nudity poster of a female behind bars, which depicted a jail cell."

Jay H. Creech, a county attorney, attacked all of the plaintiff's points. Basically he argued that McClosky ended up seventeenth in a field of forty-six candidates, not because she was a woman or forty years old, but because her skills were less competitive than those of the other candidates. Evaluations were subjective, Creech argued, but McClosky was not among the top eight on any of the lists. In fact, Sergeant O'Hagan, the only woman on the board, scored her a minus four, while Captain Speck, her adversary, gave her a plus four. "And if they're trying to say that Captain Speck is discriminating against her on the basis that she is a woman because he gave her a four where everybody else got a higher score, well, that's not true because we know that Corporal McClosky beat out nineteen male applicants."

On the question about her age, Creech said the phrasing was clearly incorrect, "but the question he was trying to get across wasn't." What he was trying to do was to get her to talk about her experience, and she did, and she gave a good answer, and everybody who testified about that answer she gave testified that it was a good answer. He pointed out that although McClosky had been turned down twice before, so had another officer named Simms (twice) and Speck (five or six times). "So it's not that she's the only one being rejected here. There are people that were interviewed in there that have been rejected eight times, and they're coming back, so it's not singling Ms. McClosky out for discrimination or anything like that. It's basically that she didn't make the top four."

As for Speck's poster, Creech handled it as best he could, saying it was hung in Speck's private office and was rarely seen by others. Besides, "it shouldn't bear in any case on what happened ten months after these posters and this calendar as to whether or not they graded Ms. McClosky impartially. We're talking about ten months later."

About the plaintiff's testimony that things were going well in her life until she was discriminated against in July 1992, "Well, it didn't sound like her family life was doing very well. Her parents were both alcoholics and hospitalized. At some point in time, she had been molested by two or three of her brothers. Her younger sister had been molested. She had three prior failed marriages. She's been in counseling with her daughter for six years, and she had previously gone into marriage counseling because of problems with an ex-spouse of Mr. McClosky."

Creech pointed out McClosky had likewise not been selected for the K-9 Corps on two other occasions, or for the Criminal Investigations Division. "Does that sound to you like a life that's going well?"

In concluding, Creech drew on his own experience as a long-distance runner and said, "I know if I could train for five years, ten years straight, that I will never win a 10K. And the thing is, Ms. McClosky doesn't accept the fact that she didn't win this one. She wasn't among the top four candidates."

Employment discrimination cases are complex, because the law keeps changing and a continual question for judge and lawyers is: What did the law say at a specific time? In her charge to the jury, Judge Chasanow focused on Title VII of the Civil Rights Act of 1964, which prohibits discrimination because of an employee's gender. "In order to prevail on her claim against the Defendant, Plaintiff must prove that the Defendant intentionally discriminated against her based on gender.... That is, you must decide whether the Plaintiff has proven by the preponderance of the evidence that she was not selected for transfer, at least in part, because she was a woman."

If the county discriminated against her, McClosky must prove that their actions were the proximate cause of her injury. "Proximate cause means that there must be a sufficient causal connection between the act or omission of the Defendant and any injury or damage sustained by the Plaintiff."

As for damages, the jury was told to consider two things: (1) mental anguish suffered in the past, which in reasonable probability may be expected to continue in the future, and (2) therapy expenses reasonably incurred in the past. Explaining the "loss of consortium" claim, Judge Chasanow said, "Consortium is loss of companionship, affection, assistance, and loss or impairment of sexual relations." She continued, "If Judith McClosky is able to prove that there was damage, but is unable to establish its monetary value, she may recover only nominal damages in the amount of one dollar." Chasanow told the jurors, "In considering damages, you must keep in mind that your award must adequately and fairly compensate the Plaintiffs, but your award should not be based on guesswork." The amount of damages must be based solely on the evidence, and the amount of money claimed by counsel in argument is not evidence and cannot be considered the true measure of damages. Lawyers sometimes go in for an astronomical sum, but will take anything they can get.

Only one count remained for the jury to decide four years after the original K-9 Corps interview and three years after the suit had been filed. It was returned in favor of the county, which two weeks later filed against McClosky for $2,614.80 in court reporter's costs for making transcripts, a final gesture from Judith McClosky's employer, but a usual one in such cases.

In 1997, Officer McClosky received a disability retirement from the Prince George's Police Department and went to work as a secretary with her lawyer's firm. She presently is suing the department for retaliation. After her experience in applying for the K-9 Corps, she never applied for any other such assignments, finishing her career on a patrol beat. "I'm glad I did what I did," she reflected. "If I had to do it all over, I'd do it again because there is no doubt in my mind I was discriminated against. They need to realize that women can make good police officers. Women don't have to use their brute strength to communicate with people and think they are John Wayne with a badge and a gun."

EDDIE BAUER AND THE GREEN SHIRT

> *"The only thing my son said to me when he got home from the store, he said, 'But, mom, it happens to me and my friends all the time.'"*
>
> *—Joyce Parker-Plummer, mother of Rasheed Plummer, Plaintiff in the Eddie Bauer case*

Eddie Bauer. "Eddie" sounds like one of the guys, but someone who has made it. "Bauer," a good, clean-cut German-American name. Mainstream. Success. The company catalogue projects images of virile young men in casual clothes, rugged, active outdoors types. Eddie Bauer threads are also high-fashion status symbols among young African Americans. But not for Alonzo Jackson, who forcibly surrendered the Eddie Bauer shirt he was wearing to a uniformed off-duty Prince George's County police officer at an Eddie Bauer floating warehouse outlet in Fort Washington, Maryland, on October 20, 1995. Jackson had purchased the shirt the previous day but left his receipt at home. Officer Robert Sheehan, moonlighting as a store guard, confiscated the shirt until the youth returned with proof of purchase.

The incident took only a few minutes, constituted only five or six short sentences and one or two actions. Its aftermath was a high-visibility civil rights suit that played out over two years, a million-dollar verdict, heightened racial tensions, widespread media coverage, a bad name for Eddie Bauer, and bitter memories for three teenaged African Americans.

During 1995, Eddie Bauer, a Redmond, Washington, corporation with $1.5 billion in sales, operated temporary floating warehouse outlets in several cities, sending in a permanent management team but hiring temporary local employees. Each outlet offered brand clothing at discount prices. After three-week stands in Toronto, Canada, and Salt Lake City, Utah, the Eddie Bauer road show and its all-white management team arrived in Fort Washington, an affluent African American suburban community on the outskirts of Washington, D.C. In October 1995, Bauer hired several off-duty Prince George's County police officers as security guards, including Officers Robert Sheehan and Wayne Pyles. More than half of the county's 1,250 officers have second jobs as security officers, making between fifteen to twenty dollars an hour. Such rent-a-cops wore uniforms, displayed badges, and were armed, following established county practice. To customers, they looked like regular on-duty police officers, although they were moonlighting. Sheehan and Pyles received a perfunctory orientation, but no one discussed Eddie Bauer's shoplifting policy with them.

Theft is a major problem for clothing stores, and Eddie Bauer University documents said U.S. retailers lose over $8 billion annually to shoplifting. Regular employees who attend the Eddie Bauer University learn to "provide the customer legendary service"—and follow a carefully worked-out policy about store theft:

"Our policy is to provide customer service and to never accuse a customer. We emphasize preventing and deterring theft—not apprehension." In encountering suspected shoplifters, Bauer employees were to do the following: "Provide them with exceptional service, commenting favorably on the merchandise they may have concealed. Step away to give them an opportunity to discard the merchandise. Alert management or your department coordinator immediately. Keep the person in sight until they leave the store. Allow them to leave the store gracefully."

The company had a well-developed list of verbal interactions employees could make with suspected thieves, such as saying to a potential shoplifter, "That (name item) is a great buy!" Or to a suspect, "I'll be close by if you need me." Bauer policy was only to have suspects arrested when there was a personal observation of that person committing the theft.

For Sheehan and Pyles, recruited with little or no orientation to company policy, such subtleties did not figure in their encounter with Alonzo Jackson, an Oxon Hill High School honor roll student, ROTC student, and basketball player, and his two companions.

On October 19, Jackson, a sixteen-year-old African American male, purchased a signature Eddie Bauer green plaid shirt at the Bauer outlet. The next day, wearing the shirt, Alonzo returned with two friends, Rasheed Plummer and Marco Cunningham. The trio had toured the store and stopped to observe a watch display near the store's front exit. Store manager Steve Markovich saw Alonzo wearing an Eddie Bauer shirt with the shirttail out. It had a "wrinkled" look, as if it "just came out of a box." Another employee said Jackson did not enter the store wearing the shirt. Markovich, according to court reports, told Sheehan that store managers had found other clothing that had apparently been exchanged.

The heart of the alleged consumer racism, false arrest, and defamation encounter took only a few minutes. At issue was a brief exchange, confrontational, if you believe Jackson and his two friends, who said Jackson was told to remove the shirt and his companions were detained against their will; conciliatory, in Sheehan's and Markovich's accounts, which had Jackson offering to remove the shirt. In a joint pretrial statement of agreed-upon facts, both sides described what happened. The plaintiffs stated, "Officer Sheehan approached Plaintiffs, stopped them, and impeded and delayed their exit from the store. At that time Sheehan wore a jacket with the word POLICE written on it and (was) armed with a 9mm revolver. While still in public view, Sheehan asked Alonzo several questions and ordered him to show the tag inside his shirt. Jackson then unbuttoned several buttons and displayed the tag at the inside neck collar to the officer. Alonzo told the officer he had purchased the shirt the previous day. Sheehan asked Alonzo to show him the receipt for the shirt which Alonzo did not have in his immediate possession."

Officer Pyles ordered Plummer and Cunningham to stand back, they said, after one of them had protested Jackson's treatment and Plummer said, "You can't prove he stole that shirt!"

"Jackson told Sheehan his receipt was at home. Sheehan ordered Jackson to take off his shirt since he did not have a receipt. Jackson asked if he could find the cashier from whom he'd purchased the shirt the previous day. Sheehan followed Jackson to that cashier, who remembered the transaction, but did not recall the details of the purchase. Sheehan told Jackson: 'To me it looks like you are trying to take this shirt.' He again ordered Jackson to take his shirt off and to leave it at the store, go home and get the receipt."[58]

Jackson sued for false imprisonment, defamation, negligent supervision, and violation of civil rights. Plummer and Rasheed sued for false arrest and assault. They asked for $85 million from Eddie Bauer, Inc. (The lead defense attorney reportedly offered to settle the case for $1.1 million, later reducing the sum to $760,000. The company's offer stayed at $160,000, an associate of the defense team said, until it was raised to $760,000.)[59]

Eddie Bauer's concise defense statement, filed concurrently with the plaintiffs', avoided the Sheehan–Jackson encounter, but tried to isolate Cunningham and Plummer from the case by calling them bystanders who were not detained for investigation nor prohibited from leaving the store. Additionally, "There is no evidence of negligent supervision by EBI of the officers." The complaint argued the plaintiffs "do not have clear and convincing evidence of actual malice by EBI to support a demand for punitive damages." It asked that "potential costs" of the case should "be assessed in favor of EBI."

That is how court documents portray the encounter. Return now to October 20, 1995. Events took a nosedive shortly after the three youths returned home. An angry Joyce Parker-Plummer, Rasheed's mother, called Eddie Bauer's corporate headquarters to file a complaint. She was put on hold and told someone would call her back. They never did. Next, she relayed information of the incident to Courtland Milloy, a popular *Washington Post* columnist, who called Eddie Bauer. "Why are you writing a story about that?" a store manager, Sherry Witlaw, asked, adding, "It's a police matter. It's not us. Contact the police. They were guarding the building." Cheryl Engstrom, a spokeswoman for Eddie Bauer's corporate headquarters, told Milloy it was typical for police to check receipts before a customer left the store and, far from apologizing, grudgingly conceded, "The amount on the receipt matched the purchase although the stub didn't specifically indicate whether or not it was the same shirt. But we gave him the benefit of the doubt and let him keep it anyway."[60]

Milloy's column ran on November 15. Other journalists and talk show hosts relayed information of the incident, which Eddie Bauer employees called "minor." Community groups voiced disapproval; racial tensions rose. Talk of boycotting Eddie Bauer was widespread. A picket line went up in front of an Eddie Bauer store in a fashionable section of Washington. A lawsuit loomed as the three youths retained counsel. Jonathan Yardley, a widely read ***Washington Post*** columnist, wrote, "The story...was infuriating. No other word will suffice. Not merely was it outrageous in its specific details—the rude salespeople, the bullying cops, the bewildered boy—but it was a classic instance of the casual discrimination to which black Americans are subjected routinely, automatically, unthinkingly."[61]

By early December 1995, as Christmas decorations went up in retail stores, Eddie Bauer Inc. sensed it had a problem. EBI hired a leading Washington public relations firm to handle the matter, issued a public apology (but never met with the three youths), and donated clothes to a homeless shelter. Company President Rick Fersch, who would later be a witness in the trial, blitzed Washington, where he had spent fifteen years with another retailing firm, meeting with the Washington office of the National Association for the Advancement of Colored People, Prince George's County Executive Wayne Curry, and other community leaders. "We blew it," Fersch said. "I'm not trying to defend what we did."[62]

Throughout the case, the teenagers said what happened at the store was a common experience for young blacks. Rasheed Plummer's mother, Joyce Parker-Plummer, said, "The only thing my son said to me when he got home from the store, he said, 'But, mom, it happens to me and my friends all the time.'"[63]

On June 12, 1997, Eddie Bauer's attorneys moved to dismiss much of the civil rights lawsuit. However, Judge Alexander Williams continued the case when the plaintiffs' attorneys said they would produce three witnesses who would testify that discrimination against minority shoppers was widespread at Eddie Bauer's stores. Some of the case's most damaging testimony came from Mary Addi, a mid-level manager who traveled with the temporary warehouse store team. In Salt Lake City, she said, African American shoppers were followed through the store even after they made purchases. Addi also said she heard the Fort Washington managers while in Toronto tell employees they needed to be aware of the "Asian problem," that Asians were known for stealing from them. Other alleged racial incidents occurred at EBI stores, Addi asserted, and Bauer management did nothing to correct the problem. (Markovich would portray Addi as an "emotionally unstable person" affected by the recent death of her mother.)

The racially charged six-day lawsuit began before Judge Williams on September 30, 1997. Discrimination suits are not easy to prove. It is not enough that someone feels discriminated against; they must be able to prove actual discrimination. For example, if a white teenager walked into the store wearing an Eddie Bauer shirt but left unchallenged, a clear benchmark would be established should a similar black shopper be stopped. A Washington civil rights lawyer said, "It was an egregious act...to have him take the shirt off. People say that would not happen to a blond-haired blue-eyed white kid."[64]

The blame game began early in the trial. EBI sliced Sheehan and Pyles off to dangle in the wind. Sheehan's actions violated company policy that prohibited confronting suspected shoplifters, Gerald F. Ivey, Eddie Bauer's attorney, argued. The two officers countered that they were only following accepted policies. The Sheehan-did-it-on-his-own approach did not go uncontested during the trial. The off-duty detective of twenty-three years said he acted only after manager Markovich signaled toward the teenager and assistant manager Jeff Linden told him the youth had entered the store wearing a different shirt. Sheehan said the youth volunteered to remove the shirt, but the teenager, an Eddie Bauer cashier, and Jackson's two friends all testified that Sheehan, who said he could not identify Eddie Bauer clothing unassisted, asked Jackson to remove the shirt.[65] The Prince George's County police conducted their own investigation and, not unexpectedly, exonerated their colleagues; county police officers threatened to boycott Eddie Bauer.

Markovich was next to fall. On January 1, 1996, EBI delivered an unsatisfactory job performance reprimanding its manager (who has since left the firm). "Steve demonstrated poor judgment in not reporting a customer service incident to corporate through an incident report. Additionally, as supervisor of the sale, Steve did not direct the Assistant Manager who observed the incident to take appropriate action, i.e., to discipline or separate the police officer."

Next, Ivey tried to split Plummer and Cunningham off from the case. They were bystanders, he said, like "the people who witness a traffic accident." Seeing something does not entitle you to recover damages, he told the jury.[66]

The lead defense attorney was Donald M. Temple, a fiery civil rights activist and former chairman of the District of Columbia Civilian Complaint Review Board, the group that reviews complaints against D.C. police officers. A colorful orator, Temple asked the seven-person jury, with three black and four white members, to "hammer home" a verdict for his clients. In cadenced speech, replete with dramatic gestures, Temple eyed the jury and said, "It is absolutely morally wrong to follow African Americans, Asians, Hispanics around a store operating on the assumption they are going to steal. It is wrong...and if you don't tell Eddie Bauer how wrong it is, they won't understand. And you are going to have to tell them in a language they understand."

If Temple was part preacher, defense counsel Ivey was all lawyer systematically summing up his case, carefully laying out his arguments, and reinforcing main points with charts set before the jury. After reviewing the firm's nondiscriminatory policies, Ivey put the blame squarely on Sheehan. There was only one question, he said: "What did Officer Sheehan do, and why did he do it?" He continued, "The Eddie Bauer management team did not authorize Alonzo Jackson's stop and did not authorize the taking of his shirt." Sheehan "made a terrible, reprehensible decision, one which Eddie Bauer did not and does not support."[67]

A mixed verdict emerged. On October 9, the civil jury returned an award of $1 million to the three youths. Although the security guard acted improperly, it was not with racist intent, the jury found. And although it rejected the claim that EBI had violated Alonzo Jackson's civil rights on the consumer racism charge, it found that EBI had engaged in false imprisonment, negligent supervision of security personnel, and defamation. The award gave Jackson $850,000 in compensatory and punitive damages, and $75,000 each to Plummer and Cunningham. Although most jurors would not speak following the trial, one, a black man, said Jackson was harassed, but that was different than consumer racism. "You just can't treat people like that," he said. The NAACP called the case a "wake-up call" to corporations "about their liability for racially insensitive acts, speech, and policies."[68] Judge Williams said later, "We have received a lot of calls from around the country asking to see the pleadings on both sides of this case. Interestingly enough, the jury did not hang its hat on the consumer racism charge. To a certain extent, both sides were victorious."

Undaunted, Eddie Bauer appealed the case to the Fourth Circuit U.S. Court of Appeals in Richmond, Virginia, claiming Judge Williams' rulings were "arbitrary, capricious, and abusive." Temple filed a counter-appeal on behalf of his clients on the civil rights count, arguing Eddie Bauer's appeal showed "they do not have respect for the black consumers who shop in their stores." Possibly in response to a renewed public outcry, EBI dropped its appeal of the jury award and settled the case for an undisclosed sum.

Cases rarely have their Perry Mason moment, TV accounts notwithstanding, but this one did. In both Judge Williams' chambers and the Clerk of Court Office are framed, media artist's colored renderings of the moment when Jackson's lawyer had the gawky youth remove his shirt in front of the jury and hand it to him. Temple asked Jackson if he ever thought about what happened at the moment when he had handed the shirt to Sheehan. "All the time," the youth replied, his voice cracking. Jackson never reclaimed it; the shirt rests in Temple's office.

CDs for Nigeria

Chief Bosah's $1.5 Million Export Scheme

> *"The largest single fraud scheme committed against mail order merchandise companies in history."*
>
> *—David Salem, Assistant U.S. Attorney, Greenbelt, Maryland*

If Wayne Mitchell hadn't spotted the stacks of CDs, Charles Bosah still might be in business. But Mitchell, who works in the Laurel, Maryland, post office, noticed the accumulation of mailed packages from record companies arriving for the same two post office boxes under various names and addresses. On November 1, 1995, he notified the Postal Inspection Service of his suspicions, specifically about the overloading of boxes 303 and 1039. Four years later, on February 2, 1998, Charles C. Bosah, a Nigerian citizen, was behind bars for his entrepreneurial $1.5 million scheme to defraud mail order houses out of thousands of pounds of records, clothes, toiletries, and other items. From 1992 to 1996, Bosah routinely loaded the merchandise into twenty to thirty suitcases and flew it to Nigeria, where he sold it in two stores, one in Lagos and one in Enugu, through the Oak Tree Outlet, Charles B. Bosah, President. A business card and refrigerator magnet advertised "clothes, shoes, CDs, books, gifts, laser discs." Back home, Bosah bought a couple of Mercedes-Benzs and was building a "Big Man's home," the residence of a chief, which is what Bosah began to call himself in prison. Abandoning unreliable Nigerian Airlines, he traveled each month on Swissair—sixty-five trips over five years—with as much merchandise as he could move. Often, the excess baggage charges were three thousand dollars a trip.

"The scheme worked generally like this," David Salem, who prosecuted the case, recalled after the trial. "Bosah or one of the codefendants—most of them were related to him—opened up post office boxes in the Maryland metropolitan area, as you can see behind you on this blown-up piece of evidence." Trim and wiry, Salem, a marathon biker and student of Russian and Chinese when he is not prosecuting criminals, pointed to an enlargement of a postal registration form for a new box, in the name of Charles Bosah. In the space listing who might access the box, at least six single names were listed: Paul, John, Ngi, and so on. Nigerians and others in the gang would periodically visit the post office, identify themselves as "Paul," "John," or "Ngi," and empty it. (The exhibit was framed and captioned, "Batting a Thousand. Our Sincere Thanks for All Your Work, Washington Division, U.S. Postal Service.")

At one point, Paul Krug, the postal inspector who investigated the case, had fifty post office boxes identified, into which merchandise flowed. The number rose to 350 mailboxes, and the stolen merchandise amounted to $1.5 million before Bosah was arrested.

Salem continued his account: "They kept it going because they closed some of the boxes, opened new ones, and switched some of the names around. And the mail-order merchandise companies at that time were not set up from a security standpoint to be able to track this in any adequate way.

"What they would do, once the postal boxes were open, is go to the back of newspapers where there are ads for twelve CDs for a dollar or four books for a buck, and they would write away to the companies in the names of these people. The ingeniousness of it was the way they would use the names designated to have access to the P.O. box. The merchandise arrives, the postal employee sees that Don Hill has access to the box and puts the merchandise in it. They retrieve it. Another application is sent out in the name of Dave Hill, or in the 'Ngi' case, they could use it as a first or last name because people wouldn't know what it was. You could have 'Ngi Dennis' or 'B. Ngi.' And so they could turn four or five names listed in the P.O. box application into thirty or forty names. And typically they would send out a series of applications all at once to these mail-order merchandise companies. They got as much merchandise back as they could and if they thought somebody was on to them, they would close the box and open another one. About once a week they traveled to all of the P.O. box locations. Every two or three weeks the whole group gathered at Charles Bosah's apartment, collected the merchandise, packed it, and he flew to Nigeria where he owned two stores. Then he converted the Nigerian naira into U.S. dollars and on some of these trips brought U.S. money, anywhere from $10,000 to $20,000 at a time, back into the United States." Then the kinsmen gathered at the apartment for their payoffs, often the cost of a month's rent or a car payment, a TV set, or a ticket back home.

"We concluded that he had no other job or means of support, that he couldn't even buy the stamps to mail the applications except through dirty money, which then helped turn this case into a money-laundering scheme," Salem noted, "and that upped the ante for Mr. Bosah, because under the federal Sentencing Guidelines, fraud, even to this extent, does not result in a lot of jail time. Only if you can take the fraud and find within it a different crime, like money laundering, do the guidelines increase the jail time dramatically. Mr. Bosah pled guilty to money laundering and got a much higher sentence as a result; I think it was fifty-eight months.

"He's a relatively young guy, and fifty months does not amount to a lot of time in his life. He will probably be in his late thirties when he is released and he will obviously have access to a lot of the money back in Nigeria. If that house is half or three-quarters built, it is built on U.S. fraud funds.

"His former girlfriend, not wanting to take the fall for Bosah, pled guilty in Maryland, which is one reason the plea-bargaining process was protracted—different lawyers, different systems—making her eligible for parole, which we don't have in the federal system, and resulting in her serving a lot less time than she might have served in the federal system. So she assisted us; she was able to tell us when Mr. Bosah left on some of his trips, and how he and his cohorts dealt with each other in his apartment. Ultimately we were able to go back to Swissair and find support for her story and trace his travels. He would check in twenty to thirty bags at a time. What is unique in this case is that in a money-laundering indictment you can forfeit property, which you can't do for mere mail fraud. We converted his frequent flyer miles into U.S. government agency miles, and, as a result, the Postal Service got a lot of round-trip business tickets courtesy of Mr. Bosah."

Bosah's enterprise began to unravel when the Postal Inspection Service arranged surveillance of a pickup of twenty-one parcels in seventeen different names at the Laurel, Maryland, post office on February 9, 1996. At 4:30 P.M. that day, Bosah's ex-girlfriend, Donnel (Dhonyale) Gibson, one of the names authorized to collect the packages, parked her red Saturn car outside the building. She carefully signed individual receipts for each package while a hidden camera rolled. Several months later, after the Postal Service began to follow the red Saturn and track Bosah's thousands of false applications to more than 300 locations, three postal inspectors visited Ms. Gibson at her modest apartment in Waldorf, Maryland. After advising her of her rights, they told her they had evidence of fraudulent activity on her part and that she faced a lengthy prison sentence if she didn't cooperate. Ms. Gibson quickly turned against her ex-boyfriend. She then surrendered thirty CDs from her personal collection as stolen goods given her by Bosah.

Bosah, she said, lived in a small Cheverly, Maryland, apartment (he listed his monthly income at $1,400 from work with a travel agency) where he warehoused stolen goods. Photos of the Spartan apartment showed minimal living space and each room, stacked floor to ceiling with boxes of merchandise. From a frail table in a windowless corner of a room, Bosah sometimes worked all night on his stack of loose-leaf notebooks with their endless lists of record companies, post office boxes, fake names, and amounts due to keep accounts open. When an account was closed by a merchandiser for nonpayment, he noted "Bad" and the date.

Bosah's original indictment came on November 14, 1996, on conspiracy to commit mail fraud, mail fraud, money laundering, and aiding and abetting (assisting others to commit a crime). The companies were a Who's Who of mail-order traders: BMG Music Service Company, Columbia House Music Club, Doubleday Direct Company, Time-Life, and Grolier, among others.

Constant paperwork was required to keep the scheme going. The trick was to keep as many applications in motion as possible in all directions while paying only the minimal amounts necessary to allow more records or merchandise to be sent. Record companies offer free CDs, such as twelve CDs for the price of one. A member who fulfills this initial obligation can leave the club or continue. Those who continue receive additional discounts on future purchases plus additional CDs when they recommend new members to the club. Thus a "member gets a member" program offers current members additional CDs once the new member pays the shipping and handling charges on their introductory and free CDs. A hundred false or altered names and addresses produced 1,200 introductory free CDs, plus those obtained from the "member gets a member" program.[69] Additionally, slightly altering the street or P.O. box address or the spelling of the name creates the appearance of a new customer in music company records, and thus a new member or referral. For example, eleven different names were associated with Box 303, thirty with Box 1039. Sometimes the box numbers were altered by placing a zero or two in front of the box number, thus changing a three-digit box to a four- or five-digit box number. Because adding digits does not materially alter the box number, the post office delivered merchandise to the same box. Mail for Bosah flowed into the Laurel post office boxes, and others in nearby

Cheverly, Clinton, and Waldorf. A check of BMG invoices to Bosah's Cheverly address showed forty-three accounts in different names. Meanwhile, the postal inspectors and merchandising companies were using newly developed software programs to track Bosah's spiderweb of transactions.

The Nigerian's arrest came on October 17, 1996. Saying he was financially unable to obtain counsel, Bosah asked for a public defender and was released on October 29, 1996, to reside at Hope Village halfway house until an electronic home-monitoring device could be installed in the home he shared with his wife, Elizabeth Hill Bosah, who then became the third-party supervisor responsible for him. (Later they divorced; Mrs. Bosah was indicted, but plea-bargained for a reduced sentence.)

Trial was set for January 28, 1997, for Bosah, his wife, Paul O. Ndibe, Ms. Gibson, and several other Nigerians. Several weeks before the trial, on December 18, 1996, the government filed a superseding indictment, increasing the criminal counts to conspiracy to commit mail fraud, mail fraud, and money laundering, expanding the case to nine defendants and extending the period from January 1, 1992, to October 16, 1996, with a dollar total of over a million dollars. To the companies already defrauded were added the names of several book clubs and mail-order merchandise houses—same scheme, but now more defendants and more charges. The trial was moved to March 19, 1997, before Judge Alexander Williams.

A week before the trial, on March 11, 1997, Bosah entered a guilty plea on two of the fifteen counts (mail fraud and money laundering) following several days of negotiations. (Court documents now listed his last employment as a Wells Fargo security guard, a job many Nigerians apply for as soon as they arrive in the United States.) On December 2, 1998, Judge Williams sentenced him to fifty months of incarceration, followed by three years of supervised release; he was also required to pay $53,176 in restitution, plus surrender his Swissair frequent flyer miles. Bosah also forfeited $43,576, including $6,800 seized at his residence by postal inspectors.

During the sentencing hearing, Bosah's brother, Ben Bosah, an environmental engineer living in New Albany, Ohio, addressed the court: "My younger brother Charles has erred and he has recognized that. Everybody in our family is suffering for it now.... With regard to getting post boxes and various CDs, he has accepted that responsibility in letters to you and to us. We pray that your Court uses leniency in dealing with him. He is sorry for what he has done."[70]

In attempting to disassociate Bosah from the leadership role in the criminal enterprise, and thus a higher sentence, his brother said, "This was an enterprise where everybody was their own leader. Nobody was responsible. Everybody was traveling." (Salem would stick throughout to the charge that Bosah was leader of the ring.)

"With regard to bringing in money, yes, he did bring in money, but he did not just bring in money from the enterprise. It's a common thing that when people travel they take money back to Nigeria and they bring back money to the United States for family, people who are in school, people like myself. I am an environmental engineer by training. That's what I practice. But I also help myself and my family sell leather goods. I buy leather goods in the United States and I send them to Nigeria. They're sold in Nigeria and the money is brought back by me.

"My wife is a physician and obstetrician. We have three children. But the family is such that everybody does everything because of the nuclear family system we have in Nigeria. You cannot just rely on one income to make ends meet. He got involved in this activity and now he realizes the folly of his actions and I think he's repentant. We have been praying for him. He's been praying for himself."

Bosah, who would answer no questions about any aspect of the case, then addressed the court: "What I have done is wrong. I know my actions have really caused a lot of people a lot of trouble. But from being incarcerated some time now, I have also, you know, learned a lot of things from it, too, and during the process I have, you know, gotten closer to God and I've seen, you know, what I've been blind to. And now, Your Honor, as I stand here before your Court I promise not to ever break the law, and I intend to keep my words. I want to thank this Court today and I hope not to come here any more, and when I come here I'll be in better circumstances."

Judge Williams then asked for the government's position. Salem replied: "This was a very pervasive, continuous fraud scheme. It is the largest single fraud scheme reported by these mail-order merchandise companies for prosecution. All that merchandise, everything that was taken from the United States, is gone. It's in Nigeria.... He's thirty-two years old. And there's approximately $1.5 million of merchandise somewhere in Nigeria."

What was the government's strategy in the case? Salem replied, "From the get-go there were two things that were foremost for us. Number one, Mr. Bosah was the principal player. Therefore any pretrial resolution to this case would necessarily require him to plead guilty to money laundering, and he was going to face more time, regardless of his lawyer's reluctance to go that route. Normally, defense lawyers like to bargain away the most serious charge and plead guilty to a lesser charge. That was not going to happen here. So that was one strategy. The other was to make sure that everyone we knew of at the lower levels was treated in a manner that we hoped would allow us to get their assistance against Mr. Bosah. Thus, the lesser players were offered better deals in the hopes that we could convert them right away into a cooperating arrangement with the government. In the end, they all told us they wanted to assist us, but they did not, except for his girlfriend, so they didn't get any breaks for cooperating with us. Mr. Bosah pled very close to the time of trial. We were preparing for him. I think he just wanted to save the additional jail time he would get by going to trial and getting convicted."

Summarizing the case as he saw it before sentencing, Judge Williams commented, "That was a pretty tough scheme and clearly you had a lot to do with it. The evidence I heard suggested that you were clearly among the leaders. It was at your place in Cheverly where they met, and you who went to the airport." Then Williams reflected, "I don't know why people do it. It's certainly inconsistent with your upbringing. You have a well-educated family, people who are successful. You have some college work. You are an educated man yourself. Why people come over here and obtain naturalization, become citizens, and then become involved in these kinds of schemes, I don't know. I don't know why people do it. You did it. You hurt a number of people. You caused a lot of companies to lose money because of that scheme. Of course, the law forces punishment on you."

Judge Williams later reflected on the case, calling it a typical example of the multi-defendant, elaborate fraud cases that appear increasingly in U.S. federal courts. "We hope these cases will remain in the federal courts," Williams, a former state prosecutor, remarked. "Generally, states simply do not have the financial and human resources to adequately investigate and present these cases. As a former state prosecutor, I understand that better than most people. It would have taken a tremendous amount of our resources in Upper Marlboro to prepare that case for trial."

From prison, Chief Bosah, as he now called himself, began to file motions on his own behalf *pro se* (by himself), *in pauperis* (without funds), denying that he had the effective assistance of counsel; for example, "My retained attorney never shared adequate information. As a result, I pleaded to a higher charge. Wood (the attorney) never filed to suppress the money laundering charge.... I was charged with a $1.2 million sum when in fact the correct amount was less than $800,000." (If the dollar amount was under $800,000, the sentencing category would be lowered, and if the money-laundering charge was dropped, he would be prosecuted on the much-reduced fraud count.)

Post-sentencing communications from prisoners are common in the court system. A few are legitimate and heart-rending, most are time-fillers asking for new trials, reduced sentences, appealing to the United Nations Charter, universal laws of humanity, and so on. Some send excrement or other body fluids in their letters to the court. Most prisoner communications are opened by a special office in Baltimore that handles *pro se* requests; some clerks wear rubber gloves when opening envelopes. Petitions flow freely from prisoners like Bosah with ample time and access to a rudimentary law library, which must be provided in prisons by statute. However, in this case, once the prisoner's court-appointed attorney responded that he had spent many hours on the case and done all he could to defend his client, the letters dwindled off.

Commenting on the case, Salem, who lectures on it around the country with postal inspector Krug, said, "This kind of fraud ring operates in many parts of the United States. If you catch a group on a particular crime, they may be very small, but they also may work together to create much larger fraud rings. Nigerian and other immigrant group fraud has been festering here in the mid-Atlantic region for a while. The Bosah scheme is different from what most people are familiar with, which is the letter fraud scheme, now endemic in the United States. A business firm or an individual receives a letter that claims the Nigerian government has some extra money it wants to share with them, and if they will just give over some information—no money—they can share in these enormous sums, nine, ten, twelve million dollars. Some people who are less well versed in this fraud, and I'm being kind to them, or who are greedy, will respond. The letter may emanate from Nigeria and put them in contact with a local person. You are asked to open a new bank account, which seems innocuous enough, into which the money can be transferred. You get a call to say that the transfer will take place at noon, then another call at 11:45 saying, 'A horrible thing has just happened. The Nigerian government has put a $400,000 tax on the transfer. We will pay $300,000 if you'll just pay $100,000.' You pay the money and everything closes up. In one of these Nigerian fraud schemes, a businessman from Germany lost $5 million. He just kept getting sucked in deeper and deeper. He was one of the victims when we prosecuted one of those schemes in this office; I was involved in that case. The Bosah scheme is just a variation. I think there are groups here now taking advantage of our system, Russian groups, Asian groups, and Nigerian groups, to name a few. There is no pattern to what the Nigerians are doing; it could be drugs, it could be anything."

What would propel a person to spend his waking hours over five years in near perpetual motion, filling out thousands of merchandise applications, setting up 350 mail drops, driving to Waldorf and a hundred other small-town post offices weekly, flying to Lagos monthly? The Oxford English Dictionary defines greed as "Intense or inordinate longing, esp. for wealth or food; avarice, covetous desire." It is what propelled Charles Bosah around Maryland, and eventually into jail.

The *Hit Man* Case

Can a Book Be Sued for Murder?

> *"Does it matter to you for what purpose your books are being ordered when you sell them?"*
>
> *"No."*
>
> *"Do you care?"*
>
> *"No."*
>
> *—Exchange between Howard Seigel, lead attorney for plaintiffs, and Peder C. Lund, Publisher of* Hit Man.

The case was called *Vivian Rice et al v Paladin Enterprises*, and it could have been the case of the century for First Amendment followers. Is a how-to murder manual, used by a contract killer to commit three murders, protected by the U.S. Constitution? A judge called the book "abhorrent," and another said promoting criminal conduct "finds no preserve in the First Amendment." But the Boulder, Colorado, publisher and more than twenty leading media and free speech groups argued that people kill, books don't. Books, the defense reasoned, "are capable of enriching, educating, and—occasionally—shocking and horrifying us. But, whatever their power, they are incapable of acting."

The case had been tried originally by Judge Alexander Williams at Greenbelt, appealed to the Fourth Circuit in Richmond, then returned to district court for retrial. It was headed for a jury trial on Monday, May 27, 1999. Judge Williams was prepared for a spectacular encounter, an artillery duel of legal experts seeking to preserve or limit traditional free speech arguments. Then, at the last minute, the case settled. On late Friday afternoon, May 24, 1999, the judge issued a settlement order, closing the case. Williams knew nothing of the last-minute settlement negotiations and had cleared his calendar for a four-week trial.

A newspaper account said the multimillion-dollar settlement was reached at the insistence of the company's insurance carriers. The case came shortly after the Littleton, Colorado, high school massacre and a recent decision by a Michigan jury ordering a $25 million payment to the family of a gay man killed by a fellow guest on a television talk show. The publisher's lawyers concluded that, First Amendment or not, the case was too risky to try.[71]

It began as a grisly for-hire murder case. Sometime after 2:30 A.M., March 3, 1993, Trevor Horn, an eight-year-old quadriplegic, was killed, his respirator yanked as the child slept in his suburban Silver Spring, Maryland, home. His mother, Mildred, forty-three, and a private-duty nurse, Janice Saunders, thirty-eight, were also murdered, each shot through the eye. A crude attempt was made to have the killings look like a robbery, but police asked, Who would benefit most from such deaths? and soon fingered Trevor's divorced father, Lawrence T. Horn. Horn lived in California and stood to inherit nearly $2 million in insurance payments. (The child had suffered brain damage, quadriplegia, and cerebral palsy; the money came from a 1988 settlement with Children's Hospital in Washington, D.C.) Horn's phone records in turn led to a Detroit ex-con and trigger man, James Perry, who, police charged, was hired by Horn and who followed the modus operandi of a how-to murder manual titled *Hit Man: A Technical Manual for Independent Contractors*, and its companion volume, *How to Make A Disposable Silencer, Vol. II*, both published by Paladin.

Horn drew a life sentence in 1996; Perry got the death penalty, but the sentence remains on appeal. Perry was no James Bond. A small-time Detroit hood who billed himself as a "spiritual adviser, case-buster, independent contractor," he bought *Hit Man* before committing the murders—the proof of purchase being his 1992 bounced check. More than 140 phone calls linked Horn and Perry in the weeks before the murder. At the trial, Montgomery County prosecutors listed twenty-two points of similarity between the Silver Spring murders and the *Hit Man* methodology. Paladin's attorneys countered that Perry, age fifty, had been convicted of armed robbery and assault in the 1970s and spent time in prison, where he would have learned techniques well-known to criminals.

The case did not end with the sentencing of Horn and Perry. Relatives of Horn's ex-wife, Mildred Horn, and her son, Trevor, and Michael D. Saunders, husband of nurse Janice, filed a lawsuit against Paladin and its publisher, a cocky Vietnam veteran, Peder C. Lund. What is unique about the case is the linking of the murders to a specific book and the action against the publisher for $50 million in a wrongful death civil suit. In a classic First Amendment free speech case, the issue would be the right to publish books, even if their content was repugnant to some audiences. But the plaintiffs argued this was a civil liability case, because the book was a how-to murder manual and was no more protected by the Constitution than a string of books on how to cheat the IRS or how to steal power from the electric company. Paladin was free to publish, they argued, but could also be held liable in civil court for damages inflicted as a result of *Hit Man* being directly used by a purchaser to murder three people. Crucial to the case was paragraph 15 of the complaint, establishing the sort of publishing list Paladin produced: "For many years prior to March 3, 1993, Paladin and Peder C. Lund had successfully undertaken to become actively engaged in the business of aiding and abetting criminal activity by providing technical information and guidance on a variety of subjects." Paladin's backlist included such titles as *Pipe and Fire Bomb Designs*; *Silencers for Hand Firearms*; *Homemade Semtex*; *The Anarchist Handbook*; *A Do-It-Yourself Submachine Gun*; *Be Your Own Undertaker: How to Dispose of a*

Dead Body; *How to Destroy Bridges*; and *Sneak It Through: Smuggling Made Easier.*

Lund, in a later deposition, said, "Paladin publishes books on an eclectic group of topics, including revenge, humor, personal freedom, espionage and investigation, explosives and demolitions." Books like *Hit Man*, he stated, "tease the reader with ambiguity as to whether they are to be taken seriously."[72] At one point Howard Siegel, a lead attorney for the plaintiffs, asked Lund, "Does it matter to you for what purpose your books are being ordered when you sell them?"

"No."

"Do you care?"

"No."[73]

The court complaint quoted from *Hit Man*. The author was an anonymous "Rex Feral" ("King of the Dead"), in reality a divorced mother of two children who was traced to a Florida trailer park and who had written a pleading letter to Lund asking for a $2,000 advance on the manuscript to pay her property tax. Parts of the book's content quoted in court documents established both its completely cynical disregard for human life and civil society and the meticulously detailed techniques of committing murder:

> It is my opinion that the professional hit man fills a need in society and is, at times, the only alternative to personal justice. Moreover, if my advice and the proven methods in this book are followed, certainly no one will ever know. (Preface, ix)
>
> Within the pages of this book you will learn one of the most successful methods of operation used by an independent contractor...Step by step you will be taken from research to equipment selection, to job preparation, to successful job completion. You will learn where to find employment, how much to charge, and what you can, and cannot do with the money you earn. (Preface, X)

> Close kills are by far preferred to shots fired over a long distance. You will need to know beyond any doubt that the desired result has been achieved. When using a small caliber weapon like the .22, it is best to shoot from a distance of three to six feet. You will not want to be at a point blank range to avoid having the victim's blood splatter you or your clothing. At least three shots should be fired to insure quick and sure death...aim for the head—preferably the eye sockets if you are a sharpshooter. [p. 24]

The complaint continued, "James Perry shot Mildred Horn and Janice Perry from a distance of three feet. He shot them each three times in the eyes, exactly as instructed by the defendants.... These manuals were published with the express intention to encourage and facilitate the commission of murder. In publishing, marketing and distributing these manuals for profit, Paladin and Peder C. Lund acted wantonly and with reckless disregard of known consequences to the public."

Paladin struck back with a series of motions, arguing that the court lacked jurisdiction in the case, that the publications are "privileged and protected...by the First and Fourteenth Amendments to the Constitution of the United States," and that the damages "were caused by the criminal acts of third persons over whom the defendants had no control, right of control, or other relationship of any kind."

Then, on April 22, Paladin filed a motion to dismiss the case on summary judgment. This was a crucial moment in the case. Such motions are routine, basically arguing that a plaintiff failed to prove a case, or that the case should be dismissed for constitutional or statutory reasons. By now Paladin was joined by friend-of-the-court petitions from more than twenty media and civil liberties groups, including the Association of American Publishers, the National Association of Broadcasters, and the Reporters Committee for Freedom of the Press.

Their basic argument was this: The "American tradition and First Amendment jurisprudence demonstrates why we do not put information on trial. Putting the information in the books on trial would spawn similar claims against publications, music, video programming, and other forms of expression. The books contain protected speech, no different from numerous other works. This lawsuit threatens entire genres of expression." In summary, Bruce W. Sanford, a leading First Amendment specialist, wrote, "A word, a lyric, a film clip—these are the living embodiments of our proud heritage of defending the rights of even the most outrageous speaker. They are capable of enriching, educating, and—occasionally—shocking and horrifying us. But, whatever their power, they are incapable of acting. To hold a word or an image jointly responsible for even the most ghastly criminal act diminishes us all, because it means that some speech surely will be chilled in the process. This case should be dismissed."

The brief also stated, "Subjecting authors of controversial books to protracted, punishing litigation and censoring their books will have no appreciable impact on the marketplace for crime. But it will have a devastating impact on the marketplace of ideas.... Imposing liability in this case would run afoul of the Constitution and our heritage of protecting even the most provocative speech. Justice was done when the jury held James Perry accountable for his actions. To hold the printed word jointly responsible for a criminal act is a step that no court in this country has ever taken, and for good reason."

Rod Smolla, law school dean and author of several books on media law, presented the case for the plaintiffs as a suit "about recompense for physical injury and death." Paladin was free to publish its murder manual, he argued, but was "not free to escape compensation for the catastrophic injury it helped cause." Smolla quoted the Joint Statement of Facts both parties agreed to before the trial, a document negotiated by both sides to reduce trial time and limit the issues brought before the court. In this case, so confident was Paladin that a First Amendment defense would trump all other legal issues, they accepted language insisted on by the plaintiffs conceding Paladin "intended and had knowledge that their publications would be used, upon receipt, by criminals and would-be criminals to plan and execute the crime of murder for hire."[74]

Judge Williams received the request for summary judgment on July 22, 1996, and a week later granted the defense motion along classic First Amendment lines. Williams wrote, "The Court read *Hit Man* in its entirety. Its content is enough to engender nausea in many readers. This Court, quite candidly, finds the book to be reprehensible and devoid of any significant redeeming social value. Nevertheless, however loathsome one characterizes the publication, *Hit Man* simply does not fall within the parameters of any of the recognized exceptions to the general First Amendment principles of freedom of speech. The Court, likewise, declines Plaintiffs' invitation to create a new category of speech unprotected by the First Amendment—speech that arguably aids and abets murder.

"In summary, the Court believes that Plaintiffs have not made a sufficient showing on this record, as a matter of law, to support their claim that the maintenance of this suit for damages does not infringe upon the First Amendment protection of speech. Accordingly, the Court will grant summary judgment for Defendants." Williams held that the book "merely advocated or taught murder, rather than incited or encouraged murder, entitling its publisher to First Amendment immunity.... The First Amendment bars the imposition of civil liability on Paladin unless *Hit Man* falls within one of the well-defined and narrowly limited classes of speech that are unprotected by the First Amendment," including obscenity, fighting words, libel, commercial speech, and words likely to incite imminent lawless action. Williams summarized, "The constitutional protection accorded to the freedom of speech and of the press is not based on the naïve belief that speech can do no harm but on the confidence that the benefits society reaps from the free flow and exchange of ideas outweigh the costs society endures by receiving reprehensible or dangerous ideas."

■

The case was appealed by the plaintiffs and argued before a three-judge panel of the Fourth Circuit Court of Appeals on May 7, 1997. Lund again was joined by more than twenty friend-of-the-court supporters, including the *New York Times, the Washington Post*, America Online, and the Horror Writers Association. The Greenbelt Court's decision was reversed and remanded for retrial in a November 10 decision written by Judge J. Michael Luttig, a passionate opinion writer whose intensity of thought is often gauged by the number of dependent clauses he piles together.

Luttig, a conservative intellectual who had clerked for Warren E. Burger and Antonin Scalia on the Supreme Court, said the issues in this case were unique in the law because of "Paladin's astonishing stipulations coupled with the extraordinary comprehensiveness, detail, and clarity of *Hit Man*'s instructions for criminal activity and murder in particular, the boldness of its palpable exhortation to murder, the alarming power and effectiveness of its peculiar form of instruction, the notable absence from its text of the kind of ideas for the protection of which the First Amendment exists, and the book's evident lack of any even arguably legitimate purpose beyond the promotion and teaching of murder."

Luttig concluded, "We are confident that the First Amendment does not erect the absolute bar to the imposition of civil liability for which Paladin Press and amici contend. Indeed, to hold that the First Amendment forbids liability in such circumstances as a matter of law would fly in the face of all precedent of which we are aware, not only from the courts of appeal, but from the Supreme Court of the United States itself." In advancing the case to the appeals court, the parties agreed that the sole issue to be decided by the Court was whether or not the First Amendment represented a complete defense. All other issues of law and fact were specifically reserved for subsequent proceedings. The appeal represented a roll of the dice by both sides. For the plaintiff, a favorable verdict would mean they could try the case again, linking the book to murder and suing for damages; for the defense, the First Amendment argument was everything, framed in classic free speech language.

Luttig demolished one of the most important free speech arguments, what had come to be called the Tom Clancy argument, that a murder manual was indistinguishable from a work of fiction, a true-crime thriller, a film, or a media presentation about crime. A clue as to how Luttig would frame the issue came early in the opinion: "Because long-established case law provides that speech—even speech by the press—that constitutes criminal aiding and abetting does not enjoy the protection of the First Amendment...we hold...that the First Amendment does not pose a bar to a finding that Paladin is civilly liable as an aider and abettor of Perry's triple contract murder.... For these reasons, the district court's grant of summary judgment in Paladin's favor is reversed and the case is remanded for trial."

Luttig, whose own father had been brutally murdered, affirmed that Perry used *Hit Man* as the model for his murders. The jurist quoted a section from the book that he said "is arrestingly effective in the accomplishment of its objectives of counseling others to murder and assisting them in its commission and cover-up":

> I'm sure your emotions have run full scale over the past few days or weeks.
>
> There was a fleeting moment just before you pulled the trigger when you wondered if lightning would strike you there and then. And afterwards, a short burst of panic as you looked around you to make sure no witnesses were lurking.
>
> But other than that, you felt absolutely nothing. And you are shocked by that nothingness. You had expected this moment to be a spectacular point in your life....
>
> The first few seconds of nothingness give you an almost uncontrollable urge to laugh out loud. You break into a wide grin. Everything you have been taught about life and its value was a fallacy. (*Hit Man*, p. 107)

Luttig concluded, "If there is a publication that could be found to have no other use than facilitate unlawful conduct, then this would be it, so devoid is the book of any political, social, entertainment, or other legitimate discourse."

The judge made mincemeat of Paladin's argument that potential readers were adequately cautioned that the books were "for informational purposes" or "for academic study" only and that "neither the author nor the publisher assumes responsibility for the use or misuse of the information contained in this book." The appeals court called such disclaimers "plainly insufficient in themselves to alter the objective understanding of the hundreds of thousands of words that follow, which in purely factual and technical terms, tutor the book's readers in the methods and techniques of killings."

Separating the content of *Hit Man* from the work of news reporters, Luttig wrote, "It will be self-evident in the context of news reporting, if nowhere else, that neither the intent of the reporter nor the purpose of the report is to facilitate repetition of the crime or other conduct reported upon, but, rather, merely to report on the particular event, and thereby to inform the public."

Once the Fourth Circuit's decision was handed down, Vivian Rice, Mildred Horn's sister, and Michael D. Saunders reopened the case on May 13, 1999. This time a resounding appeals court opinion supported their position. The defendants, whose attempt to take the case to the Supreme Court was turned down, argued Paladin did not have the specific intent to aid and abet James Perry in committing the murders of Mildred Horn and Janice Saunders, that it had no knowledge of James Perry's and Lawrence Horn's criminal plans, that Paladin markets books to a wide readership of law-abiding citizens and, as such, is no different from other booksellers, publishers, and distributors. Turning to Perry, Paladin's attorneys argued Perry did not receive substantial encouragement from Paladin or its publications, that he knew "most if not all the contents of *Hit Man* from his military training and service in

Vietnam, his prior violent felonies, his incarcerations at the Jackson, Michigan State Prison" and "that the techniques Perry purportedly learned from *Hit Man* are widely known and a part of popular culture in films, literature, and news." Finally, "the Plaintiffs' claims are barred by the First Amendment to the United States Constitution."

Paladin next filed a motion for continuance, asking that the trial be postponed sixty to ninety days because of "the potential ramifications that the recent shootings at Columbine High School in Littleton, Colorado, may have on Paladin's ability to receive a fair trial" and submitted a list of more than 440 news reports and editorials in regional publications on the Littleton shootings and the culture of violence they reflect.

Smolla countered, calling Paladin's motion "a desperate last-ditch effort to delay these proceedings. It lacks legal foundation, runs contrary to common sense, and should be summarily rejected by the Court.... As one of the country's major traffickers in training manuals that instruct criminals and would-be criminals in the manufacture and use of bombs and firearms, Paladin is understandably uncomfortable these days."

Then abruptly Paladin called it quits. Part of the multimillion-dollar May 24 settlement included surrendering the remaining 700 copies of *Hit Man* and Paladin's making annual contributions to charities of the plaintiffs' choice, one for the victims of Oklahoma City (Timothy McVeigh was a Paladin book purchaser), another for the victims of Littleton.

Few cases in recent times have so stirred the interest of media lawyers, First Amendment scholars, gun and grenade enthusiasts, and free speech advocates. The lines were drawn, the classic arguments made, and some new ones as well. What court watchers sensed coming was another case like those bringing the tobacco companies and gun manufacturers slowly but inexorably to public accountability in the courts. It didn't happen, however, because of the eleventh-hour settlement.

Although the Fourth Circuit's opinion is binding only on the courts of the states within its jurisdiction, other circuits traditionally give great respect to precedents established by sister courts. Significantly, the Supreme Court did not accept the appeal, finding no constitutional issue meriting its scrutiny. The case was like an intensely interesting play, only three acts of which were completed. It is shelved now, to be finished in another time, another place.

Judge Williams' face lit up when I asked for his comments on the case. "I've always enjoyed First Amendment issues," the law school professor began, "because of the importance of a free press to America. There has been a paucity of Supreme Court First Amendment cases as of late. This is a subject the Supreme Court is going to have to address in the years to come, because there are a lot of copycat issues out there. The question is, Where are we going to draw the line on some of the media violence questions and bring defendants in under some causation linkage, versus the First Amendment which says people have the right to think, express ideas, and promote views that may be different from what we like to see, which is the whole essence of what is America, as stated in the Bill of Rights.

"That was a very exciting case for me to look at, a once-in-a-lifetime case," he recalled of *Hit Man*. "It was a well-argued case on both sides. The lawyers were geared up for one tremendous trial. I ruled according to my understanding of the law. Then the Fourth Circuit basically said that particular act went far beyond what was anticipated by the framers in the Bill of Rights. I was looking forward to trying the case under the narrow issue of aiding and abetting under Maryland law, but the defendants settled.

"There was not much out there in Maryland law as to whether the conduct in this case would fit a definition of civil aiding and abetting. As I read the cases, it was a tough standard, almost like the criminal standard. You had to prove it was done intentionally, purposefully, and knowingly—but you never know what a jury would have done. This is a case that would have been decided by the

Fourth Circuit and probably the Maryland Court of Appeals. What I probably would have done, had we gotten a verdict, and all the post-trial motions were completed, is to have certified the question to the highest court in Maryland. I would have gotten an opinion from the highest court of Maryland as to whether or not the conduct the jury found occurred here would fit into civil aiding and abetting.

"The Fourth Circuit could have done it also, they could have certified it 'across the street,' as they say, to the highest court in Maryland, and asked, 'Under Maryland law, would this have been civil aiding and abetting?' Ultimately, the Supreme Court would have had to face the critical issues as to whether or not a jury verdict saying someone was aiding and abetting under Maryland law and awarding damages was contrary to the protection provided by the First Amendment. A great issue, and I think all of us were looking forward to that day."

Mr. Mature and the First Amendment

Free Speech vs. Pornography

> *"I think he crossed the line here.... There were no notes, no research, no drafts—nothing.... The question for me is, when was he going to start writing?"*
>
> *—Judge Alexander A. Williams Jr.*

The lavender-colored folder has a white sticker on which a clerk had typed *United States of America v Lawrence Charles Matthews*, and stamped "Date opened: July 28, 1997." That was the date a federal grand jury returned a true bill against Larry Matthews, a fifty-five-year-old, second-tier Washington, D.C., radio journalist, for the interstate transmission of pornography by computer. The issues were starkly contrasting: Matthews, a veteran WTOP and National Public Radio journalist and investigative reporter, claimed he was researching a story on child pornography on the Internet. Downloading and transmitting picture files of children engaged in sexual acts was designed to create rapport with sources of information on the industry, he argued. It was a free speech issue. If convicted, Matthews would be the first journalist to be sent to jail for accessing child pornography.

The government saw it differently: receiving and transmitting pictures of child pornography was a clear violation of the law. If Matthews wanted to pursue a story, they argued, there were other ways to do it.

It all began at about 11:50 A.M. on the morning of December 11, 1996, when the Matthewses' cleaning woman answered the door of their two-story home at 2514 Locustwood Place in Silver Spring, Maryland, a middle-class Washington suburb. FBI agent Nick Rodriguez and two U.S. marshals handed her a search warrant. They were there to seize Matthews' computers and to look for evidence of child pornography. It was not an impulsive raid. For several months Matthews had been entering preteen chat rooms on the Internet, which alerted the FBI's Innocent Images program, an around-the-clock group of agents that monitor pornography traffickers from an unobtrusive Calverton, Maryland, office building. Given the volume of activity, it is the repeat inquiries that attract police attention.

An FBI memorandum noted, "A computer was located on a desk in the upstairs rear bedroom. A second computer was located on the desk in the basement office, and a third computer, a laptop, was found in the file cabinet drawer in the office area. These computers, with peripheral equipment, were seized.

"The residents, Mr. and Mrs. Lawrence C. Matthews, returned to the home during the search and were interviewed by Special Agent Ferrante and Detective Rodriguez. A copy of the warrant was furnished to Matthews during the interview. The Matthews departed at about 2:15 P.M. Upon completion of the search an inventory of the items seized was left on the dining room table. The premises were left secured at approximately 2:47 P.M."

It is a federal crime for any person to knowingly receive or distribute child pornography that has been mailed, or that contains materials that have been mailed or shipped or transported, by any means, including by computer. In its affidavit supporting the search warrant, the government argued, "The ability to produce child pornography easily, reproduce it inexpensively, and market it anonymously (through electronic communication) has drastically changed the method of distribution of child pornography. This pornography can be electronically mailed to anyone with access to a computer and modem."

The FBI had been tracking Matthews from July to December 1996, during which time, "the defendant did knowingly and willfully transport and ship, in interstate commerce, via computer, a visual depiction, to wit: a graphic file identified as 'ZBRDANCE.JPG,' the production of which involved the use of a minor engaged in sexually explicit conduct and which depiction was of such conduct." Details of Matthews' AOL account were obtained, and the government alleged that, under the name of "Mr. Mature," Matthews transmitted numerous image files through the computer company's bulletin board service, including one "depicting a girl in her early teens who is facing the camera. She is wearing a T-shirt and tennis shoes, but nothing else. She appears to be seated on a table with her left leg raised so that her foot is resting flat on the table. Her legs are slightly spread, giving an unobstructed view of the genitals. This image file was received one time and forwarded 7 times by Mr. Mature."

Another file "depicts a naked girl, approximately 7 or 8 years old. She is standing, facing the camera at about a 45-degree angle, and leaning back on a piece of furniture. Her legs are slightly spread. Crouched in front of her is a female of undetermined age who is performing cunnilingus on the young girl."

The indictment contained fifteen such counts. The files had such names as ZZ5&COCK.JPG, 9JERK1.JPG, 10YANKIT.JPG, 10DAD.JPG, JANEDAD.JPG, 6YRSUCK2.JPG, 1BRO&SIS.JPG. Other files had such names as Stargirl, Tanlegs, Natasha, Blondie, Oldie but Goodie, the poetry of pornography.

Matthews was arraigned before Magistrate Judge William Connelly on August 27, 1997, a month after the grand jury had found a true bill. He pleaded not guilty. Connelly released the journalist, but he was ordered to surrender his passport and was forbidden from entering a chat room that allowed sexual contact with minors. The case entered the court's computerized assignment process and was designated for Judge Alexander Williams Jr. and set for trial on March 10, 1998.

The lines were clearly drawn. The defense was arguing free speech, a reporter taking on the protective coloration of his craft to obtain a story on a subject about which he had previously written.

For the prosecution, the issue was not free speech but the committing of a crime, repeated examples of laws being broken on the sending and receiving of child pornography. Reporter Ruben Castaneda, who covered Maryland courts for the *Washington Post*, wrote, "Federal prosecutors have said the case is about a child pornography aficionado who happens to be a reporter. They say they do not believe Matthews' explanation that he was researching a story when he received and transmitted images of children in lewd poses or engaging in sex acts with adults."[75]

The heart of Assistant U.S. Attorney Jan Miller's argument was that the defense case was based on "the proposition that a member of the media has the right under the First Amendment to violate criminal law if his purpose is to gather information in order to write an article. The defendant does not, and cannot, cite any support for this dangerous proposition." The prosecution would agree that Matthews' motive was not a legal issue in the case, that it was irrelevant to the charge. In explaining this position, Deborah A. Johnston, one of the prosecutors, later drew an analogy. "You could put on evidence that you were acting in self-defense if you were involved in a murder case, but you wouldn't put on a self-defense if it was a theft case. We do not have to prove motive; in a case about distribution of child pornography, all you have to prove is that someone knowingly distributed it."

Meanwhile, the defense unleashed its big guns in an *amicus curiae* (friend of the court) filing by National Public Radio, the American Federation of Television and Radio Artists, and the Radio-Television News Directors Association. The document was filed on March 2, 1998, and written by David B. Isbell of Covington & Burling, a First Amendment specialist, and Kurt A. Wimmer, a well-known lawyer in the field. Their argument: "Journalistic speech occupies a privileged position under the First Amendment. This protection extends to the newsgathering process by which the information on which journalistic reports are based is sought, for without some protection for seeking out the news, freedom of the press could be eviscerated.

"The government's stance fundamentally misconstrues the nature of the First Amendment defense in this case. For it is no part of that defense that the content of the pictures here are protected under the First Amendment. Matthews claims protection not for the content of the images at issue here but for the activity of news-gathering. The protection afforded to the latter under the First Amendment is as broad as the protection afforded to the former is narrow.

"The balancing required by the Court in this instance is straightforward—the First Amendment defense cannot, of course, automatically trump any prosecution of an individual who may have violated Section 2252 (a) (nor do we understand Matthews to argue that it does). Rather, due process and the First Amendment merely require the Court to permit Matthews to present evidence for the consideration of the Court or jury to be permitted to argue in favor of a First Amendment defense."

Enter the seventh-floor Pennsylvania Avenue space of Covington & Burling, from whose front offices partners can invite clients and family to watch the inaugural parade, turn left past the vase full of fresh roses, stroll across the Oriental carpets, past the grandfather clock. In the reception room where a clerk leafs through a mail-order catalogue, not one but three firm pamphlets are easily available on a coffee table: *In the Supreme Court, Recent Litigation Successes*, and another that says, "Our lawyers are typically high-ranking graduates of the best law schools. Many have advanced degrees in other fields. Many have been clerks to leading judges, including justices of the United States Supreme Court. Others have taught law or other disciplines, or have served in significant government posts."

Bursting through the floor-to-ceiling glass doors is Kurt Wimmer, young, trim, and one of the firm's leading media law specialists. He wrote the brief supporting Matthews on behalf of several professional broadcast associations. A journalism graduate of the University of Missouri and a Syracuse University Law School graduate, Wimmer follows libel and broadcast regulatory laws closely. It is unusual for groups to file an *amicus* brief at the trial court level; generally they wait until the appeals court level or until the case reaches the Supreme Court, where the issues have focused. To file such a brief in district court, consent of the other side must be obtained (not granted in this case) or a motion must be made to the court (made and accepted in this case).

"It's a difficult case," Wimmer reflected, sinking down into an ancient leather chair. "On the one hand, you have a reporter investigating a story using investigative tools that in his mind are appropriate and necessary to develop the story, and you have the tension of a statute that is being interpreted in a very rigorous way, potentially making part of the newsgathering process illegal. So the question really is: How do you interpret the statute? If the newsgathering activity is breaking the law, then it is clear the First Amendment doesn't provide him with a defense for that. All sorts of content-neutral statutes are applied to limit newsgathering. You have to obey trespass orders; if you are at a crime scene you have to obey law enforcement officers who tell you to stay away from the evidence. The question here really is not, can a reporter get away with breaking the law, but should you interpret this statute in a way that makes this behavior contrary to law? It is a fine distinction, but an important one for our clients."

Why did the U.S. Attorney's Office move to limit any free speech defense by Matthews from the beginning? Wimmer saw it as the government's effort to obtain a tactical advantage and field position. "Child pornography is such a horrible thing and an area where we have zero tolerance. While I am sympathetic, especially as a parent, to really vigorous enforcement of child pornography laws, it struck me that what they did was overzealous advocacy. I can understand why they did it. They are good advocates, and if you have someone on the other side knowing there will be a bunch of media companies weighing in on the defendant's behalf, you can expect them to take the position 'Let's frame the issues in the best possible way for our side.' This is done all the time. It obviously was a strategy that worked for them. But it puts Mr. Matthews in a very difficult position with no journalistic arguments at all."

Why didn't Matthews opt for a jury trial? "It's a tough, tough call. On an issue as sensitive as child pornography, you cannot expect a jury to necessarily be sympathetic to a defendant. But once it became apparent that his entire defense was going to be ruled legally irrelevant, he had no choice but to plead guilty, be sentenced, but nonetheless challenge the basis of the sentencing."

Why was it that, within a three-day span, the defense entered a lengthy plea to the judge on Matthews' behalf, the prosecution responded lucidly and point-by-point a day later, and on the next day both sides signed a guilty plea agreement that had obviously been the product of negotiations? Wimmer did not find the arrangements unusual. Recalling the saying "In the halls of justice there is no justice but in the halls," he added, "It goes with our system of advocacy. No one really wants to settle until they see what their chances are going to be, and in our system of justice sometimes you just don't know that until the last moment. My sense is there would have been negotiating throughout the entire time, narrowing gradually until the last moment."

Wimmer threw up his hands and laughed when I asked if his research had turned up any previous cases that clearly supported his line of argument. No such cases exist. "The best support comes from the legislative history of the statute," he continued, referring to the brief filed by Leslie McAdoo-Brobson, Matthews' main attorney during most of the case. "This was not originally a cyberspace statute, it was a trading-in-pornography statute. It was strengthened by Congress on the basis of a reporter's work in investigating these child pornography rings and getting the stuff.

"I've never had a case like this one," Wimmer said in conclusion. "In the case of a journalist it is appropriate to look at the larger First Amendment issues, because once you annex the press as an investigative part of government, the whole newsgathering process suffers, the openness and freedom of expression being promoted by the First Amendment suffers, and ultimately society itself suffers because you cannot get the sort of reporting we have become accustomed to under the First Amendment."

Three months later, on June 29, 1998, Judge Williams issued an opinion denying a defense motion to dismiss the case. "The law is clear that a press pass is not a license to break the law," Williams concluded, stating he ruled on behalf of the government because of its "surpassing interest in protecting children from harm caused by the spread of child pornography." Williams amplified his views in another opinion a few days later. "Even assuming that the Defendant's exploration would in some way advance his investigation, the degree to which a reporter gains knowledge about the general subject matter by committing his own violations is insignificant compared to the government's interest in preventing the exploitation of children.... It is the Defendant's actions which contribute to the very problem he wanted to investigate." Additionally, Williams acknowledged that the availability of material over the Internet "may not be an easy matter to explore. However, it does not seem substantially different from other means of distribution, such as mail received from overseas providers."

In the *Matthews* case, the prosecution had covered all their bases. They wanted to keep the case limited to receipt and transmission of pornography—that was the crime. Consequently, they preempted Mathews' use of a free speech defense by filing a motion to exclude any evidence, testimony, or argument concerning a journalistic motive.

Undaunted, one day later, Matthews' lawyer filed a motion to reconsider the court's order of June 29, to which Williams replied, "The Court does not believe that the First Amendment provides a defense when the production and dissemination of the pictures at issue causes the overwhelming harm to the children identified by the Supreme Court in *Ferber*.... Because the Court does not believe that the Defendant is entitled to a First Amendment defense concerning his alleged proper motivation in using the pictures," the motion for reconsideration was denied.

Assistant U.S. Attorney Miller replied with equal speed on July 1: "Whether the defendant's position is viewed through the lens of the Free Speech Clause or the Free Press Clause, it still boils down to an unfounded assertion that the First Amendment somehow allows members of the press to violate the law in order to gather information on which to base an article." Referring to Williams' earlier ruling, he argued, "The Court correctly held that the First Amendment does not provide such a license to violate the law to members of the press. The Court's ruling should stand."

The guns on both sides were silent now. The entire defense had been predicated on a journalists-in-the-act-of-newsgathering-are-protected argument, which the court did not allow. Larry Matthews, ex-WTOP reporter, was being tried like any other interstate trafficker in child pornography. The trial was scheduled to start in a few days.

It was at that point that Matthews' attorneys folded their cards and decided to enter a guilty plea. The journalist would plead guilty to two basic charges, and thirteen other similar charges would be dropped. His long shot was that the free speech issues would prevail with an appeals court. Explaining the decision, Matthews' attorney said it was the "most efficient and practical way of getting the issue before the Fourth Circuit Court of Appeals."[76]

On July 2, 1998, a plea agreement, drafted by Assistant U.S. Attorneys Miller and Johnston, was sent to Michael V. Stratham, Matthews' current lawyer, for Matthews to sign with his spidery, bunched-up signature. The key sentence was, "Mr. Matthews, your client, agrees to plead guilty to counts one and nine of the indictment" charging him with receipt of and transporting child pornography. The letter noted, "The defendant is free to present evidence to support and seek a downward departure based on his alleged motive of conducting research for a news story. The government is free to present evidence to refute the defendant's claim regarding his motive."

Judge Williams sentenced the veteran reporter to eighteen months in federal prison on March 8, plus a $4,000 fine payable in $150 a month, and three years supervised release. (The sentence was on the low side of the Sentencing Guidelines range; the top-side would have been twenty-four months and $40,000.) Matthews was allowed to remain free on bond, pending an appeal to the Fourth Circuit. He continued to work as a shift editor for National Public Radio. Pointing out that Matthews spent nearly two years contacting Internet "chat rooms" and exchanging child pornography with pedophiles and federal agents posing as teenage girls, Williams said, "I think he crossed the line here.... There were no notes, no research, no drafts—nothing.... The question for me is, when was he going to start writing?

The lead prosecutor, Jan Paul Miller, was quoted in the press as saying, "This was going on a daily basis, sometimes several times a day, with hundreds of pictures going back and forth. It does somewhat stretch credulity to suggest somebody could be investigating something for this long, with this intensity, and have nothing to show for it whatsoever."[77]

The case was argued before the U.S. Court of Appeals for the Fourth Circuit on December 1, 1999, and on April 13, 2000, Circuit Judge Diana Gribbon Motz, writing on behalf of a three-judge panel, affirmed Judge Williams' earlier opinion, stating, "Congress enacted a statute that would subject to criminal prosecution not only child pornography dealers, but also those who lack a profit motive, including individuals, like journalists, whose professional standing might help to disguise a fetish for such material. Matthews' version of the facts, which we accept as true at this juncture, present what initially appears to be a close question. But, at end, after careful review of Supreme Court precedent and the legislative considerations underlying 18 U.S.C.S 2252, we are persuaded that Matthews' asserted First Amendment defense simply enjoys no support in the law. Accordingly, we must reject it."

THE HIGHER LAW AND THE PAINTED BOMBER

"The five defendants approached the B-52 bomber in this context, symbolically poured blood and hammered on the plane with household hammers, prayed, and then explained to the group the meaning of their actions."

—David Walsh-Little, Defense Counsel,
USA v Frank Cordaro, et al.

Sometimes the higher law is in conflict with ordinary law. Henry David Thoreau made such a case in *Civil Disobedience*. Dietrich Bonhoeffer invoked a higher law to resist Nazi Germany; so did Martin Luther King in the United States in his "Letter from Birmingham Jail." So did two nuns, two priests, and a grandmother at Andrews Air Force Base on Sunday, May 17, 1998. It was 9:30 A.M., and the U.S. Air Force was showing off its planes on Visitors' Day, designed to build community support for the large suburban Maryland base from which presidential flights originate. Later there would be flight demonstrations, band music, and other festivities for several thousand people.

Methodically, the five peace activists, part of a loosely organized group called Plowsharers, entered the base and headed for the flight line where, with hardware store hammers, they pounded on the bomb bay of an aging B-52, poured blood on it, unfurled a banner, and let themselves be arrested.

Air Force security reacted quickly, but there was no resistance. The FBI was called in and Father (religious titles were not used in the court documents) Frank J. Cordaro, forty-seven, Sister Ardeth Platte, sixty-two, Father Lawrence A. Morlan, thirty-eight, and Sister Carol Sue Gilbert, fifty, were arraigned before Magistrate Judge Jillyn K. Schulze, as was Kathleen A. Boylan, fifty-four, a Washington, D.C., grandmother. On May 18, they were charged with attempting to "willfully injure or commit depredation against property of the United States." The original felony counts of property destruction were later reduced to misdemeanors. In a courtroom filled with peace activists, Judge Schulze released the five persons on bond and held them over to trial. In signing the court papers, Platte added in her own hand, "I acknowledge that the judge told me the orders, not that my conscience—or God—allows me to comply."

A two-day bench trial was then scheduled before Judge Alexander Williams on September 22 and 23, the defendants having waived their rights to a jury trial. At the trial, *USA v Frank Cordaro, et al*, AW 98-0237-001, and during preliminary motions throughout the summer, both sides took the positions they would hold until the end—the higher law versus domestic statutes. Were they prophetic heroes in the Martin Luther King tradition, or anachronistic throwbacks to the Vietnam protest movement? Let the reader decide, in this case about different issues than those that usually come to court.

David Walsh-Little, a Columbia Law School graduate whose office is located above a Baltimore soup kitchen and who founded a not-for-profit law center for poor neighborhood people, the Sowebo (South West Baltimore) Center for Justice, argued the charges were unconstitutional, the case violated international law, and the defendants did not have the requisite *mens rea*, or criminal state of mind, to merit conviction. Walsh-Little filed a wide-ranging brief appealing to morality, history and international law. A poor person's lawyer by choice, he was taking his first foray into international law.

He described the five as follows: "Together, they call themselves the Gods of Metal Plowshares," a reference to a phrase in Leviticus 19:4, "Do not resort to idols or make for yourselves gods of cast metal"—namely, the B-52s.

"The B-52 is a nuclear weapon intended to unleash vast heat, blast, and radiation which cannot be controlled in space and time. They are intended, designed, and built to threaten, start, and escalate a nuclear war," the defense argued. "Each B-52 is equipped and intended to threaten and use twelve air-launched nuclear cruise missiles and eight short-range attack missiles. Each nuclear bomb is eight times the explosive force of the bomb dropped on Hiroshima and could destroy everything within thirty square miles."

"International law, as such, binds each of us," Walsh-Little argued. "Acts adjudged criminal when done by an officer of the government are criminal when done by a private individual. The guilt differs only in magnitude, not in quality. Failure of a citizen to prevent known, planned, and threatened violations of fundamental and binding law of his or her government makes that citizen culpable." Linking international law to domestic statute, the defense counsel argued, "The defendants ask only that the Court not allow a criminal prosecution under a statute that conflicts with established United States commitments under international law. Therefore this criminal prosecution should be dismissed."

Walsh-Little's final argument was about criminal intent. Specifically, the statute under which the defendants were charged with a misdemeanor posited that each person must act "willfully," or have *mens rea* (criminal intent). "The undisputed facts of this case indicate that none of the defendants specifically intended to injure the B-52 as property of the United States. None of the defendants believe that the B-52 is property. Instead they all believe as a matter of law that the B-52 is illegal under international legal principles."

The prosecution would not accept any of the international arguments.[78] Patrick E. DeConcini, special assistant United States attorney, argued, "This case involves a violation of domestic law, and has nothing to do with international law. The defendants in Nuremberg were charged with violations of international law. Violations of domestic law are resolved in domestic courts under principles of domestic law, and violations of international law are resolved in international courts under principles of international law. If this were not so, the sovereignty and laws of all nations would be subservient to the laws of international courts, making all domestic laws essentially meaningless."

The prosecutor zeroed in on the question of intent. Here the defendants claimed they lacked traditional criminal intent, since their purpose was to halt gross crimes against humanity. DeConcini responded, "Application of this principle would create a defense for any person who, for whatever reason, thinks that the U.S. is in violation of some international law, regardless of whether we are or not. This is clearly an unacceptable, anarchistic principle that cannot be tolerated by a civilized society." Clearly, two different language systems were in conflict, one moral and historical, the other traditionally legal. There was a certain unity to the argument line Walsh-Little devised. The question was, would Judge Williams, minister and ethicist, buy it?

The answer was no. On January 5, 1999, Judge Williams gave each of the accused minimal sentences. Boylan received a ten-month sentence, based on prior convictions—as pacifists and social activists, the defendants had been encountering the legal system for decades—Cordaro, Morlan, and Platte received six months; Gilbert, four months.

"They had a different reason for doing what they did than most people who appear in this courthouse have," Assistant U.S. Attorney Jack Geise, who helped prosecute the case, reflected. "People have different motivations for what they do. You treat people differently depending on their motivations, even though it may still be technically a crime. A person going seventy mph in a thirty mph speed zone to take their child to the hospital is going to be

The courthouse at Indian Creek,
Greenbelt, Maryland

Jurists of the courthouse on Indian Creek: (left to right) Magistrate judges Charles B. Day, William G. Connelly, Jillyn K. Schulze; District judges Deborah K. Chasanow, Peter J. Messitte, Alexander Williams Jr.; Bankruptcy judges Paul Mannes, Duncan W. Weir.

(Photography by Don Patterson/Patterson Video-Photo)

treated differently than someone who is going seventy mph in a thirty mph zone for the fun of it. That's what prosecutorial discretion is about."

Reflecting on the case, he continued, "There are lots of reasons why people appeal to higher law, and there are lots of higher laws out there. Such cases are not as common as they were thirty years ago. Whatever their legal arguments might have been, they are not the ones that will be honored in a court in the United States.

"The other thing that struck me about this case," he said, in an office strewn with stacks of legal briefs, a shelf full of stuffed animals, and an ornamental tree badly in need of water, "is these were people who were interested in social justice. They were doing some very good things; they really weren't Dr. King going to jail—and this is my personal view—they were not going to change anything by throwing blood on a B-52. I think the strategy they chose, which was to promote disarmament, was fairly silly. Part of the reason civil disobedience works is it resonates with people's feelings, that it really is right, as in the case of Gandhi, and in the South on racial desegregation. I think they would have a lot more influence doing good works in their communities rather than spending the time in jail."

Later Judge Williams, who teaches courses in ethics and the law, reflected on the issues in *Cordaro*. "That was a difficult case, because these were not like the sorts of criminals we imprison daily," he observed. "These were people acting out their political views. They may be moral views, but they are also political views. You have a right to vent such views to a legislative body. The government took the position you just can't destroy a bomber and you can't throw blood. That constitutes malicious destruction of property no matter who does it. Because the defendants had records and said they wouldn't cooperate with the probation people, and stated they wouldn't return to court, there was nothing to do but to detain them until their sentence was executed. I think I gave them all the minimal sentence that I could."

Was there any moral dilemma for a judge who is also a minister? "Yes. I was convinced those people were acting under moral principles. They believed in their case, the idea that aircraft had the potential for mass destruction. They asked me to look at the situation as being the same as Martin Luther King faced when he was in prison. He was attacking an unjust law. There were certain aspects that I agreed with, but I told them that even Martin Luther King went to prison, and he gave us an argument as to why and when you should disobey a law—when it was unjust. But I didn't feel this particular case went that far. I told them they had an avenue to express their frustrations and concerns through Congress and politically, and that is the difference that I saw."

Williams reflected, his usual precise manner trailing off into speculation. "I guess if I get there one day to the point that I do believe that a law is immoral, even though I have taken an oath to uphold the Constitution and the laws thereof...you can only go so far in your own conscience if you believe that a law is unjust, not just in its enactment but in its application. I haven't reached that decision yet and it did not surface in this case."

Of all the cases I encountered at Greenbelt, this was the only one that had any ideological basis. I could accept Geise's point that the protagonists were "no Martin Luther Kings." Such people come along once in a century. Yet, in their own eyes, was the collision with the law inevitable? Or was this history's late, late show, a rerun of the Vietnam War protests? (I had sat in on part of the Chicago Seven trial in 1968, where the defense's side of the courtroom looked like the chorus from *Hair* and chunky Chicago police officers erected wooden barriers around the courthouse to keep the protesters back.) How would the "painted bomber" defendants represent themselves? I called Kathleen A. Boylan at the Dorothy Day Center in Washington, D.C.

The large, run-down, blue house in a once-prosperous, now-transitional neighborhood in Washington, D.C., is home for several families and single mothers with children living through stressful times. A Dorothy Day Catholic Worker Center, it is one of several such islands of hospitality welcoming the poorest of the poor, providing a temporary safe haven, hot meals for the needy once a week, a neighborhood food shelf on Wednesdays, and a continuing witness to peace and justice issues. The "Plowshares" movement, of which Boylan is a part, takes its name from the biblical verse in Isaiah 2:4, "He will judge between the nations as arbiter among the peoples. They will beat their swords into plowshares and their spears into pruning knives." I asked Boylan how many members there were in Plowshares, but she didn't know, because it is a "spirit-led" organization whose numbers and structure keep shifting.

In her mid-fifties, Kathleen A. Boylan is a mother of five and grandmother of two. She has lived in community with several other peace and social justice activists since 1988. Her moment of truth came during the 1968 Catonsville Nine draft protest when Fathers Daniel and Philip Berrigan and others burned draft cards with homemade napalm and were arrested. "I was a young twenty-four-year-old mother of two small children. I turned on the radio that day and heard the news and it changed my life," the former South Bronx schoolteacher recalled. "I was touched with what they did. It was miraculous." Since then Boylan has been arrested six times. I asked if she would be jailed again. She hesitated, then said, "I cannot say where my conscience will lead me." Going to prison is "a difficult experience, but if I can do it, anybody can do it."

Prophets on the cutting edge or throwbacks to an earlier era? I asked Boylan. "Nothing I am doing will make any immediate change," she answered. "It's a long process, like the process that ended slavery. I'm just one of the millions of people doing something to end war. I can't show any results for my work, but that's fine with me, because it is part of opposing weapons of annihilation and mass destruction.

"It's biblical what we are doing," she concluded. "Jesus spoke of people picking up the cross. Picking up the cross, I understand to mean, is to do the kinds of things that will get you in trouble with the oppressors, the people in power. The cross was a method of execution. I believe we are nonviolent revolutionaries called to transform the earth. We all have a common vocation to cry out against and resist death and injustice. That's the human vocation."

Impulsively, that Saturday morning I took some groceries to the Dorothy Day Center. A sign in English and Japanese said at the door, "Peace be to all who enter here." Although I had interviewed Kathleen Boylan on the phone, I did not know what she looked like. The three-story, turreted Victorian house was filled with people, and the garden brimmed over with flowers and vegetables. (She was in New York visiting her son, so I missed her.) At Dorothy Day Center, a Salvadoran resident, wearing a New York Yankees jersey, helped me carry the bags inside. His manner was intent as he picked through our conversation in English.

"What does Ms. Boylan look like?" I asked.

"Tall, but not as tall as you."

"Thin?"

"Thin."

"White hair?

"White hair."

"What is her face like?"

He exploded in a smile. "She has the face of an angel."

Part III

The Article III Judges

Peter J. Messitte

The central figures in any courthouse are its judges. At Greenbelt, there are three Article III federal judges (appointed under that section of the Constitution), three magistrate judges, and two bankruptcy court judges. And because Greenbelt is a relatively new courthouse, its judiciary is relatively young. All were appointed at about the same time; thus the court does not have entrenched Ancients vs. Moderns, Democrats vs. Republicans, Old Timers vs. Newcomers to the Block—colorations that affect some courts. Of the three federal judges, Peter J. Messitte was the older of the two appointed on the same day, and thus became the de facto leader of the new court division. The chief judge of the district, Walter Black (and later J. Frederick Motz), was in the northern division in Baltimore.

Peter J. Messitte was born into the heady world of the late New Deal. His father, Jesse, was a product of the Harvard Law School Class of '32. After six years with a Wall Street firm, Jesse came south as one of the Roosevelt Brain Trust, young lawyers who were changing the face of government. Jesse's father had been, among other things, a New York City street car conductor, but Jesse, whose parents had grown up in what was then Austria (now Ukraine), went to City College of New York before heading north to Cambridge. "When you grow up the son of a lawyer, you're exposed to how a lawyer thinks," Peter recalled. "My father was the sort of person who would say, 'There are four responses to that. First....'

It was so typical of him. It got rather poignant. At one point I remember I was fourteen or fifteen and having romantic problems and said, 'I don't know what love is.' He was temporarily working out of the city, and I still have what he sent me, a dozen pages with sixteen points on 'What is love?' One, two, three...It was so characteristic of him to be analytical that way. There was also a tender side, which was another quality he had, but it was that rational side that showed me how lawyers think."

Peter's mother, Edith, said Jesse put family first; she recalled him taking Peter down to the Library of Congress to do research for a term paper on Saturday afternoon because the local library was inadequate. Out-of-town offers came his way, including one to move to Hollywood as counsel to Sam Goldwyn, but he much preferred the stability of a high-level government job to the roller-coaster life of private practice on the outside.

The portrait on Peter's mother's living room wall is of an intelligent, energetic, smiling man, of medium height, with lively eyes and a warm manner, ready to shake hands with a visitor or engage in a conversation on FDR's latest New Deal initiative. As part of life in the sprawling, tree-lined suburb of Bethesda with its solid 1930s homes, Peter attended Bethesda-Chevy Chase High School, in those days one of the country's premier academic institutions. A young, already on the move senator, John F. Kennedy, was the commencement speaker the year Peter graduated. Speaker Sam Rayburn had a niece in the graduating class; several other Washington luminaries had offspring there as well. Debate and public speaking were in the air.

"I suppose I discovered early on that I could say things that people responded to in class or otherwise. I liked to stick up for the underdog, and somehow speaking out and seeing that lawyers did that probably led me along the path to law. I don't know there was much doubt I would do something like that. In eleventh grade, I was chief justice of the student court (it never met) and in twelfth grade was president of student government." (In 1999, four graduates of the B-CC Class of '59 were among twenty-five attorneys named by the Montgomery County Bar Association as the best Montgomery County Lawyers of the Twentieth Century. Peter was one. Another was Jim Thompson, who used to down milkshakes and cheeseburgers with Peter at drive-ins after B-CC games, and who is now president of the Montgomery County Bar Association and a major state political-legal figure.)

Recalling the 1950s, Messitte remarked, "I have a fairly clear memory of the McCarthy days. I must have been ten or eleven. In my class, there was a girl whose father was the Washington representative of TASS, the Russian news agency. I don't think there was any question he was a Communist. The daughter was the brightest girl in our class. It was clear that some parents told children to shun this girl. People were being accused of having a sympathetic association with Communists, so it was a difficult time. I remember both my mother and father saying quietly but firmly, 'Pay no mind to that.' My mother used to bottle preserves with this girl's mother, a severe-looking Quaker woman, but very, very nice. My parents didn't socialize with them at all, but they never, ever said anything to me about being careful in my dealings with this girl."

Public appearances came naturally to the young Messitte, who was a regular panelist on the TV show *Youth Wants to Know*, featuring "the searching and provocative questions of today's youth, and broadcast live from Washington, D.C." During high school, Messitte was a regular, asking questions of Hubert Humphrey, Wayne Morse, and other leading figures—even the comedian Jerry Lewis. "Do you have any good jokes?" Peter asked him to open the show. "If I didn't, I'd be out of business," the veteran performer replied. "This was a serious program," Messitte recalled, "and it fired my enthusiasm for politics. Law and politics go hand in hand."

In high school, Peter won several oratorical contests as well. "That pumps you up. You think, 'Hey, maybe I can do something with this.'"

The subjects were Americanization and democracy, and Messitte made his way from Rotary to Optimist clubs for the creamed-chicken-peas-and-biscuits luncheons and a civic talk—a practice he continues now, though the menu has changed. Thus student politics, oratory, and national TV all pointed toward a career in law.

Peter and Susan Messitte's spacious waterfront home in St. Mary's City, Maryland, is filled with Brazilian and American art, plus Maryland memorabilia. It all started with political buttons. "In 1952, I was excited about politics. I saw all the buttons. Washington was the place to be because everyone was running for president. Ike, MacArthur, Richard Russell of Georgia, there were people coming out of the woodwork then. My brother and I would take the trolley downtown from Chevy Chase on Saturdays with shopping bags. We would go from headquarters to headquarters and collect handfuls of buttons." At the 1952 Bethesda-Chevy Chase Harvest Show, Peter entered his political buttons in the special collections category and won first prize. After he left for college, his mother cleaned his crowded room, discarding most of the political button collection and the 300 baseball and 300 football cards, including three 1951 Mickey Mantle rookie cards. "When I last looked, in mint condition they were worth $18,000 each." Peter remembers having to purchase loads of bubble gum, "that pink stuff that had the white sugar on it that tasted like wallboard. I threw away enough to construct a small city."

Yale, Williams, Wesleyan, Bowdoin, Dartmouth, and Amherst all accepted Messitte, and several offered scholarships. Preferring a small liberal arts college, he picked Amherst, where he majored in history. Focusing on Latin America, he wrote a thesis on "Social Aspects of the Nitrate Industry in Chile." He spent part of his junior year in Chile, learning vernacular Spanish and working for a paper products company. Returning to school, he thought of becoming a Latin American specialist and an academic, but his father's Socratic method of questioning kicked in once more. "Do you really want to do that? If you become a lawyer, you can still deal with Latin America, but if you become an academic, you don't have that flexibility. Why don't you think about it?" Peter picked law.

"I didn't particularly like law school," he recalled three decades later. "I didn't find it an experience that was all that pleasurable. By my third year, I was only a sometime student in class. By the end of the final term, I was full of legal education. I was just tired of being in school. I wanted to do something. Since then, I have thought of how well the film *Ferris Bueller's Day Off* captured my mood as a student, watching the clock which is not moving at all, or when you look at it, the hands move back." But he did win first prize for best overall team and brief in the 1965 Moot Court Competition.

Were there any positive memories of three years at the University of Chicago Law School? "I do have positive recollections of my first-year contracts course taught by Professor Malcolm P. Sharp, who was an almost inscrutable fellow. He seemed to talk in riddles all the time, but if you listened carefully, he was telling you to be alert to all things at all times. His favorite line, and it is one I use often, was, 'Everything is like everything else and nothing is like anything else,' which seems to me to be a fairly good way to summarize potential legal cases. Even for a case just coming into your office. Someone is telling you a story. It doesn't leap out and say, 'This is a contracts case, a problem of offer and acceptance.' It is just someone talking, and if you don't leap in and try and shape the story too quickly, you will begin to see its legal dimensions."

From September 1966 to October 1968, the Messittes were Peace Corps volunteers in Brazil. Peter had met Susan, a tall, lithe young lady, while visiting the White House one summer. Both were from the University of Chicago (Susan was working on a master's in political theory), and they were married during Peter's second year of law school. Both were eager to see something of the world, and the Peace Corps was the experience of a lifetime. They were originally slated to work with youth groups in São Paulo through the local Young Men's Christian Association, a middle-class movement working with less-privileged neighborhoods. Peter coached soccer (reading the coaching manual as he did so) and taught basic hygiene, while Susan worked with a girls club and taught English. The Messittes had a simple apartment in the middle-class Pinheiros neighborhood, slightly outside the central city of São Paulo. "We had friends in the Brazilian and American communities who lived out that way. We got to know some Brazilians fairly well, people who are now judges, law professors, and leading lawyers thirty years later."

As a young lawyer, Peter met with members of the local bar and soon was asked to give a course on the Anglo-American legal system at the University of São Paulo Law School, the country's leading law school. He taught in Portuguese, which by then he spoke fluently. Simultaneously, his connections with law professors led to work with legal aid groups in Brazil. In the mid-1960s, many young American lawyers thought poverty law was a high calling. In Brazil, "there were programs through law schools, and through labor unions, and a few bar associations; but they suffered from the same ills legal aid programs everywhere still suffer from today—limited funds, young lawyers with limited experience—although that is changing in our country. You tended to get a less than satisfactory product. I published two articles on the subject of legal aid in Brazilian law journals that are still cited." From a bookcase he produced two recent books on Brazilian law reform still quoting his 1968 surveys of the literature. "There really hadn't been anything written about the history of legal aid in Brazil until I wrote it," he said. "They gave me open access to the stacks of the University of São Paulo Law School, so I just started pulling things off the shelves where I thought something might be. It took me months to gather material."

Messite continued his recollection. "A criminal law professor of mine at Chicago, Norval Morris, a distinguished international figure, had been the director of the United Nations Institute of Criminology in Tokyo. When I told him I was going to São Paulo, he put me in touch with another branch of his UN program in Brazil. These people had fine quarters with three or four empty offices. They weren't doing much of anything, but they said, 'You can have an office here.' So I had an office downtown that I went to two or three days a week. I was writing, teaching, and visiting legal aid programs. In fact, USAID (U.S. Agency for International Development) funded my travel around Brazil to visit legal aid programs all over the country. They got interested in what I was doing."

One friend, whom the Messittes knew as a neighborhood newspaper editor, "always used to run funny things in the paper about us. We lived very modestly in a simple apartment, with simple furniture. When we were leaving in 1968, he ran a banner headline: 'American Couple to Move, Assets for Sale—Great Opportunity.' We must have had 250–300 people outside our door to buy our junk—I mean junk. I think some people must have wanted things just because they were American. They even took our cat, which had been born a block away."

But it was time to come back home and practice law. "And we had a child, the first Peace Corps baby born in Brazil, our son Zach. It was time to get started in life. We were pretty antsy to do what married couples do—settle down, get a job with a law firm, buy a house."

After returning from Brazil in the fall of 1968, Peter worked as an associate with the Washington firm of Zuckert, Scoutt, and Rasenberger, until 1971. The practice was largely administrative law, and the restless young lawyer, eager for more varied fare, struck out on his own, taking the risky leap of setting up a one-person office in Chevy Chase, Maryland. "I hoped to cultivate my Brazilian contacts," he recalled, "to get to know the people in the Brazilian Embassy. I'd like to say I was discovered by them, but the truth is I was laying traps everywhere. One way or another, the Brazilian consul, who eventually became a good friend of ours, told the Brazilian community there was a lawyer in town who could help them and could also speak Portuguese.

"There was a celebrated case I had in 1977 that got front-page coverage in the *Washington Post* and the *Evening Star*. It involved a significant money judgment against the Diplomat Hotel in northeast Washington, where two Brazilian women were staying. They were brutally raped, sodomized, and threatened with murder. I sued the motel on their behalf for insufficient security. A dummy security camera in the lobby was not hooked up to anything, but more than that, they were tolerating prostitution in the back. I put an expert on who talked about prostitution and crime and then showed prior crimes there. U.S. District Judge Thomas A. Flannery let me put in evidence the computer printout record of all the prior crimes there. The pages began to flap down; there must have been twenty pages of crimes at the hotel. We got a $530,000 verdict, which in a security case of that era was a huge verdict."

Messitte recalled how it felt to strike out on his own. "Was I nervous? Yes! First day. What do you do? Who calls you? How do you keep busy? I had an uncle who had a small publishing company. Just before I went into practice, he sent me a check for $500 and said it was a retainer. He didn't call me for three years. He more than got his money back over time because I rarely billed him after that, but I was so touched by his giving me that vote of confidence when I started. You just go out; it's one of those things where you have friends, you have family, your mother is telling everybody, 'My son is a lawyer and he's got this practice and he can do work for you,' and that's how it starts."

As a lawyer, Messitte did the spectrum of solo practitioner law—wills, contracts, litigation, domestic relations, commercial and corporate work, and real estate transactions. It was a solid general practice with frequent court appearances, including some high-visibility, complicated cases. "The biggest case I tried was against Clint Murcheson, owner of the Dallas Cowboys, in the U.S. District Court in Dallas. The case lasted two weeks. I got a $3.3 million verdict against him in his home court. The plaintiff was a former employee of one of his computer companies who felt that Murcheson had reneged on stock options. The verdict was later reduced and reversed, but I was out of the case by that time because I had gone on the state bench.

"By 1971, I was into politics. I was the Montgomery County Lawyers for McGovern chairman, which was a committee of one. In 1980, I was an uncommitted delegate to the Democratic National Convention in New York City, the only uncommitted delegate east of the Mississippi." Messitte organized the uncommitted delegates' caucus, representing 300 delegates out of 1,500 at the New York City convention. At the time, it was basically a contest between Jimmy Carter and Ted Kennedy. "I was getting urgent calls from both sides. *The Baltimore Sun* ran a series of articles about my position, and at the convention, I was followed by National Public Radio. The first night of the convention, which was a Sunday night, we were the only event, so we were the main subject. In the end, I was not prepared to sign on with either candidate. I was hoping someone like Mondale or Muskie would step in and run."

After 1980, a key Democratic leader in the county sent feelers Messitte's way indicating that, if he wanted to run for the Maryland House of Delegates, the party would support him. Peter and Susan discussed their future at length; the clear preference was to stay with the law. "Earning income was our livelihood. I didn't think I could do justice to my practice and be in elective politics, too. So I chose to practice law but keep my hand in by helping my friends in politics." In 1982 several vacancies occurred on the Circuit Court for Montgomery County. "I thought I could qualify for one of those seats. I had had some prominent cases and had represented some condominium associations and tenant associations, and some of my friends had been elected to high office. In Montgomery County during that time everyone sort of knew whose turn it was to be the next circuit judge. In fairness, there was a blue-ribbon commission that selected the candidates, but still...you almost knew who'd get the seat. My wife was a member of the commission, and when I decided to apply she stepped aside. The procedure of the commission was to vote on sending three names to the governor. I was not on the lists they sent up, and on one list they only sent one name. I didn't like it. The candidate was a nice fellow, but it seemed to me to be very undemocratic. I had some contacts at the state level, including the governor and the attorney general, so I thought I'd be a contender. But you had to get through the gate, and I couldn't do it. I also saw that in the last seven or eight nominations to the circuit court, the candidates had to do a stint on the district court, which was like peoples court. There was a tradition in place, which seemed to me to be inappropriate. If you were forty-one or so, which I was, and said, 'I'd like to be a candidate for circuit court,' many lawyers would look at you as if to say, 'Who do you think you are?'

"I decided to run and in 1982 went on the ballot for an opening on the circuit court. It was an active campaign with some prominent people supporting me. I lost two to one, but must have run a decent race. It was the first time in a long time anyone had challenged the system. There was some sorting out afterwards. I continued to practice law and get good results. I think in the long run people thought it was a gutsy thing to have done and that it was done honorably, even if it upset some establishment folks. But then the membership of the commission changed and the chairman of the commission, whom I knew well, said, 'Apply again.' I applied and was eventually nominated. In 1985, the same day he interviewed me, the governor's secretary called and said, 'The governor is appointing you to a circuit court vacancy in Montgomery County.' In Maryland, judicial appointments are made by the governor, but the candidate must stand for ratification by the electorate at the next general election."

The circuit court is a court of general jurisdiction, covering commercial and criminal cases, plus ruling on estates and contracts and convening a lot of jury trials. Messitte had some big trials, including the First Maryland Savings and Loan case, a complex multimillion-dollar commercial fraud case that lasted for months. A $367 million verdict was returned in the case against the company's officers for risky lending practices. Another significant case involved a police officer who said his gun went off accidentally, sending twenty pieces of shot into a woman's body near Gaithersburg, Maryland. The case was tried without a jury. Messitte found the officer guilty of involuntary manslaughter and gave him a year in jail.

How did he move from Rockville to Baltimore and the federal bench? "I thought that some day there might be a possibility of being an appeals court judge in the Maryland system. There were Democratic governors but Republicans in the White House when I was on the county bench from 1985 to 1992. It wasn't until the fall of 1992, when all of a sudden it looked like Bill Clinton might win the presidency, that I thought to myself, 'There are vacancies on the federal court and it looks like a Democrat might win the presidency.' The idea of a seat on the federal bench, which had never seemed possible, suddenly did. I was for Clinton. I'm sure I thought, 'I'm the sort of person he may be looking for.' But in all candor, he had been saying, 'I want to put women, persons of color, and minorities on the bench.' I'm thinking, 'This may be an uphill battle for appointment.' And maybe it was. President Clinton had five appointments to the Maryland bench, including two women, two African Americans, and one white male—me. What was gratifying was that I had very broad-based support of Republicans and Democrats in Montgomery County for the seat, the bar leadership, and letters signed by all the state senators, delegates, and members of the county council. They contacted Senator Sarbanes and said basically two things: 'Montgomery County should have a representative on this bench' and 'This is the guy we would like to have.' I had known Sarbanes from politics, but he was very deliberate. He didn't do anything automatically. He went carefully through the list of candidates. He probably had a list of from seventy-five to a hundred applicants for these positions. He had us fill out forms and interview with various bar associations. It was about professional qualifications, not about ideological stands. I don't know how it winnowed down in the end. When I finally heard about the nomination, I was at my thirtieth-anniversary reunion at Amherst. I'm waiting for the Friday evening reception to start and someone says, 'There's a long-distance call for you from Washington. Senator Sarbanes' office is trying to reach you.' I went to the Alumni House and got Sarbanes, who informed me, 'I'm sending your name to the White House.' I called my mother, who said, 'Don't worry if you don't get it.' I said, 'Mom, I'm calling you to tell you I got it.'"

Later Senator Sarbanes discussed his judicial selection process. A former Rhodes scholar and member of a blue-chip Baltimore law firm who had once clerked with a federal judge, Sarbanes takes the process of selecting Article III judges seriously. He knows each of the Baltimore and Greenbelt judges personally. "Maryland is a small state," he explained. He personally interviewed fifty applicants when the Greenbelt openings became available. "You're looking for ability, experience, and obviously character," he began, adding, "I have very high standards as to who should go on the bench. A district judge sits alone. The only check on them is the appeals process, and that in reality is a limited check. No one checks them for temperament, demeanor, the courtesy they show toward litigants once they are on the bench." Of Messitte, he said, "He had done a great job in handling complex cases. Among all the judges there (in Montgomery County), he was the one most able to handle matters of consequence."[79]

Next Messitte was interviewed by the Justice Department, and his name was submitted to the Senate. Unlike the situation in the Reagan days, there were no ideological litmus tests. "If you were a former Peace Corps volunteer from Brazil, I suppose they could draw certain inferences from that, and if you've done work with tenants groups and victims of sex crimes, they could probably guess who you were. I also had some very nice support from the NAACP,

Hispanics, and women's groups. My friend and mentor Steve Sachs, a former Maryland attorney general and a great lawyer, got off some funny lines at my investiture. One of them was 'Judge Messitte's nomination was met with a great deal of enthusiasm, some of it spontaneous.'"

The hearings were a non-event. Messitte was among the first group of Clinton presidency nominations to the federal bench. After the FBI and Department of Justice investigations, the Senate Judiciary Committee had done its investigation. They basically say to Justice, "O.K., this person is acceptable." Democratic Senator Carol Mosely-Braun of Illinois was presiding. "There may have been one other senator present for part of the time," Messitte recalled. "Also, Democratic Senator David Boren of Oklahoma, who had been a high school friend at B-CC, came to present me, along with Senators Sarbanes and Mikulski of Maryland and Connie Morella, who represented Montgomery County in Congress. The hearing went without a hitch."

On October 20, 1993, the White House confirmed the appointments of Judges Messitte and Chasanow after the Senate vote. The older of two judges confirmed on the same day, according to Department of Justice practice, gets seniority. If both were born on the same day, they choose the person born earlier, but it didn't come to that. Messitte was older, so seniority went to him. Chasanow was sworn in November 1, Messitte on November 15. The new judges headed for Baltimore, where space was at a premium because several senior judges had kept their chambers, and were given temporary space until the Greenbelt Courthouse was completed a year later.

Messitte's hope was to "make the Greenbelt court user-friendly while not being too informal. I have to be frank about it. To many Montgomery County lawyers, Baltimore was cold and distant, more than forty miles away. It was a respected court, but one we didn't feel part of. The idea was to come here and maintain the high quality of the product that came out of Baltimore, but be more involved in outreach to the bar through talking to the lawyers, opening the courthouse to the arts, and having contact with community groups. That's something we're working on all the time."

Messitte's international interests remain strong. A while back he had lunch at the Supreme Court with Justice Sandra Day O'Connor, who had recently returned from a speaking tour in Brazil. In asking the Library of Congress about Brazil's legal system, she was referred to Judge Messitte, who prepared a briefing document for her, and in Brazil she met judges who had worked with Messitte since his Peace Corps days. "Your footprints are everywhere down there," she said, and invited the Messittes, the Brazilian ambassador, Dr. Paulo Bekin, a leading Brazilian jurist, and his wife, to lunch in a private dining room at the Supreme Court, along with Justices Scalia and Kennedy. Over pasta prepared at home by Justice O'Connor, they talked about international judicial exchanges. (Both Scalia and Kennedy do a lot with international colleagues). "That morning I had talked with my mother and told her, 'I'm going to the Supreme Court for lunch today. I'm afraid that is as close as I'm ever going to get.' And my mother said, 'That's not what I'm telling my friends.'"

No question has been more blurred in the judicial system than the dividing line between state and federal jurisdictions. To begin with, the Founders never solved the question satisfactorily, nor could they. States wanted to retain their sovereignty and only grudgingly conceded certain powers to the new national government in 1787. As for the courts, more than 90 percent of cases are dealt with in state and local courts. The federal cases are ones under the growing body of federal law or disputes between citizens of different states, such as a citizen of New Jersey suing a contractor incorporated in New York.

These "diversity of citizenship" cases enter the federal courts if the sum in dispute is more than $75,000. Admiralty cases, suits between states, international disputes, and suits in which the

United States is a party are the other cases that find themselves in federal courts.

How does this state-federal divide affect a sitting federal judge? Most criminal and civil cases, like murders, robberies, and rapes, are state matters. That is a basic tenet of federalism. "Federal courts are courts of limited jurisdiction," Messitte reflected. "I could get a case, an automobile vehicle accident case, if the sum involved was more than $75,000, and one citizen was from Maryland and the other from Virginia. I would apply Maryland law, just as I did when I was a circuit judge in Montgomery County. Much civil litigation is also diversity litigation, and it can involve torts, contracts, other commercial matters, plus disputes with local and state governments. Judges do that as well. Historically the reason for bringing such cases to federal courts was there was some feeling a litigant might get a home-court advantage if they sued in their state. The out-of-state litigants might find themselves at odds. People now say, 'Diversity litigation is a thing of the past. Why do we need it in federal courts? The idea that one state might discriminate against an out-of-state litigant doesn't happen any more.' Some people respond, rather persuasively, 'Let's think about a New York stockbroker being sued in a rural Alabama county for breach of fiduciary duty. How do you think the Alabama jury is going to look upon this stockbroker in a state court?' Well, maybe a federal forum in a more cosmopolitan setting is going to give this person a better chance. There is, I think, an argument to be made for retaining diversity jurisdiction. Still, it is mostly limited jurisdiction.

"All the time people are trying to bring a state case to a federal court. I had a case recently from Calvert County, essentially about unpaid hospital bills. And they added the patient's employer as a party, saying it was a cause of action that arises under the Employment Retirement Income Security Act and tried to get it up here. In fact, my analysis was it doesn't belong in federal court. Parties can't confer jurisdiction on this court and say, 'Well, O.K.,

Judge, we agree it should be here.' If we don't have jurisdiction, we don't have jurisdiction and the case gets remanded back to state court.

"Sometimes people will bring a civil suit based on five causes of action, only one of which is based on a federal law, while the rest are based on state law. Well, if they are purely state law cases and do not involve diversity of citizenship, there is no jurisdiction for a federal court. But they say, 'What gives the court federal jurisdiction is the one federal cause of action there.' And that may be true. If there is a legitimate federal cause of action, a federal court can exercise jurisdiction over state causes of action using the theory of supplemental jurisdiction. (On the other hand), the judge can dismiss all those state causes of action, and if they want to file in state court they will have to refile that part of the case in state court.

"If there is a pending state proceeding and someone wants to bring a comparable proceeding in federal court, what do you do? There are abstention doctrines where in deference to the state proceeding, the federal court defers. Abstention is one of those practices that federal judges have engaged in which has become a doctrine, supported now by case law, without ever being defined in a statute. Basically, it means deferring to state law as a way of avoiding unnecessary conflict with state law and courts or avoiding error in interpreting state law by leaving it to a state court to decide. There is nothing magic to the doctrine, however, and a federal judge could just as easily decide that federal law trumped state law in a particular case and apply it instead.

"The fact that we traditionally defer to the states in the criminal area is another manifestation of federalism. But what's happened in recent years, and there is a great debate about this, is that much crime has been 'federalized,' especially drug crimes. It is easier to prosecute them in federal courts, especially cases that cross state and national boundaries. Also, the federal sentencing guidelines are stiffer. Crimes have been defined that are federal in nature. The Parental Kidnapping Prevention Act is classically something that should have state involvement, but you have interstate and international boundaries being crossed. Domestic violence laws are also getting federalized. There is much Congress has done that dumps a lot of cases into the federal system. I'm not arguing whether they should be there or not. It is a legitimate legislative call, but many more cases are being assumed by the federal courts that used to be in the state courts.

"Federalism is alive and well. That concept is not missing in either the civil or criminal context. When I was a state judge, I don't think I had much sense of the federal courts at all. There was little if anything that we did not do in state court. Even, for example, federal civil rights litigation, race and gender cases...the classic case might be excessive police force, a violation of one's Fourth Amendment rights to be free from unreasonable search and seizure. That is basic stuff in federal civil litigation and a classic example of a federal case, but interestingly those cases can be tried in state court, too. They aren't as a matter of preference, again perhaps as an example that the local jury might be too sympathetic to the police, as opposed to a federal jury more diversely drawn; but that's debatable. I tried cases like that as a state judge, and I did so because, if you look back historically to the Nixon and Reagan-Bush years, the federal government wasn't all that hospitable to some civil rights litigation, and with the changing of complexion of a number of the U.S. federal circuits now, there really has been a serious retrenching of view of what kinds of rights the Fourth Amendment provides. So there was a swing there for a few years back to state courts as a more hospitable forum to try these cases. The point is you can go through your life as a state judge and not feel much encroached upon, doing much the same work as any judge. Obviously, the big difference is if you are a federal trial judge, you can sometimes speak to the entire state, not just to the litigants in a particular case.

"You are always dealing with a concrete case between specific litigants over specific claims, and you have to find the right law that applies, and hopefully you do, intelligently, sensitively and with a certain amount of savoir faire. That doesn't change from state to federal courts; but the scope of the law you are applying is larger, and the impact of what you decide is far greater as a federal judge, and you sense that. One federal judge can make a decision involving an executive department of the government, and the government takes it seriously. One circuit can take a position, and the government can say, 'We want to take this to the Supreme Court.' Also, because you are dealing with complex cases involving a great deal of money, typically they will involve a higher degree of lawyering and better-developed cases.

"The quality of the judges is high in the federal system. I never thought it was anything less in Montgomery County; they were always first class. But if you were to ask most lawyers around the country to compare the quality of federal judges with the overall quality of state judges everywhere, there would be a qualitative difference there.

"You write more as a federal judge than as a state judge. You probably have more bench time as a state judge trying cases; here you have more chambers time. By multiples a federal judge spends more time in chambers than on the bench. In a typical day, you may have a sentencing for half an hour followed by three or four motions that are argued and decided from the bench, on the spot. If it is a trial, we will sit from Tuesday to Friday from 10:00 to 4:30 with breaks in between. But if I don't have a trial, it gives me writing time. I will come in and draft some opinions and motions. Some of these are routine or are moot, but you need to keep the papers current.

"I do most of the writing of opinions myself; certainly any opinion of any length or complexity I will write myself. I ask my clerks to prepare a bench memo on the issues. They may be able to draft a short opinion or memorandum on a regular issue. I like to write; I write a fair amount, and I've got my own style.

"My organization of chambers is, you manage your own cases as a federal judge, a case comes in with a docket number, either odd or even. I give all my odd-numbered cases to one clerk, the even-numbered ones to the other. I don't try and divide them up among types of cases; that just doesn't work. In the end, it is basically an equal distribution. Now Robyn Ryan is my odd-digit clerk, Chan Park is my even-digit clerk. I'll know just by looking at a docket number who to give the case to. I make them fully responsible for the cases. They note when the case is opened, and when any information comes in pertinent to that case, she or he will process whatever that paper is, such as a motion. We communicate through case notes, kept much like a doctor's hospital record where you enter every visit, prescription, etc. So if there is a matter to be ruled on, there is a note entry and my response. We go back and forth. That's the way we process papers.

"Today my desk is fairly clear because I've had a few days to clean it up. I have five general piles on my desk; the first is all recent minutes and notes pertaining to the court in general; then in the next pile are the Greenbelt missives, notes or E-mails between me and the other judges here, administrative matters about this particular courthouse, the Joint Advisory Committee, etc. In this middle pile, I keep materials on the Disciplinary and Admissions Committee of this court, of which I am the chairman. We meet monthly to vote on admissions, renewals, and disciplinary matters. In the pile next to that are all my papers pertaining to an exchange of judges with Brazil. In the pile next to that is the International Judicial Relations Committee. And there are various boxes around on cases and projects. These are all active piles," he said, gesturing to a Maginot Line of white cardboard boxes piled along walls and under tables and constituting a distinct safety hazard to anyone who walked near them.

"I usually get in about 9:00 or 9:15 A.M. and usually stay until 7:30 P.M. Almost never do I take home things in the evening, and only on weekends when there is something critical coming up on a Monday. Most likely I take home reading material—books and law review articles to catch up on, that sort of thing— rather than particular case material."

Deborah K. Chasanow

A political science major at Douglass College, Rutgers University, Deborah Koss did not know what she wanted to do next, so, like many young people, she applied to law school. Being a woman at Stanford University Law School in the 1970s was not easy. Of the 150 students in her class, only twenty to twenty-five were women, and some of the older professors were uncomfortable with women. One teacher made all the women sit in the front row. Picking her words carefully, she recalled, "He was a gentleman with failing eyesight, and we heard different versions of the reasons why he did this. One was that he had once called on a woman who had burst into tears, and he did not want to call on any, and, because he couldn't see too well, he wanted us in the front row. The more benign explanation was he couldn't see very well, but he could see the first row, and he would rather look at the women than the men. Either explanation is somewhat sexist...but we put up with it, we did it. There was no refusal on our part. It was a different era." And she encountered the face-to-face objection many women law students of that era encountered in the form of the question, "What are you doing going to law school, taking the place of someone who needs to support a family?"

While at Stanford, she participated in a clinical program with the Public Defender's Office in San Jose County, representing juveniles in difficult situations. "It was an eye-opener in terms of the world out there," she recalled. "It was a very important experience for me. I was not going to be a trial lawyer, I concluded; it was too hard. But if I was going to be a lawyer, it would be to help people. I wanted to defend them rather than be a prosecutor, but in the early days of clinical programs they were only done in criminal law. It was my attempt to get some practical experience while at law school."

Of medium height, with short black hair, Chasanow has an intense manner, and her speech is thoughtful. Ask her a question, and she will reflect on it, then reply with carefully chosen words, staring intently at the speaker so that no nuance is lost.

She spent a summer working in the county attorney's office, which led to a clerkship when the county attorney became a judge. Another summer was spent with a small law firm in Washington, D.C., that did a lot of government contracting work. Engaged to a classmate who was stricken with leukemia, she quit the job to move to Cleveland, Ohio, his hometown, and took a year off from law school. While in Cleveland she found work with a firm doing criminal defense and personal injury law. After her companion's death in January 1973, she returned to Washington and worked for a variety of firms that needed short-term help before returning to Stanford Law School for her third year. "I was the original temp," Chasanow recalled.

After Stanford, she clerked with a judge and completed the clerkship still with no clear career prospects. A single application to the Maryland Attorney General's Office "was the sum total of my job search during my clerkship." After a wait of several months, the Criminal Appeals Division called her in for an interview. "I think they needed a woman. There were eighteen lawyers in the division, and I was the only woman. I stayed there eleven and a half years. It was the best decision I ever made. I had an amazing amount of responsibility and was enjoying it. Steve Sachs was elected attorney general and made me chief of his division. I supervised the staff in addition to carrying my caseload.

"I got to argue in the Supreme Court of the United States. It was a case about pornographic magazines. It was funny. The defendant was a clerk in an adult book store. The police went in and bought two magazines they thought looked obscene, took them out to the parking lot where they looked them over, and decided they were obscene. They went back in, arrested the clerk, and took back the fifty dollars they had used to buy the magazines. Now the magazines had cost twelve dollars, so the police paid for them and had gotten thirty-eight dollars in change, went back, and got the fifty-dollar bill. You can see what's going to happen. The defendant was a little miffed: 'Not only am I arrested, but you netted thirty-eight bucks!' Anyway, the defendant moved to suppress the magazines, contending that the purchase was an illegal search and seizure, and he won in our state court. He was convicted. But the appellate court found it was an illegal search and seizure, so the state was the petitioner. We took the case to the Supreme Court and we won—I think it was 6–3, although it might have been 7–2.

"It was not a difficult case to win, it turned out, but it was a wonderful experience. I had both formal moot courts and informal discussions with anybody who would listen to me. The National Association of Attorneys General had a Supreme Court liaison, and in an effort to increase the professionalism of appearances by attorneys general, provided an opportunity for a formal moot court before very, very good lawyers. The proceedings were videotaped, and you were given the tape and you could learn how to appear more professional. We had a similar session back in the office. Steve Sachs was an incredibly wonderful teacher, and he said that before you argue before any appellate court, and especially the Supreme Court, you must know your case and the law better than any other human being. There is nothing called too much preparation. I bought a new navy blue suit and a white blouse. A lawyer who is not with the U.S. government wears a business suit. The government lawyers wear cutaways. There were a couple of questions, none of them particularly hostile. I didn't take my full thirty minutes. I'm probably one of the few lawyers who argued before the Supreme Court who sat down with time left. I said what I had to say. This was a very simple case. All I could do is lose it if I kept talking, so I sat down. One of the few questions was, 'What are the names of the magazines?' The defense attorney was a specialist in representing the industry on First Amendment issues, but this was a Fourth Amendment issue, and not a particularly difficult one."

Now a senior partner in a major Washington firm, Sachs, Maryland's attorney general from 1979 to 1987, recalled Chasanow as both a legal scholar and someone with a practical bent who could run a complex office and also balance relations with the twenty-four state's attorneys who were the chief elected legal officers in each county, plus the City of Baltimore. "I wanted to upgrade the office," the former state's attorney general recalled, "and Debby was the logical choice to head it. She became the head of my Criminal Appeals Section literally from the first day I took office."

It was a demanding fifteen-lawyer office charged with both criminal appeals and correctional litigation, a unit that appeared often in federal court on prisoner's cases. "She mastered the intricacies of the law and was very thorough in her preparation of briefs," Sachs continued. "She had a proactive relationship, which I encouraged, with the state's attorneys. Her role was to handle the appeals that came from them. It was very important to have a relationship of trust with them, because sometimes you had to tell them that their case could not be defended. That is an enormous thing to say to a prosecutor. It didn't happen often, but occasionally it happened. Debbie won that trust. Also, she was nonpolitical. The state's attorneys were politically elected, so was I. It was very important that the criminal appeals process not be political, and Debbie kept it that way."

"In March 1987, I was selected to be a magistrate judge in this court," Chasanow recalled. "Two years before there had been a magistrate judge's opening in nearby Hyattsville. Since I had always lived down here, I applied for it. Because the position was down here, there were just a few of us. I don't remember the process as being particularly onerous. There were a lot of criminal and misdemeanor cases, and because of my background I hoped I had the credentials for the job. I made the list and was interviewed by all the judges. I was not selected, but was encouraged to apply the next time, which was two years later when there were two vacancies—one was when Judge Smalkin, who had also been a magistrate judge, became a district judge and one when a new position was opened. I applied; it was the same process, including a merit selection board. I don't remember asking for much outside support. I think that I had come in second on the Hyattsville list, so I had some visibility.

"The philosophy on applying for a judicial appointment is that it is a fine thing, but there is no way of ever guaranteeing that it will happen. You try for it but can't ever invest too much in it; it may not happen, through no fault of your own. The first time it was Judge Kaufman calling me to tell me I had not been selected; the second time it was Judge Harvey calling me to tell me I had been selected.

"I was a magistrate judge from March 1987 until I became a district judge on November 1, 1993. The Maryland Attorney General's Office is in Baltimore, so I had been commuting to Baltimore for nineteen years before we opened down here. I knew every way to get into Baltimore from the south. I still don't know where anything is north of North Avenue. Becoming a magistrate judge in Baltimore resulted in a 180-degree turn in my practice. I was at the trial level now, not the appellate level, doing civil rather than criminal work, and I was in federal court rather than state court; so what I didn't know about what I was doing was huge. Fortunately, there were a lot of people willing to help me learn. The most important thing is that even if you are the person in the judge's seat, you are not alone. You have a lot of resources and you can ask. Judge Fred Smalkin sat down and told us his technique in approaching settlement discussions. Paul Rosenberg was very helpful on criminal procedure. Dan Klein and Chick Goetz shared their experience on how to handle discovery disputes. Ed Northrup, one of our senior judges, would say, 'Come up for coffee,' and he would just talk about things. It is a wonderful place, and everyone was extraordinarily willing to give. It is, I've been told, one of the most collegial courts in the nation, and from my experience that is true. There isn't a single person I've come in contact with there who hasn't been helpful to me.

"A lot of the skills I had developed stood me in good stead. I know how to research and find an answer, if there is one. I know how to assess a legal problem, but in terms of the substance and the rules of procedure, I had to learn it all. Maybe that was good; maybe I didn't have any bad lessons to unlearn. I learned that after having read hundreds and hundreds of transcripts of trials, I had a pretty good feel for what ought to be going on in the courtroom.

"I had no independent ambition to become a district judge; it was not professionally something I thought about, except when we were going to open this building and we had two vacancies on the bench. Although I knew I could be here as a magistrate judge, it was really the opening of this building that made me decide that I wanted to apply to be a district judge in order to be one of the, at the time we thought, two judges down here."

What was her political backing? "You'll have to ask Senator Sarbanes how much political backing goes into the process, because it is he, as senior senator in the state from the president's party, who ultimately makes the recommendation to the White House. Senator Sarbanes does it all by himself; he does not have a panel screen for him. He personally interviewed everyone who applied. I'd like to think it was my credentials as well as geography that gave me the nod. I had known the senator through my mother for a while. (Her mother was a reform-minded member of the Maryland House of Delegates.) I am certain there were others who supported my candidacy. But I have not been a political person.... Steve Sachs, while he was a politician, prohibited us from participating in his campaigns for state attorney general. We couldn't even contribute. I was not involved in politics, although years before I had been a Democratic precinct chair. My mother had been very active in politics, but I had not been.

"The only hearing I had was before the Senate Judiciary Committee. Carol Mosely-Braun was the only one there by the time my name was up, and she wasn't feeling very well and wanted to finish things in a hurry; so I don't think she asked more than two questions and we were done.

"I kept my old chambers in Baltimore for one year before we moved down here, same secretary, same clerk. But within one week of being sworn in, I had 150 cases, so we spent the first week going through files and trying to figure out what was going on.

"There aren't the significant differences that you might think between a magistrate and a district judge. The biggest difference is that I do felony criminal work, whereas as a magistrate judge I only did the preliminary proceedings in felony cases, but tried misdemeanor cases. So obviously I have to deal with criminal law cases with serious charges, but I was a criminal law practitioner, and there is nothing I'm seeing now that I didn't deal with as an appellate attorney."

During one summer, the Chasanows (at the time, her husband was a judge on the Maryland State Court of Appeals) team-taught evidence law at the University of Maryland. The class met from 7:00 to 10:00 P.M. each Monday and Wednesday evening, and also involved grading exams for fifty-five students. "It was exhilarating; I learned an incredible amount, and I hope we imparted some evidence law, but I am still exhausted. I used to teach constitutional criminal procedure and criminal law, but I haven't done that for fifteen years."

A member of two Inns of Court, Chasanow joins groups of about sixty judges and lawyers who meet five or six times a year to act out real-life legal issues the group members might encounter. Recently they presented a skit about attorneys who are "running afoul of virtually every rule of professional responsibility you can find. We try and do it in a humorous way, but the idea is to generate discussion and make sure all of us are sensitive to what we should and shouldn't be doing as lawyers." She is also a member of a law club that meets for dinner once a month. One member prepares a paper to generate discussion. The topics can range from a current book, such as Jonathan Harr's *A Civil Action*, to why the Maryland State Court of Appeals wears red robes. About twenty years ago, they went back to wearing red robes. Judges in this country used to wear robes of every hue until Queen Anne died in 1714. They donned black in mourning for the queen and never switched back to the multicolored robes worn by English judges. (The Maryland Appeals Court is an exception.)

Chasanow's hobbies include travel with her husband (who has retired from the Maryland State Court of Appeals) when he teaches around the country, and participating with him in collecting oriental jade and ivory. The Chasanows have a daughter, a University of Pennsylvania English major and dog lover who one summer returned home with Sukoshi, a pug, and later Pavlova, an abused dog of mixed ancestry and complicated history from Prague. If Messitte's chambers resemble materials gathered for a museum of popular culture, and Williams' are the quintessential judge's chambers from central casting, Chasanow's are a work in progress. She alternates between two desks, one next to the other, each with its chair and spread-out collection of briefs and books. Tables and chairs are stacked with cases under review or opinions being written. A vase of artfully arranged dried grasses is crowded by a sea of law books marked with paper clips or papers with notes. Museum-quality oriental pottery is tucked furtively on shelves among crowded rows of law books. Hers is the only chambers with a stereo set sandwiched among the law books. Judge Chasanow, a former amateur oboe player, also keeps a stack of Baroque records on a bookshelf.

One of the most demanding challenges she finds on the bench is ruling on employment discrimination law cases. "Employment discrimination litigation is a continuing issue facing the courts. It is fascinating to look at twists and turns of the cases, the laws, and Congress's responses to court cases. The challenge is to know where the issues are and to deal with a case under existing law but recognize that it might be interpreted differently next week, so you don't want to start all over again. The Civil Rights Act of 1991 allowed a jury trial as a right under certain circumstances, but we did not know when it would trigger. You try it both as a bench trial and a jury trial at the same time because that is something you can do. You try to figure out a way to accommodate alternatives. If you deny a jury trial and if you're wrong, you have to try it again before a jury. In some of the evolving areas of law, you are trying to anticipate the uncertainties and to accommodate them."

As for clerks, "I have 300 applications for two positions a year. I keep each clerk one year. I'm always looking for some connection to Maryland, and in particular the counties we serve. I give a priority to people who come from here and want to come back here. We're a new federal court building in this part of the state, and we need to develop a core of good federal practitioners here. Right now a lot of our lawyers come from Baltimore and Washington, but I want to see them come from Lanham, Greenbelt, Bethesda, and Rockville. I have never been disappointed. I have always found ten to twenty possible clerks who have the Maryland credentials. Beyond that, it becomes a question of how the person fits in. I do read their writing, but I'm looking for someone who writes well because I have such a high volume of work to do I don't have a lot of time for editing."

ALEXANDER WILLIAMS JR.

Among Washington Redskins' fans, season tickets to the old RFK Stadium were a coveted item, passed down in wills. (The normal wait was otherwise twenty years.) In the early 1960s, Alex Williams, then a high school student, assembled his entire savings and purchased a ticket (one that he still had thirty years later). Like other Redskins' season ticket holders, he fell into conversation with the person who regularly sat next to him, an elderly white-haired man who came into town each Sunday from distant Prince George's County. Except for a few glory years, the football wasn't that good, and in the course of conversation, young Williams talked about possibly studying law. His neighbor's interest quickened. Ralph Powers was the chief judge for the Prince George's County Circuit Court. (He is now deceased; his son inherited the ticket.) Over several seasons, he gave the younger man advice on courses, invited him to see a courthouse and a judge's chambers, and encouraged him to "come across Eastern/Southern Avenue," in those days the Berlin Wall of Washington's black-white societies (along with 16th Street to the west.) "I got in on the ground floor," Williams recalled. "He was a tough guy; he was tough on me because he wanted me to understand excellence."

Williams had always been adventurous, and the law kept intersecting with his life. Career days at Washington's Theodore Roosevelt High School, a predominantly black, middle-class school, brought lawyers to describe their work, and a grandfather who was an elevator operator at the D.C. superior court recounted cases in graphic detail for the family. Alex's career hopes were encouraged by a devoutly religious mother and a supportive father, who was unable to finish high school and who spent thirty years as a clerk at the Navy Yards, one of the few government jobs available to African Americans in the 1930s. His older sister, Diane, an ordained minister and pastor of the New Genesis Baptist Church, was another early influence.

The family made it out of the projects to a home they bought at 7th and Webster Streets, NW, an African American working-class neighborhood, where they stayed until the neighborhood was razed by the government to build a school just as Alex was headed to college.

Recalling the home where they grew up, Alex's sister said, "It was a very warm home for our family. We got along really well; we had dinner together as a family every day; every person would talk and share in the news of the day, but our external trappings were few. We didn't decorate our home the way the four of us do now. My brother gets his frugality from my mother. She always prepared just enough, she didn't cook too much, so we were not overweight children. We had a piano because my mother loved music, and she taught us all music. Alex could read music and sing fairly well." From the father's side came an interest in public life; from the mother's, a precision of speech, an emphasis on good writing and careful expression. Diane was proud of what her generation had achieved, the first Williamses to have the benefit of college educations. Of the relatives who helped Alex and her make it up and out of working-class Washington, she reflected in long-drawn words tinged with memories: "If they had had the same opportunities we had, they could have done even more."

The family watched early television news programs together, like *Agronsky & Co.*, and subscribed to three newspapers. Alex had a paper route, delivering the now-defunct *Daily News*. "We were the only ones on the block who went to college," his sister recalled. "We were well disciplined. We didn't hang out at night; we had to be home at dark. We were not disrespectful; there was no acting up when you became a teenager, so nobody got in trouble. It was a good life. We didn't deal with racism because there were no white people around, although we watched the news about it on the television," she recalled.

It was a solid place in an era before drugs and crime, a stable neighborhood where everyone knew everyone else, groups of children shot baskets or played on front porches together. A good high school was within walking distance. At school, teachers told students their educations would be their tickets to being somebody and called home if there were problems with a child's homework. All four children grew up to professional careers. In addition to Alex and Diane, a sister, Joyce, became a music teacher and later a real estate dealer; a brother, Michael, earned a doctorate in sociology, taught at several universities, and became an educator in Ghana and a novelist.

Attending Howard University opened new doors, and Alex became intensely involved in student politics, sports, and courses in law and religion. Those were heady days for the Howard law faculty. Some of the civil rights legal pioneers, "warriors in the civil rights struggle, were at the tail end of their legal careers," Williams recalled, including James Narbrit of *Brown v Topeka Board of Education* (1954) fame. The memory of Thurgood Marshall was still fresh, and other professors, such as Herbert Reid, Adam Clayton Powell's lawyer during the congressman's legal battle on Capitol Hill, told their students to turn on the jets and work harder than the whites they would encounter in courts and in Congress.

Williams made law review, and when he graduated with honors in 1973 got attractive offers from firms in the District of Columbia and as far west as Seattle, Washington. Instead, he headed east into Prince George's County and clerked with Judge James H. Taylor, the only African American circuit judge in the quintessential southern county seat of Upper Marlboro. "It was a tremendous experience. Things you couldn't get from the classroom. I got to write for a judge, see the cases firsthand, and see how a judge reaches his decisions, his thought patterns, why he ruled the way he ruled. I began to handle the lawyers as they came in chambers. The clerks did most of the administrative work. I got to know at least half the litigators in Prince George's County. I became a part of the family of the judicial system there in Prince George's County. When I would walk into court with a client, the clerk would say, 'How are you doing, Alex?' It was invaluable."

Williams knew that Prince George's County was growing and African American attorneys were underrepresented. So he opened his own one-person law practice, not in one of the conventional black-belt communities but in Hyattsville, where he stayed from 1974 until 1986. The practice grew quickly. "Word got around. As African Americans moved in, they knew there was a black lawyer there. My practice developed quickly. I did everything—wills, contracts, leases, personal injuries, domestic cases, and a lot of criminal defense work. The judge's old clients came to me; my family and friends spread the word. Some of the Prince George's politicians I knew felt comfortable enough and confident enough to recommend me to clients. I shared an office with another guy, but we were not partners."

These were also years to raise a family. Williams' wife, Joyce, a former teacher, presently runs a child-care center. They have three sons: Johnny is a high-tech computer specialist; Alex III, a graduate of Morehouse College and a law student; and Algernon, a high school student.

Williams became municipal attorney for the African American towns of Fairmount Heights and Glenarden, Maryland, two expanding suburban communities, from 1975 to 1987, and added other part-time positions that would increase a young lawyer's income and contacts, such as becoming an assistant public defender for the county. Gradually, he worked his way to the top. From 1986 to 1987, Williams was chairman of the Washington Suburban

Sanitary Commission, the powerful regulatory body that controls water and sewage rights in a two-county area. The commission, with an annual budget of over $500 million, is the nation's seventh largest water, sewage, and storm water removal system. Appointment to it was the pinnacle of Prince George's County non-electoral politics.

In 1978, five years after he graduated, Howard University Law School invited him to return as a faculty member, and within a decade Williams was a tenured full professor. Even after becoming a federal judge, he still remains an adjunct professor at the law school, teaching courses in business law and criminal law, plus a seminar in public ethics. Howard University and its law school are one of Williams' two great interests, the other being Walker Memorial Baptist Church. Located on 13th Street in Northwest Washington, Walker is one of the post–Civil War anchor churches of Washington's African American community, an offshoot of the large Shiloh Baptist Church, with only two pastors in the last fifty years, both of them college educated. Williams was christened there, met his wife and married there, and ran the Sunday school. He is also an ordained minister and helps the pastor at Sunday services, delivers the message several times a year, and teaches an adult Bible class. His sister said, "It was an educated middle-class church, and its members modeled for us. It was a church with a couple of Ph.D.s, and when they got their degrees, the church made a big thing out of it; plus several public school teachers, an architect, people of achievement. Not only did the church promote these people, but these people were constantly asking us, 'What are your college plans?'" When Williams was sworn in as a federal judge, Walker sent two busloads of members to Baltimore for the ceremony. "Our first pastor took an interest in Alex. He was a very wise man, very calm and reflective, and Alex got that from him," his sister commented.

Two generations of Williamses were preachers, and Alex learned the cadences and speech rhythms of Baptist preachers. "I never wanted to be a pastor myself. I separate church and state; it doesn't influence my decisions, but I have always been interested in religion, especially ethics. When I was the state's attorney in Prince George's County, I made the decision to attend divinity school as well. The idea was to assist me with ideas of justice."

As chief law enforcement officer, he played a major role in determining the course of justice in Prince George's County. Williams also taught one of the country's first law school courses in public service ethics—conflicts of interest, improper gifts, the conflict of legislators as attorneys, campaign expenditures, gifts, the revolving-door syndrome, honorariums, moonlighting, and the role of the independent prosecutor.

By 1991, he had completed a Master of Arts in Religious Studies and Ethics at Howard Divinity School and then entered a Ph.D. program at Temple University in Philadelphia. "I knew that after two terms that would be it for me, and if I went back to some faculty somewhere with a joint appointment in religion and law or if I wanted to be president of a college I would need a terminal degree."

But although he commuted between the worlds of rural courthouses and ivy walls, Williams liked the active life. "It was time for the professor to come out of the classroom and put his theory into practice," he said. Instead, he walked into a buzz saw. Arthur "Bud" Marshall had been the county prosecutor for twenty-four years when Williams took him on in the 1987 Democratic primary. Marshall was well wired with the county Democratic machine and was a fierce competitor and an able prosecutor whom, Williams argued in his primary campaign, had lost touch with the times. Notwithstanding, "he was a real fair guy," Williams recalled. "He fought for fair housing long before that was popular, and he hired the first African American on his staff. It was not a racial thing, it was a personal thing. There was a lot of tension between the old-line white community and the newly emerging African Americans that wanted political representation. We didn't have one county-wide elected official, never had one before, and Marshall was the most vulnerable of the five elected Democrats on the ticket—county executive, sheriff, clerk of the court, register of wills, and state's attorney."

Williams found a place on the ticket, but it wasn't a comfortable relationship. Meanwhile, his opponent continued to self-destruct. When Len Bias, a University of Maryland basketball superstar died from a drug overdose, Marshall jumped on the case, appearing on the TV news each evening, lecturing the public on the case, but alienating voters. "I remember the Greenbelt parade on Labor Day in 1986," Williams recalled. "There was tension in the air. I picked up endorsements from the *Washington Post* and the *Baltimore Sun*. When I was in this parade with Marshall, white people were coming up to me saying, 'Are you Williams? You've got my vote.' I had 11 percent name recognition before that."

Williams squeaked out a victory in the primary, winning by fewer than 2,000 votes out of 60,000 cast, then became the first African American to win the general election. Four years later, in 1990, the aging Marshall made a comeback, running now as a Republican, and lost to Williams, 70,000 to 48,000 in the general election. Like the campaign four years earlier, this one was hard-fought, but by then the tide had turned.

In 1994, Williams ended his seven-year tenure as state's attorney.[80] Calling the 120-employee office "the largest law firm in Prince George's County," Williams added Hispanic, Indian, Korean, and Chinese-American staff attorneys in response to a changing demographic profile. Combating the spread of drugs became a high priority for the office. Five additional attorneys joined the staff to work solely on drug cases. A 1991 Maryland Nuisance Abatement Law, passed in 1991, made it easier to evict occupants of a suspected crack house and seize drug dealers' assets. Williams pushed legislation for a victim and witness protection program, much like the highly successful federal witness protection program, and an anti-stalking law carrying a five-year prison term for violators. Plus there were the usual county problems, including endemic "casino" nights, when churches and volunteer fire departments held their cards-and-dice fund-raisers, with their skimming and payoff problems. (A drive through the county will sometimes show a fund-raising tent or tents nearly as large as the sponsoring church or fire department. Williams, as a federal judge, recently sentenced two casino night organizers to prison terms for skimming nearly $1 million from a volunteer fire department.) Left unsettled were minority communities' complaints of excessive force by law enforcement officials, which continued to plague Prince George's County.

Opportunities for African Americans opened up in the county, and after being state's attorney for six years, Williams ran for Congress in 1992, when the old congressional district was restructured to reflect the region's population shifts. One of ten Democrats running for office, he took his home county, but lost in populous neighboring Montgomery County, losing the election by about a thousand votes. In 1994, when word of a federal judicial opening was raised, he decided to go for it.

The Clinton Department of Justice actively sought to change the racial and gender mix of judicial appointments. This included naming more African Americans and women to the bench. For Maryland's three vacant judgeships, they selected Williams; Deborah Chasanow, already a magistrate judge well-known throughout the state; and Peter Messitte, a respected figure in heavily Democratic Montgomery County. "I was Clinton's first African American judicial appointee to the federal court," Williams recalled. "There must have been a hundred other lawyers around the state who wanted the position." From political events Williams knew Maryland's two senators, Paul Sarbanes and Barbara Mikulski, both Democrats from Baltimore. "Sarbanes recognized that one-third of the state's population was African American and we had to have some people from two of its largest counties, Montgomery and Prince George's, on the new court," Williams recalled.

All three judicial nominations were forwarded to the U.S. Senate after FBI background checks; only the customary American Bar Association evaluation of nominees remained. In Williams' case, it was the battle of his life over the next several months, for the ABA declared the law professor/attorney/public defender was "unqualified" to be a federal judge. At the June 30, 1994, hearing, the ABA accused Williams of lacking the necessary qualifications, lacking familiarity with trials, and misstating his experience. For good measure, they called his prose pedestrian and his analysis of legal issues shallow. "There was no effort to puff or hide," Williams said of his record, with Maryland's two senators and three members of its congressional delegation sitting with him at the hearing table. Williams' supporters said the "ABA's findings reflect a subtle bias toward the silk-stocking lawyer over someone who has spent their career in public practice."[81]

"I'm a realist," Williams said. "I suspect that some of the people who wanted this job got to the ABA, some of my political enemies developed from my term as state's attorney, and others. I suspect there was some jealousy and that was the way they dealt with it, but I wasn't to be denied." Marshaling his own considerable forces, Williams took the offensive. The National Lawyers Association, the preeminent African American bar association, gave him a strong endorsement, arguing he was an elected prosecutor in a major jurisdiction. Howard faculty and students, many of them well placed by now, supported Williams, whom the Student Bar Association had named Professor of the Year in 1979–1980. "You can't say you didn't have the experience in federal cases, because we all come from different backgrounds and you want people from different walks of life on the federal judiciary. That's the beauty of the bench," Williams said.

Both at the three-hour Senate hearing and in a *Washington Post* piece, his supporters countered the ABA accusations. The president of the Howard University Law Alumni Association of Greater Washington wrote, "Even one of the ABA investigators, William

Brennan III, testified in favor of Williams' nomination.... His investigation revealed that Williams had not inflated or exaggerated his trial experience. To the contrary, Brennan concluded that Williams had significantly understated his trial experience."[82]

Noting the ABA's long ban on African American membership, the NAACP concluded, "Williams' career as a law clerk, a lawyer in private practice, as assistant public defender, a law professor, a community leader, a writer of numerous law journal articles, and Prince George's County state's attorney from 1987 to the present is probably more broad and varied than most of those appointed as federal judges since the mid-1980s."[83]

By the time the Senate Judiciary Committee reported the nomination to the full Senate, opposition had dissipated. After both majority and minority reports were received, Williams passed the committee 16–0, and recalls its chairman, Republican Orrin G. Hatch of Utah, saying, "From what I know about this young man, he is going to make us proud." Williams was confirmed by the Senate 98–0 on August 17, 1994. "I have no bitterness; life is like that," he reflected, adding, "It was a hurting thing." Williams said that twice, in the measured voice of the preacher, teacher, judge; but if not bitterness, his voice betrays memories of a bruising ordeal.

Senator Paul S. Sarbanes, his sponsor, reflected on the nomination battle several years later: "Williams had a different sort of legal route. He set up a solo office and began serving the people directly. He also spent a lot of time at public interest law. Fortunately we are getting some more judges out of that field, so the prototype is no longer a partnership in a large firm doing corporate practice. The ABA has moved away from its opposition to such lawyers, and I think the Williams nomination had something to do with that."[84]

Of the three judges on the Greenbelt bench, Williams' chambers are closest to what a film director would choose for a judge. Everything is neat, the thick case folders carefully aligned in rows on tables, the massive desk flanked by the national and state flags, the thick red leather swivel chair—what you would expect for someone who spends long hours poring over law books and case filings. The wall of respectability is well aligned, with rows of signed photos, degrees, and plaques. Of medium height and leonine in bearing, with his former Afro having given way to a trim beard and haircut, Williams still has the fire in the belly, as evidenced in his energetic, yet controlled, manner. Speaking with precise, carefully composed sentences, his voice rises and falls to emphasize a point or pause over an illustration, hands gesturing to reinforce a point, the craft of someone who has spoken in courtrooms, classrooms, and from the pulpit. He also teaches a course each semester at his alma mater.

It is 8:00 A.M. on a foggy November morning on the second floor of Holy Cross Hall, a vaulted Gothic building in upper Northwest Washington, D.C. Once a Roman Catholic girls school, it is now Howard University Law School. Where nuns once told young Irish ladies how to meet suitable young Irish men, Alex Williams is now moving back and forth from the lectern, building his sentences around words like *authority* and *reasonable*. Williams explains what constitutes a power of attorney, peppering his remarks with "you know about that" or "you remember that equitable estoppel is..." In front of him is a thick, well-thumbed folder of notes; after poring over them like a pulpit Bible, he uses different tones of voice for each participant, then the omniscient voice of Abraham to interpret the law, while hitching his wide suspenders and trousers, which periodically sag from the weight of a cellular phone.

By now the twenty early-morning students are chiming in, fortified by carry-out coffee and high-energy breakfast bars. The case is about a real estate agent who goes beyond the explicitly agreed-to terms discussed with the client. What is "express authority" and "implicit authority"? The students, who may be drafting real estate contracts next year, are in a lively discussion in the course on business organization. Several crowd around the podium at the class's end, asking questions.

Later, back in chambers, Williams reflected on the most important lessons learned in five years on the bench. What were they? "Patience, above all patience," he answered immediately. "You need to show patience, temperament, and understanding. Those things are real. When you have vociferous lawyers going at each other and emotions are high, they sometimes say things that are disrespectful to judges and each other, and you've got to maintain order. There is a tendency for judges to lose it sometimes. I may have lost my temper once or twice with a couple of lawyers who wouldn't shut up and take no for an answer, but by and large I think I am pretty patient.

"I grew up understanding that as lawyers we were gentlemen and ladies. We have to work with one another. You can respect each other and not compromise your advocacy for your client. You can do both. A lawyer's word historically has been his bond. If I told you I wouldn't oppose something, I stuck to it; but in the last years we are angry at one another, we don't respect each other, we bicker all the time. It's just not right.

"I try to be compassionate and understanding in the courtroom," he said. "I want to put the contending viewpoints out in public, look at all sides, and see what the law says. You want to ultimately see a fair result. You don't know which side will win, but when the lawyers, the litigants, and the jurors leave the courtroom, your hope is that they believe a sense of fairness pervaded, that everyone got a fair shot. I also want people to feel at home in court. Some witnesses are testifying for the first time, and sometimes new lawyers are frightened to death. I try to put them at ease. 'Slow down, settle down, and we'll hear from you,' I tell them. I never make anybody look bad, I never belittle anyone. Everyone is important to me.

"Also, you have to work hard in this position. These are tough cases or they wouldn't be here, and you face some of the best legal talent you can see anywhere from the strongest firms around. The briefs and the quality of representation are superb, and it brings the best out of lawyers."

The judge takes work home with him every night and especially the night before a case is heard. He arrives early most mornings, except when teaching. "I review the files first on a case and pretty much have an idea of the direction I want to go before I give it to my law clerks. I prepare a basic memorandum on where I see the case going and questions for research and ask them to prepare a bench brief or memorandum in response." A docket of about 270 civil cases awaits the judge at any given time, with thirty-five to forty-five new civil cases a month. He has about fifty criminal cases pending, with five possible additions each month.

"Case management is the most critical issue I have learned. Don't let a motion become stale; get your responses out as expeditiously as you can. And when motions are ripe and ready for ruling, rule. Lawyers are not that much concerned as to whether a motion is for or against them as they are to getting a decision. That's the key, and that is all part of case management. You really have to close the same number of cases that you bring in. If you are bringing in forty-five cases a month and closing seven, you're not going anywhere; you're soon going to have 500 cases."

In conferences with attorneys, "The idea is to simplify the issues and narrow down the inquiry. I tell both sides, 'I want to know every objection that is going to be made, and I want the case to run smoothly without a lot of interruptions with the jury.' In conferences before the trial, we try to resolve any issues or disputes so we won't take away precious time with the jury, keeping them in a back room while we are conferencing. I don't like that to take place in the courtroom, so I use the conferences to resolve any issues that are going to require an early ruling or that I am going to have to work on. I try to let the lawyers know, 'No surprises, ladies and gentlemen. I don't want that. The other side is entitled to know where you are coming from and I need to know.' I don't really have a problem with the lawyers, most of them. They are quality people who assist in the civil operation of the court for the most part."

What are the most agonizing questions facing a federal judge? "By far for me the most difficult questions have to do with the Sentencing Guidelines. You want to help some people whom you think don't deserve incarceration, but sometimes the amount of time you have to give them is high. Sometimes you disagree with the guidelines, but Congress has mandated them; but it doesn't leave the judge with much discretion and it takes away the compassion you may have for a circumstance. Prosecutors have the authority and power to structure pleas and recommend sentences. That is one of the most frustrating, difficult things. There has been a lot of politicizing of the entire sentencing process, what judges are doing or not doing; it is just not fair.... I don't like drugs or what they do to society, but there is a discrepancy between the sentences for the first-time drug dealer and the first time someone embezzles or steals, and I don't think the sentences are fair from that standpoint.

"I don't know how we can stay out of social issues. I don't get into them that often, but they are there. You are beginning to see in Prince George's County the same problems you are seeing in the District of Columbia. Who is going to correct them? I don't ever want to take over a prison system, take over housing, take over a budget, or social services, or a school system, but a judge has the authority to do what is appropriate. If the agency is losing public funds and not discharging its responsibilities, you have a problem."

How does Williams, federal judge and Baptist minister, feel about the death penalty? "It is not the problem for me it is for some people. I can see cases where it could apply, and I have written to this effect. As the state's attorney, I had the obligation of determining when to file a request for a death penalty. I think I had about fifteen occasions to do it, and I did it about four or five times. The jury repudiated a couple of times. I've handled that. I did support the death penalty, even though I had reservations about its effects. But as an elected prosecutor in Prince George's County I was there to represent the people, and the majority of citizens in the country support the death penalty. As a federal judge I have had one habeas corpus case. I had a case just three weeks ago of a guy on death row. I found some problems with it and ordered a resentencing."

An abiding concern for Williams is that all who appear before him are satisfied they have had their day in court, that both sides are patiently and thoroughly listened to, the facts presented, the law laid out. One of the dilemmas he finds, as do other judges, is that one side in a case makes a deeply felt and convincing argument, but the law just isn't with them. "It is one of the most difficult moments I face as a judge," Williams reflected. "Here are people who have put heart and soul in a case, but the law just isn't on their side. You have to be strong as a judge. Everyone who comes here wants to have their day in court, usually before a jury. If it is a criminal case, there is a jury, but that is not always so with a civil case. It can be difficult for a judge to have to rule against someone on summary judgment simply because their case did not measure up to what the law required."

With such an extensive caseload, Williams finds, that in about 90 percent of the civil cases, half will settle and the other half will be dismissed on summary judgment or motions to dismiss. The settlement process is not automatic. For a judge, the time and effort spent in pretrial actions can be as much as or greater than that involved in a trial. Sometimes the effort to settle starts with the parties, sometimes with the judge. One or several conferences are held to narrow the issues, or to say to one of the parties, "This or these claims are not likely to survive. The law is against the litigant." Often settlements take place early, because one or both parties want to avoid the costs of prolonged litigation. At other times, once they have survived the request for summary judgment or a dispositive motion, one of the parties will not want to risk a large judgment or no judgment, and will settle. "I call it bending but not breaking," Williams reflected. "Sometimes in my opinions I give them language or a signal that this is a case that ought to be resolved. Or if I believe that one side is being unfair or has misconstrued some of my rulings, I may bring them in and suggest to them that every case has a settlement value. And there are times when you have to tell the plaintiffs, 'You've been successful up to this point, but there is no guarantee you're going to win your civil suit.' While they may have some difficulty in hearing that from their counsel, sometimes hearing it from a judge will help." The moment for a summary judgment motion comes after the plaintiff's case has been made. Usually the defense counsel will ask that the case be dismissed, chiefly arguing that the facts in the case are lacking or do not meet the law's requirements.

The judge added, "The vehicle of summary judgment is a powerful means to dispose of cases in federal court. More so than in the state system. The law is so clear, and the appellate courts have encouraged the district courts to look at whether or not the plaintiff has met the burden of surviving summary judgment. We do a lot of disposing of such cases as a matter of law. Usually they originate with the defendant."

The problem of increasing costs of litigation, especially for America's middle class, is a continuing concern of jurists. "I'm concerned about how the middle class and citizens with no means can make their way through the maze of legal papers in the courts. I think you have two types of people—those who can afford litigation expenses and those who can't. Some are entitled to a public defender or legal aid representation, and they get good, competent representation. I used to be a public defender, and I gave my best every time. I have found that the public defenders in this building and in this district are super. They don't compromise on anyone's case, and they mount an enthusiastic, strong defense.

"So that leaves the great middle class of America that is increasingly being denied access to courts because they can't afford it. They work, they have contract issues, or family fights. Their children get into difficulty, or they face other kinds of financial problems that end up in bankruptcy or with lawsuits. These are the sorts of court issues the average middle-class person faces. My concern is that most people don't have the kind of money needed to obtain the representation they would like. It is very difficult to maintain a suit in court. If you feel you are the victim of discrimination in your job, it may take

$50,000 or $100,000 over two or three years for legal fees, including the heavy costs of taking depositions or hiring expert witnesses. That may consume most of a person's life savings. Today lawyers can change $200 an hour on an average. It is totally different from the days when I was out there as a small practitioner; you would charge $500 or $750 for someone who got in difficulty on a drunk-driving case or with an uncontested divorce. Today, there are lawyers who won't take a case like that unless you come up with a retainer of $10,000 to $15,000. Most people don't have money like that."

Part IV

Other Players

The Court from Tim Maloney's Window

Who knows the Greenbelt Court inside out? Tim Maloney's law office sits on the hill overlooking the Greenbelt Courthouse. The twenty-two-lawyer office of Joseph, Greenwald, and Laake is an all-purpose regional firm that does everything from large consumer product liability cases to the filing of wills. A local product (Georgetown University, University of Baltimore Law School), Maloney grew up in Prince George's County and for sixteen years served in the Maryland House of Delegates before retiring from politics at the relatively young age of forty-three to practice law. The gregarious Irishman clerked with Judge Chasanow's husband, Howard, now retired from the Maryland State Court of Appeals. Maloney presided at the bar association roast to say goodbye to Howard Chasanow. (Once, in introducing the Chasanows, he spoke of "the very distinguished Judge Chasanow and her husband, Howard.") Former Maryland Attorney General Steve Sachs called Maloney "the Mozart of the Muldoons," a Baltimore term for perennial politicians, and said Maloney was the person most knowledgeable about the Greenbelt Courthouse because he was always trying cases there.

As we spoke, Maloney observed, "It's 7:30 P.M. and Judge Williams is still there. I can see the light on in his chambers. He is the last of the three to leave. They all work pretty hard; they have a pretty strong work ethic over there." Two TV vans were outside the courthouse; a guard at the Food and Drug Administration had just been arraigned for murder.

Maloney reflected on the three judges and how they differed from one another. Because he had clerked for Howard Chasanow, he rarely appears before Judge Deborah Chasanow, but has known the family socially for many years.

"Debby should be on the Supreme Court. She's smart, hard-working, meticulous, like her mother before her. Her mother was in the House of Delegates and chairman of the Constitutional and Administrative Law Committee. Debby used to be assistant attorney general in charge of the Criminal Appeals Division. She expects lawyers to be prepared—all three judges do. She is very clear, very direct, I think very well respected within the Fourth Circuit. If you do a Westlaw search on Maryland criminal cases, Debby was probably the leading criminal appellate lawyer of her day. She is a very kind person, a thoughtful person, but a bit shy.

"Alex is a very well-prepared judge. His opinions are very well written, very practical. He is able to get at fine distinctions quickly in a case. He is considerate of lawyers. I had a case last summer and the other lawyer couldn't come to court for a couple of days. I thought of some of the federal judges in the older days and what would happen, but he couldn't have been more considerate and thoughtful of this other lawyer. He is a lawyer's judge.

"I first met Peter in the early 1980s. He is very bright and has been a real leader in establishing the Southern Division. He has been great with the wider community, including the arts community, in hanging local artists' work and giving them some recognition. He did a masterful job in the Prince George's County school desegregation case. He took a case that had been festering for twenty-six years. He brought closure to it and did it in a way that allowed everyone to be a winner."

Of the Greenbelt Court, Maloney had this to say: "It's not as stuffy and reserved as many federal courthouses, and it's not as informal as many state courthouses. I think it struck a happy medium. I think the practitioners like coming there. It also has a nice culture among the magistrate judges. I think we have some of the best magistrates in the country; and because of that, a lot of people will try a case in front of a magistrate if the judge is too busy and they can't get an early court date.

"The only downside of the courthouse is it has become too popular. They are running out of room and are now leasing space in other buildings, like over in Hyattsville for the minor misdemeanor Washington Parkway cases. There are so many cases that a lot of them are being assigned to the Northern Division. I just had a case Thursday assigned there, just because they are running out of judicial capacity. They could almost use another judge or two."

Was a new courthouse justified at Greenbelt after all? Maloney recalled the sharp battles before it was built: "It was very controversial, but you couldn't imagine going back to the old days now. It wouldn't make logistical, geographical, or political sense. There was a piece on Chief Judge Fred Motz's Website talking about the day when they might consider having a Southern district, not a division. I don't think there is any big push for that right now, but the volume is building down here. We're seeing a lot of law firms putting up satellites on Ivy Lane" (the street across from the courthouse).

THE FOURTH U.S. CIRCUIT COURT OF APPEALS

A BRICK WALL

Any party in a federal case can appeal the court's verdict to one of thirteen federal appeals courts where the judges may affirm or reverse the district court's opinion, remand the case for reconsideration, or issue a simple unpublished opinion saying they see no issues in the case meriting further action. In the case of the Greenbelt Court, the route to filing an appeal is the road to Richmond, Virginia, the site of one of the most controversial appeal bodies in today's judiciary, the Fourth Circuit Court of Appeals.

There is nothing subtle about it. When federal cases from Maryland, Virginia, West Virginia, and the Carolinas go up on appeal, they hit a brick wall that is the Fourth Circuit Court of Appeals. Called "the boldest conservative court in the United States," the Fourth Circuit has been identified as "the black hole of death penalty cases" and a court that has "blazed new trails in striking down laws that a majority of its judges say improperly enhance federal power at the expense of the states."[85] At its core are a handful of Reagan and Bush-era judicial appointees who actively manipulate the judicial process in legal ways to force their distinctive agenda on the district courts under them.

Its rulings are binding on only the five states under its jurisdiction, but the Fourth Circuit has consistently supported states' rights to restrict abortions and limited criminal defendants' rights. And in February 1999, it ruled that federal law-enforcement officials are not required to follow the long-established *Miranda v Arizona*

Supreme Court decision requiring criminal suspects to be notified of their legal rights. For good measure the court also ruled that the Food and Drug Administration did not have the power to regulate nicotine as a drug, and rejected complaints from gay rights advocates challenging the Clinton administration's "don't ask, don't tell" policy on homosexuals. In December 1998, the court dealt the Clinton administration's wetlands policy a major setback in *USA v James Wilson*. In this case, it narrowed activities of the U.S. Army Corps of Engineers by overturning a lower court's conviction of a Maryland residential developer sentenced to prison and fined $1 million for "knowingly discharging fill material and excavated dirt into wetlands on four separate parcels without a permit, in violation of the Clean Water Act."

The court's chief judge is a godson and former clerk of Justice Lewis F. Powell Jr., J. Harvey Wilkinson III (known as "Jay"), son of Powell's longtime Richmond business associate and friend, J. Harvey Wilkinson. The Cardinal Ratzinger of the court is Judge J. Michael Luttig, whose consistently conservative opinions are clothed in the rhetoric of states rights, and who has frequently called the court's positions "courageous." And when the court sits in three-judge panels, Luttig is quick to ask that key cases that may go against him be heard en banc, meaning that the case is important enough to be heard by the full court, which usually votes 7–6 conservative. Luttig is no aging Neanderthal: vigorous, intellectually sharp, and in his mid-forties, he gained his spurs by clerking with Chief Justice Warren E. Burger and Justice Antonin Scalia, giving him ideological credentials to fine-tune his conservative cast of mind. (Luttig also has a high batting average in placing his clerks with Supreme Court Chief Justice William Rehnquist and with Justice Scalia.) Although the Reagan-Bush appointees only slightly outnumber their Carter-Clinton counterparts, they are mindful of their majority and know how to protect it.

A law school professor who has followed the Fourth Circuit, Arthur Hellman of the University of Pittsburgh Law School, said, "There is a conservative majority on the full court, and if they see a panel decision they don't like, they just take it en banc and reverse it. No other circuit enforces majority rule the way the Fourth Circuit does. It's gotten to the point that if there is a 2-to-1 liberal panel decision, you can predict with almost perfect certainty that it will go before the full court and be reversed. Liberal panel decisions are not allowed to survive."[86]

What this means for the Greenbelt Court is that its judges stand a reasonable prospect of being reversed on key cases that go against the ideological stance carved out by the appeals court. "The precedents of higher court decisions that shackle district judges is something we can't do anything about," Judge Williams observed. "I've made some careful decisions down here that have been overruled. The Fourth Circuit that this district sits in is a pretty tough court, depending on your persuasion. In my background I represented the little person in private practice and as a state's attorney was in support of the underdog, but I have been reversed by panels of the Fourth Circuit that seem to side with the big interests.

"The Fourth Circuit has had a lot of criticism as one of the most conservative courts in the country. If I have a criticism of Clinton it is that he has not done a good job of getting different points of view on these circuit courts. I consider myself a moderate. I think most of Clinton's appointments as district judges have been moderates, but it is the appellate courts that pretty much run the country and make the law. Most of the appellate court decisions are never appealed, or if they are, are not taken by the Supreme Court."

The Fourth Circuit regularly asks judges from elsewhere in the region to sit as guest panel members, and Williams has done so. He notes with irony that the conservative court has constantly resisted suggestions that its numbers be expanded, claiming it has enough judges to do the job, yet it frequently borrows members from district courts to sit with it on cases when it does not have enough of its own judges.

At present, there are three vacancies on the Fourth Circuit, which comprises five states. Traditionally, there are three seats each for Maryland and West Virginia, four each for Virginia, North Carolina, and South Carolina. A possible African American nominee, a federal judge from North Carolina, experienced the familiar Jesse Helms stonewall. James Beatty had sat on the Fourth Circuit, as Williams is doing, in a rotational panel that vacated a murder conviction. This turned the opinionated Helms against him, and because a state's senior senator must forward a judicial nomination to the White House, Beatty's proposed appointment went nowhere.

Magistrate Judges

The First Line of Defense

Three magistrate judges provide a first line of defense for the three federal district judges in Greenbelt. Their basic role is to lighten the burden of the federal district judges by doing much of the judiciary's pick-and-shovel work, such as handling misdemeanor cases, ruling on motions, issuing bench warrants, responding to requests for bail review, appointment of attorneys, telephone taps, and so on. Sometimes litigants will agree to appear before a magistrate judge because they can get an early trial date. Until about twenty years ago, magistrate judges were simply called "magistrates," secondary court officials, but with the steady rise in demands on the federal judiciary, they have taken on an increasing part of the judicial burden. Many eventually go on to the district bench.

The magistrate judges are appointed by the district court bench. The process starts with an ad being placed in the paper when there is an opening, as when a previous magistrate judge retires, joins a private firm, or is elevated to the district court bench, or when a new position is created. The educational and professional requirements are listed and writing samples solicited from the more than 100 lawyers who ordinarily apply for each opening. The numbers are winnowed down to ten to fifteen candidates by an interview board of state civic and legal leaders; the board's membership changes frequently to ensure impartiality. The ten-member panel rank-orders the candidates, after which the district judges conduct the final interviews and pick one judge to join their ranks as a magistrate judge. A full field investigation of the candidate by the FBI completes the process. A magistrate judge serves a term of eight years and may be reappointed.

CHARLES B. DAY

"I was terrified," Magistrate Judge Charles B. Day of Greenbelt recalled, in describing himself sitting on one side of the table with ten federal judges on the other trying to be informal yet probing. "But when it was over it seemed like a pleasant experience. I felt prepared. I thought about the kinds of questions they might ask and I prepared for them."

The magistrate judges, like the bankruptcy court judges, are appointed under Article I of the Constitution, Section 8, a brief provision allowing Congress "to constitute Tribunals inferior to the supreme Court." The other federal judges are appointed under Article III, Section 1, which states, "The judicial Power of the United States, shall be vested in one supreme Court, and in such inferior Courts as the Congress may from time to time ordain and establish."[87] From these fewer than fifty words in the Constitution, the whole American federal judicial establishment has sprung.

On the day we first talked, Day was holding court at Andrews Air Force Base in the military courtroom, just off the wing where presidential flights originate. The courtroom had been recently remodeled, and in the rear several church benches were filled with defendants in T-shirts and gym shoes, and one or two in suits. The docket may have started with sixty cases, but most of the defendants pleaded guilty, and some asked for a continuance of the hearing. Most of the charges were driving violations: a driver had backed his truck into another motorist; several persons were charged with driving under the influence; a woman who worked at a day care center and made six dollars an hour was arrested for leaving her four children locked in a car in the base Post Exchange parking lot.

Judge Day explained carefully, sometimes two or three times, defendants' rights and options. The prosecutor and public defender moved up and down the corridors like emergency room medics. The steady stream of humanity congregated in the corridors and during breaks in the trial day; lawyers and clients gestured like subjects in a Daumier etching. Judge Day was like a bandleader, keeping the whole scene moving, shifting colored folders from one pile to another as cases were disposed of, peppering his commentary with remarks like "My heart tells me to do one thing and my mind tells me to do something else." "Quite frankly, I am not a gambler. I want you to know exactly the situation you face." "Has anyone made any promises to you about what I will do? Do you understand you are giving up your rights to a trial?" "Do you plead guilty because you are guilty and for no other reason?"

Charles B. Day, now a magistrate judge, spent his formative years torn between wanting a career as a saxophone player and a career in justice. Music was a powerful attraction in the Baltimore where he grew up. Jazz greats like Lionel Hampton and Dizzie Gillespie would drop by to visit with faculty friends at Douglass High School and hold concerts. At the same time, the truck driver's son had a keen interest in street justice. "If I saw a bottle of soda not filled to the top being sold for full price, I was indignant," he said. His father could "drive anything that moves," including coast-to-coast tractor-trailers that crossed the United States in four days. Charles sometimes accompanied his father on such journeys. His dad wanted him to be a lawyer. "He was sneaking it in on me," Day says. But that had to wait. "I thought I was the best alto-sax player in the city. I learned I was a fine technical player. I wanted to be an interpretive jazz artist but didn't have the gift." About that time, college interfered with a musical career. Charles picked the University of Maryland at College Park, a journey of only fifty miles, but light-years away from Baltimore.

Life at College Park was a cornucopia of choices, plus parties and a beautiful young woman who had grown up only six blocks from where Charles had lived. "I was attracted to criminal justice. I wasn't a theoretical person; I was a practical person and criminal justice held an attraction for me. I thought about law but didn't say anything to anybody. I was scared! *The Paper Chase* thing, the competition. I almost chose a career in law enforcement, except that I didn't want to get shot at.

"Then I entered a graduate program at American University. It taught me that I could survive. I went to classes at night. I had to get a job during the day but kept getting turned down because I didn't have a car and lived in Ellicott City. I finally got a job. I would hitchhike from Ellicott City to Baltimore, take a bus to College Park, then another bus across town to Adelphi and get a bike from a friend. I would peddle all over town during the day investigating criminal cases, then straight up the hill by bike to AU. Each evening a cabinet officer's daughter would pass me as she was being delivered by limo. I'd sit in the classroom on one side, sweating profusely from 6:30 to 10:30 P.M. and then reverse course."

Next came a job in Rockville as a victim witness coordinator in the Montgomery County State's Attorney's Office. Day also organized a program for juvenile burglars that reduced the recidivism rate by 73 percent. "The kids came from all over, rich homes, poor homes, stable homes, broken homes. We set up one-on-one interaction with prison inmates. There was an educational component; they saw courtrooms and went on police ride-alongs. We told them they had a choice: they could be part of the community, but if they fooled around with a life of crime, the prosecution was going to do everything it could to put them away."

Meanwhile, Day started attending law school at night at the University of Maryland, Baltimore. By now he had graduated from a partial interest in a rickety car to full ownership of his own none-too-reliable vehicle. "There were lots of fast-food meals at traffic lights," he recalled. How did he keep up such a demanding pace for six years? "Sometimes I had headaches when I was working and attending law school, but I didn't believe God had brought me that far to drop me. I was fully prepared to be kicked out of class by the gurus who ran it, but I was never going to fail because I wasn't trying. My old man had no quit to him. I was living at home. He wouldn't let me quit."

Day's next job was as an assistant state's attorney for Montgomery County. Soon after joining the office, he became part of a felony trial team going after large-scale drug dealers. Day co-prosecuted the largest PCP case (involving thirty-five gallons of PCP "angel dust") ever tried on the East Coast, complete with police chases, shoot-outs, and roadblocks.

Work as a county prosecutor is good training for young lawyers who are given important cases and spend lots of time in court—experience that a medium-sized Washington, D.C., law firm found attractive in Day. Sherman, Meehan, Curtin & Ain, P.C., is a niche-market firm of twenty-five lawyers specializing in domestic law and litigation. Day enjoyed his eight years there. "I wasn't happy unless I was in a courtroom," he said. He made partner and the money was good. Like many lawyers who became judges, Day took a substantial cut in pay when he became a magistrate judge in February 1997, but gained a prestigious position with long-term stable income and benefits.

"For a number of years, friends had been urging me to prepare for a position in the judiciary," he recalled. "On the federal side you have a wonderful blend of civil and criminal cases, small and large cases. You are in court enough to stay sharp, but also face a lot of fascinating legal problems. I'm not interested in being on an appeals court; I like it where I am. I get in and try and mix it up and try to get it to move along."

Shortly after taking the bar examination in 1984, Day married the young woman who had seen him through his two-career roller-coaster ride. Cheryl Day raises their three active children while working four days a week with a locator service for business executives who move to Maryland and want to find child-care facilities. The Days live in a comfortable western Montgomery County suburban complex about an hour's drive from the court. Spare time is spent with the children and at church. "I got started on the Baptist track when I saw my father's dog tags from Vietnam. I said, 'I'm a Baptist' when I was asked my denomination." Day sometimes prays silently in between cases or when he reaches a difficult point in a case. "I end up praying on the bench more times than I admit. Sometimes I'm on the fence. Usually, there is some merit on both sides. They wouldn't bring the simple issues to court; they bring cases because they want answers.

"As a judge, you are supposed to sit real high but serve real low. People are looking to you for the right answer. I don't always get it right, but I try. People criticize us; they say, 'We don't have a justice system, we have a legal system.' I sit up there and try and find the right answers. That's important for judges, because if people don't feel they can get justice, they will find it other ways."

Day reflected on his life as a judge. "You have to push hard. There are people who have the gift of being able to shoot from the hip and shoot accurately, but I'm not one of them. It is hard for me. I have to work hard. A court is like a bank. So much goes on after the door is closed. There are laws to check, cases to consider, endless papers to fill out.

"I've not had a difficult time determining guilt or innocence. The question is what do you do afterwards. That is what I agonized about as a prosecutor and as a judge. It's real difficult to say to someone, 'For the next eight months, I'm in control of your life.' The whole Bill of Rights is slanted to protect the accused. I was no angel growing up. I think of the breaks I got along the way. Is this the time to help someone or to say, 'It's over!'? In America we lock up more people than anywhere else in the world. Very few people want to see the first-time drug user in jail, but if crimes are more serious, you want to see the person removed from society."

Is it easier for an African American to be a lawyer or a judge in Maryland now than it was twenty years ago? "Twenty years ago you could count on one hand the number of African American lawyers, and there were two Hispanic Americans and no Asian American lawyers in Montgomery County," Day reflected. "The base is changing constantly, and there are more lawyers of color moving with it. I was the first African American magistrate judge in Maryland and the first African American to make partner in my firm."

JILLYN K. SCHULZE

Jillyn Kaberle Schulze was the first of Greenbelt's three magistrate judges to be appointed, and is senior magistrate judge for the Maryland district. She is a petite, long-haired woman whose eyes suggest a physician's concentration, yet who is given to bursts of ready laughter. As an assistant attorney general for the State of Maryland from 1981 to 1991, she worked in the criminal appeals division writing appellate briefs and arguing them before the court. Next, she was appointed as legal advisor to Governor William D. Schaefer, serving from 1991 to 1994. "That was a neat job, the most interesting legal job I ever had. I was involved in many lawsuits filed against the state that affected policy issues. A lot of litigation was going on with the State Health Department over its treatment of disabled people and mentally ill people. My marching orders from the governor were to try to not have judges telling him how to run the state. 'Settle the case if you can,' he said, 'so I don't have some judge telling me how to run things.'"

She graduated from Western Maryland College in 1973, and from the University of Maryland School of Law with a J.D. degree in 1980. Her husband has a Ph.D. in human development and works for an urban public school system. The couple has two children, a profoundly autistic son and a daughter. When she is not in court, Schulze enjoys a variety of activities. "I garden a lot. I have a house in the woods, and I spend a lot of time in the woods and hiking. I'm also the manager of my daughter's soccer team. I read novels. My favorite author is John Barth. I love all of his books."

Of the Greenbelt bench, she said, "I was hired as a magistrate judge on October 24, 1994. We were all new and every single one of us came from a completely different background and came to the job in a completely different way.

"I was looking at the end of Governor Schaefer's term and therefore the end of my job. Debby Chasanow had been my supervisor in the Attorney General's Office, and she suggested that I apply for this. It was her job, actually; it was the job she vacated when she became a district judge. As part of my work for the governor I went to a lot of functions and got to know a lot of people I hadn't known before, and that was certainly very helpful. I had people in all the counties of the state who knew me, and I was able to ask people to write letters on my behalf and to get letters from all over the state, which seemed like something that would help me get this job."

How was she attracted to a career in law? "I had been out of college four years and worked at a number of jobs that required a college degree down to waitressing, which was my last job before going to law school. I thought that I might have an aptitude for it. I took the Law School Admissions Test and got a very high score on it, which encouraged me to apply, and that's how I got into it. My father was a law-school graduate, but he had never practiced law. I was surprised by the courses that I liked; the courses that I thought would be most boring turned out to be the most interesting, like civil procedure. The ins and outs of what you can do and when you can do it—I loved it."

Judge Schulze learned a lot from clerking with Judge Roszel Thomsen, a senior Baltimore judge, just after law school. "He was eighty when I clerked for him. He was patient with me as well as with the lawyers; I and his other clerk were young upstarts, but he always listened carefully to us. I learned something about the decision-making process, but more about how you should conduct yourself.

"I always seem to have a docket of about eighty civil cases at a time. The district judges may get 300 cases, but most of them don't need any attention; but every case I get needs attention or otherwise I wouldn't get it. It is so hard to say how long a case will take; it can be half an hour or a week. I've had some that go on for years with a new motion you have to deal with every month. Others, you spend half an hour with them, and the case goes away."

Regarding the off-site criminal dockets, she said, "You go for a day and you may hear seventy or eighty misdemeanor criminal cases; 95 percent of them are guilty pleas or dismissals by the prosecutor. They don't remain on your docket. About three or four days before you hold court you are brought a stack of about eighty files, and someone says, 'These are the cases you will have on Friday.' You read through them, you go on the bench, and there they are."

What has she learned since coming on the bench? Judge Schulze laughed in response. "I think I am more patient in my interpersonal relationships. I think I am more tolerant of statements that people make to me that I don't agree with. I think it has made me more open-minded and more easygoing. It was my biggest concern when I got this job. It was something I worried and worried about through the whole application process, because I always considered myself an intolerant, impatient person. I just worried and worried about how I could sit and listen to something I disagreed with and still give it due consideration. It turned out to be a lot easier than I thought. I guess I got into the mind-set of 'this is my job and this is what I should be doing'; when you force yourself to do it, it becomes natural to you eventually. I guess that is what happened to me.

"Also, I would say that when you come out of law school, you know a lot of legal theory and very little about how to actually handle a case and how a case gets decided. A judge should focus narrowly on the facts that are in front of them and narrow their issues down to one specific issue...work with that...and run with it. Don't try to make a law review article out of every case."

What are the hardest questions a judge faces? "Sentencing decisions in criminal cases. That's one reason why I like my job so much, because I don't have to make at least major sentencing decisions. I don't have jurisdiction to impose sentences of more than one year on anybody. I don't have the kinds of issues the district judges have to deal with, and I'm very happy about that."

Judge Schulze, like the other Greenbelt magistrate judges, spends one or more days each month holding court in different parts of the judicial district, such as in a county courthouse or on a military installation where misdemeanor cases are tried. One particular trial made a lasting impression on her. It was "a dumb little bench trial that I did at the Pautuxent Naval Air Station. Two women had gotten into a fistfight as they were putting their kindergarteners on the bus; they got into this drag-down, hair-pulling, scratching, kicking, biting fistfight, and one of them ended up with an assault charge. There were about eight witnesses who testified, an equal number of witnesses on each side. The defendant was on crutches at the time. Someone said the defendant had actually swung a crutch and tried to beat the plaintiff with it. There was a seven-year-old child who testified. She had been coached on what the parent wanted the child to say. That's probably the one trial I will never forget. It ended with a not guilty verdict because there was no way I could decide who started that fight after I heard all the witnesses."

WILLIAM CONNELLY

"The car was going 138 mph on the Baltimore-Washington Freeway, and to avoid the U.S. Park Police, the driver turned off his lights while driving." Judge William Connelly was describing one of the 11,000 misdemeanor cases that come to the Greenbelt Court each year. The Greenbelt Court differs from many of the ninety-four other federal district courts because it has three major federal highways and several federal installations within its territory, giving the federal courts jurisdiction over any legal disputes occurring on federal property. "A lot of the issues we deal with are life-skills issues," Connelly observed. Referring to a case just heard in the courtroom across from his chambers, the judge remarked, "This fellow obviously had a drinking problem. He lost his Maryland license and his West Virginia license. He has shown a pattern of sobriety for a period of time and ought to have been able to find ways to obtain at least a limited driving permit from West Virginia, until this incident."

Hanging up his robe and switching to a neat dark blue suit coat, Connelly observed, "People feel almost compelled to drive. When you look over his record, there are four prior 'driving while intoxicated' offenses. When he gets here, people think, 'These are not serious infractions, no one got hurt.' I'm a fellow who believes the first time you give a person a break, but after the second, third, or fourth time, I'm far less likely to give breaks. Many times in these kinds of cases I give someone a short period of incarceration. A short period is a long period for someone who hasn't previously been to jail. I can also confine people in their home and test them for alcohol. We need to tell these drivers that changing their ways will be beneficial to them and their family. There is some social work that goes with the misdemeanor docket. We have a good probation department, we have a number of agents, and we are well-funded. I have money for detoxification and drug treatment programs, and for mental health treatment."

Connelly reflected on the public's view of the judicial system. "Based on my fourteen years in private practice, and having a lot of clients who would come to the courts for a divorce or on a contract dispute, I concluded most people often will have only one experience in a courtroom, and they will judge the entire judicial system from what happens then. People want to be treated thoughtfully. People expect not always to win their case, but they want to be treated with respect. For many, this is their one encounter with the judiciary. You want to be prompt and well prepared, and be thoughtful in conducting the case. You're there almost to sell the judiciary system to the people. It's the idea that everything you do is important and it should be done as well as you can do it."

Tall, thin, sandy-haired, with a warm handshake and an alert manner, Connelly could be a bank vice president welcoming a client into his office. I asked him how he chose a career in law. "It is a simple story. I grew up in Prince George's County and went to an all-boys Catholic school. I was a debater. My father had a high school education, but he rose to a GS-18, the highest civilian rank with the National Security Agency, in a senior managerial job. My father didn't want his children to work for the federal government as he sometimes had to deal with a twenty-nine-year-old whiz kid who maybe didn't have the experience he had. I wanted to get a good occupation. I stumbled through math and sciences, got by in Latin and French, but knew I was not a linguist. That left law."

Connelly majored in government at the University of Maryland, College Park, earned a J.D. degree from the University of Maryland, spent four years in the Air Force, and received an LLM from Georgetown University Law School. He was a lieutenant colonel in the Air Force Reserve, assigned as a judge on the Air Force Court of Criminal Appeals.

Connelly has four brothers and sisters, two of whom are lawyers with large downtown law firms. On Saturdays he coaches soccer for various teams on which his four daughters play; a memento on an office shelf shows a soccer ball and the caption "Time Spent Coaching Is Never Lost." His wife, whom he met at the University of Maryland, is a former government manager. The Connellys are active in their Roman Catholic Church in Bowie, where he is a lay lector, she a lay Eucharistic minister, and the girls are altar servers. Otherwise, "There are probably two or three bar events I attend each month. I could be out a lot more than that."

Connelly clerked with two circuit judges. One was Judge Howard Chasanow, then a circuit judge, later a Maryland State Court of Appeals judge. "He suggested I contact a lawyer who was looking to expand his practice. We found a good location in Camp Springs, across the street from Andrews Air Force Base in the new credit union building. We thought we would pick up some business from the base and, if we rented from the credit union, they might need a lawyer and consider us, which they did after a couple of years." While in practice, he had a separation agreement, which he negotiated with a Montgomery County lawyer named Peter Messitte, and a couple of cases with a Prince George's County attorney, Alexander Williams, when the latter was in private practice.

Active in county politics as a young lawyer, Connelly ran for the state legislature in 1981, spending each afternoon going from door-to-door, avoiding dogs, and leaving literature or talking with voters. "We went through this tremendous effort, and I lost. I did reasonably well—I got maybe 50 percent of the vote. People said, 'He's a good candidate, but he's not from the state Democratic machine,' so I learned a little bit about politics. I ran shortly thereafter for an Orphans Court judgeship but lost. Most of my time was spent managing campaigns for circuit court judges. I managed seventeen judges in six campaigns and didn't lose one."

When two vacancies for magistrate judges were advertised during late 1993 and early 1994 after Judge Deborah Chasanow was elevated to the federal bench, Connelly pursued the position. "I had attempted to get on the circuit court in Prince George's County, and I got through the merit selection commission and was interviewed by Governor Schaefer, who is a very pleasant person. But there were other considerations, such as diversity of race and gender, and I couldn't contribute to that." From the more than 100 applications the citizens commission reviewed, the number was narrowed to twenty-eight who were interviewed, then to five, whom the district court judges interviewed before making their selection. Judge Jillyn Schulze was appointed, "but Judge Fred Motz (head of the Maryland Federal Court) called each of us and encouraged us to apply again. I applied four or five months later and was selected. The FBI and IRS did their reviews, and I was appointed to an eight-year term on March 31, 1995."

Connelly works long hours, "often from 8:30 A.M. to 7:30 P.M., but I live not far away. I put in five hours on Sunday as well. On many evenings when I've left, the green jeep (Judge Messitte's ancient wagon) is still here. I'm blessed to have a good clerk and a good judicial assistant, who was Thurgood Marshall's secretary for thirteen years. I have to keep reminding her this is not the Supreme Court."

The stacks of red, yellow, and brown case files are piled in neat foot-high stacks on his desk; as soon as one stack is disposed of, another appears. Many are routine, some are colorful, some pose knotty judicial issues. Criminal cases are generally more colorful than civil cases, which are often more substantive, Connelly reflected. "I remember one day I had signed two search warrants in drug cases. When the FBI entered the house, the person said, 'I'm out of here' and jumped out of a third-story window and was taken to the hospital. I had to go there for the initial appearance because, until it was held, he was still in custody of the FBI, which did not have provisions to watch him during a ten-day hospital stay. Once the hearing was held, he was in custody of the U.S. marshal, which usually assumes custody of charged people. That is why in the courtroom arraignments the defendants are brought up by one agency and taken down by the U.S. marshal. Later that afternoon, the FBI called to say they were serving the second warrant and another drug suspect jumped out of a fifth-story window. He smashed his ankle badly, but they brought him here and we had the hearing."

A magistrate judge does not rule on requests for wiretaps by federal agencies; these are done by district judges. But magistrate judges can do pin registers—placing devices on phones that record incoming and outgoing phone numbers and the calls' duration.

Search warrants also come to magistrate judges. Usually they are drafted by the FBI or the Secret Service and must show probable cause. "Last week I looked up and there were two investigators from Kenneth Starr's office and a senior FBI agent who showed up with no advance warning. They wanted me to issue a search warrant allowing them to search a lawyer's office in Montgomery County, the lawyer for one of the principals in the expanded Whitewater investigation. They were looking for evidence of obstruction of justice; their witness complained of tires being cut, intimidating phone calls, that sort of thing. I was concerned that, if they went into the lawyer's office and seized the computers, as often happens in such cases, a lot of protected lawyer-client information would be compromised, so I limited the terms of the warrant. What you do in such cases is to send someone not connected with the investigation to go and look through the database for the specific information you are looking for."

Another case involved the admissibility of state secrets in a civil case. "I had a case, a dispute about software data-mining technology, involving state secrets. A major corporation was being sued by a small software provider who alleged its work was being misappropriated and wanted compensation for it. The large corporation responded to the software company's officers, 'You did not develop it; you took the technique with you when you left the CIA. You can't claim we stole it because it was never yours to steal.'" The U.S. attorney general wrote the judge saying state secrets were involved. A safe was set up in his conference room and several hundred pages of classified documents placed there. "The arguments were convoluted, but I concluded the information was too sensitive for use in a trial. This may mean that information is not admissible in a trial, even if it could clearly affect the outcome for one of the litigants. It's a difficult decision, but ultimately it's like saying to the people who invented the technology that broke the Japanese codes during World War II, 'We are suing you. Tell us what your technology is.'"

Much of a judge's time is spent not in the courtroom but in chambers negotiating settlement of a case or attending to motions of various kinds. What does Connelly try to do in a settlement meeting? "First of all, I carefully read the details of the case. I want both parties to know that I am familiar with the issues in their case. Then I bring all parties here with their lawyers. Sometimes you need time for the plaintiff just to tell the judge what happened in their language. They need that before you can move ahead. At times you have to get the attorney to realize that he has committed an error but not embarrass him in front of his client. I will also try and figure out what really motivates the parties. It is your job as a judge to figure out what they really want. Some people want an apology.

"Depending on the issues, I'll put the two parties in two different rooms and shuttle back and forth to see where they are in their deliberations. If you keep at it, people will see it as an investment of time and will want the results to be successful. Often they just need a neutral person like me to say, 'I understand what you are saying but here are the possibilities.' Sometimes when they come to this building it makes a difference. It is a beautiful building, and they say, 'Wow, this is serious stuff.' There is also a bit of the Stockholm syndrome that comes into play. Many times someone will think the other side is the devil incarnate, but after they have spent some time interacting with them, they see there is another side. It may be that the plaintiff has never heard the defendant's attorney tell them what they are going to do to their case if it gets in to court, or vice versa, and that comes from their getting together in a controlled environment. This is true of almost everyone except construction people. They are just tough guys; these are diggers and concrete men. You're not getting any signs of progress until one says, 'Let's take it outside.' Then we're making progress. And there is a lot of pretty uncouth language, but it comes with this particular niche of industry."

How does he control a courtroom? "I've never had a gavel, don't want a gavel. I've never had a problem in court. If you treat people with thoughtfulness and are polite, they will respond. Frequently, when I run a misdemeanor court, there may be a hundred people waiting, including some with significant mental health issues, some with alcohol or drug problems. They are all there, and I used to have no contempt authority. If you are on time and prepared and have respect for all parties, you will not have a control-of-court problem."

BANKRUPTCY COURT

Less well known, but no less active than the other courts, is the federal bankruptcy court, whose two judges have chambers in the Greenbelt Courthouse, and which has one of the highest volumes of bankruptcy cases of any court in the United States. It is in bankruptcy court that the blood and guts of the citizenry are spilled daily. A nervous couple in late middle-age, shoulders stooped; a young man with a nervous look; a single mother accompanied by a child—they are part of the steady stream of persons who come into the Greenbelt Court's Bankruptcy Clerk's Office each day, filing for personal bankruptcy, along with lawyers from the growing local bankruptcy bar, who deposit similar documents on behalf of other individuals or corporate clients. The District of Maryland has the sixth highest caseload of all the nation's bankruptcy courts, rivaled only by such populous centers as Los Angeles and central Florida.

The numbers tell the story. In 1982, the filings statewide numbered only 4,398. A decade later, the number was 16,740. There were 17,000 cases in 1995; 36,000 cases in 1998. Why is there such an astronomical rise in the number of bankruptcies? People live off credit cards. "This is as true of the person with one credit card who pays the outstanding balance every month as it is of the person with fifteen credit cards who pays only the revolving minimum," Bankruptcy Judge Duncan W. Keir reflected. A former Baltimore bank deputy general counsel, Keir became a judge in 1993. "You figure you're going to get your paycheck by the time the bills come due. Meanwhile, the bill arrives for the patio furniture and the trip to Hawaii. That makes people more vulnerable when something else happens to interdict their income, like job loss, or a significant loss in job benefits, as when a former manager becomes an hourly worker without benefits or when someone is hit by catastrophic illness or divorce." Such events create an enormous strain and lead people to file for bankruptcy. Also, the stigma once attached to bankruptcy is gone; bankruptcy is a way of life in modern America.

The debate continues among legislators: Is consumer credit too easily available and should large credit card companies bear some responsibility for it? Credit card companies want no restrictions and argue increased personal bankruptcy reflects people not taking responsibility for their actions. Companies are often perfunctory in their credit checks, calculating that profits will outweigh bankruptcy losses.

Three types of bankruptcy filings are widely used. Chapter 7 allows consumers with heavy debts to obtain a fresh start, free from creditor harassment. This is done through an orderly liquidation of the debtor's assets and the distribution of nonexempt assets to creditors. Businesses don't get a fresh start—they have to be liquidated.[88] Chapter 11 allows a business to reorganize and restructure its finances, to operate, to provide its employees with jobs, to pay its creditors, and to produce a return to its stockholders. Chapter 11 provides a breathing spell for a troubled business to work out a plan for reducing its debt, eventually returning to a viable state. Many large construction companies also file under this chapter, as do large businesses, plus mom-and-pop stores. Chapter 13, often called wage-earner bankruptcy or the "save the home" statute, allows individuals with regular incomes, under court supervision and protection, to develop a plan for the repayment of debts. During this period, creditors may not harass the debtor to seek to collect debts, but receive payments paid to the trustee by the debtor, who in turn pays the creditor. Debtors continue to support their families while repaying at the same time.

Pressured by the credit card industry, Congress has progressively taken steps to make bankruptcy filings easier. The word *bankrupt*, with a Dickensian opprobrium to it, was replaced in the Bankruptcy Code by *debtor*, as in "forgive us our debts as we forgive our debtors." Such an enlightened view of bankruptcy comes relatively late in world history. In ancient Greece, the Draconian division of the debtor's body was a distinct possibility. Shakespeare's Shylock, reflecting sixteenth-century commercial practice, could exact a pound of flesh as payment for a debt providing no blood was shed.

Bankruptcy law is relatively recent in American legal history. In 1973, the Rules of Bankruptcy Procedure created the position of bankruptcy judge, until then called "bankruptcy referee," and the U.S. Trustee program, which leaves judges free to be judges. On average, about 10 percent of the cases make it to the court hearing stage because of disputes that require court intervention to settle.

A staff of 100 clerical employees (forty-two in Greenbelt, the rest in Baltimore) field hundreds of inquiries each week. A sore point is that many of the applicants believe they can file the applications by themselves; it is possible, but technical or legal questions soon arise, and the clerk's staff is prohibited by law from providing advice. As a result, a lawyer is usually retained, but people's frustrations are real.

Greenbelt has a reputable bankruptcy bar, but there are plenty of shysters who advertise on buses and in telephone directories about how a call to them will prevent a bankruptcy foreclosure. Bankruptcy law is a respected and generally well-paying profession in the United States, but it does not lack for piranhas around its edges looking for a bite. Yellow-page solicitations and bus ads compound the problem.

In most bankruptcy cases, emotion or fault are not the issues. Creditors want to recover as much money as they can; debtors want to retain houses, vehicles, clothing, and sufficient cash to meet their basic needs. Basically, what happens in a bankruptcy case is that the instant the case is filed the clock is stopped; an automatic stay goes into effect, stopping most creditors from suing or foreclosing against the debtor or taking any collection efforts, such as repossessing a car, without permission of the bankruptcy court. This allows the bankrupt person or firm a breathing spell and a chance to get back on their financial feet; it is not intended as a way of allowing a debtor to strategically escape creditors, although some calculating persons and their attorneys try to manipulate the law to that end.

Predatory credit card companies will systematically argue that bankruptcy filers are committing fraud and thus force them into a separate settlement with the company. It works like this: The company knows a debtor has difficulty in raising the lawyer's fee, say $600, for a filing. By asserting the bankruptcy is fraudulent, the company has a fair chance at jack-hammering a settlement through in which the debtor agrees with the company to retain part of the credit card debt. This is a cheaper resolution than fighting the company's challenge in court, and the company knows it. But it circumvents the purpose of bankruptcy.

"I see certain credit card companies who file a large volume of complaints objecting to dischargeability on what appear to be very few, thin facts," Judge Keir noted, adding, "I see many of those Chapter 7 cases settled because the debtor does not have the money to pay a lawyer to contest them. So the debtor may have been actually entitled to discharge that credit card debt but ends up submitting a consent order to this court. Faced with $1,500 or $2,000 worth of attorneys' fees to defend a nondischargeability action or an agreement where $1,000 of the credit debt paid over two years is something they can do. The debtor will often elect to agree to the settlement. They may struggle or go without food, but they can't afford the lawyer who wants the fee in one lump sum. When that complaint is filed for that reason, to leverage that settlement, I consider it improper," he remarked.

Judge Keir added, "I do not see what I have seen characterized in press reports as a tidal wave of cases filed solely to allow debtors who are living the good life to escape too easily their obligations. Come in and sit in on one of our hearing days on Chapter 13 cases and listen to the stories we hear. Many people sit there with their head down in their hands, some in tears, embarrassed to be in this circumstance. This may be someone who has no ability to control the circumstances that forced them into that decision."

On the larger picture of what is happening in bankruptcy cases, Judge Keir concluded, "We have to be careful not to let the pendulum swing too far in any given direction or we will destroy something. If it swings too far in the direction of a person or an entity being able to escape their responsibility under contracts, then the problem will be enormous. If it swings too far into not allowing relief to persons who simply cannot pay debts which have been incurred no matter what happens and who cannot feed themselves or their families to any reasonable level without some relief, all we have done is created a class of desperate people without any benefit to society."

The Section 341 meeting of creditors is a central event in any bankruptcy case. At the Section 341 meeting, named for a section of the Bankruptcy Act, the debtor testifies under oath about his or her financial circumstances. Creditors rarely attend such a meeting, but this is the point at which creditors can object or claim fraud. A typical case will close within four months, but for a seven-to-ten-year period, the person will have difficulty in obtaining credit. However, auto dealers and department stores will renegotiate loans and let the person keep the merchandise for assured payments. I watched as two attorneys from Sears, most likely dressed in suits from the company they represent, darted like dragonflies through the several rooms full of bankruptcy trustee hearings, asking people, "Do you want to keep your TV, stereo, boom box, etc.? Well, step outside." In the corridor, they would peel an agreement form off a clipboard and get the debtor to sign, agreeing to fixed payments over a certain period.

A key figure in most bankruptcy proceedings is the U.S. bankruptcy trustee. Clifford J. White III is the assistant United States trustee who, with a small staff, keeps the high-volume program moving smoothly in the Greenbelt district. The U.S. trustees, named by the attorney general, supervise the administration of bankruptcy cases and the individual case trustees, freeing the bankruptcy judges from the day-to-day administrative tasks of appointing individual case trustees, and conducting the meetings of creditors. Greenbelt at present has ten such Chapter 7 trustees, to whom cases are assigned on a blind rotational basis. Generally, each carries about forty-five cases at a time. A case trustee has a fiduciary duty to act in the interest of the bankruptcy estate. "Our role is to ensure that the trustee is acting appropriately," White noted, adding, "We do not substitute our business judgment for that of a trustee. But we see to it that the funds are properly accounted for and that the case is moving forward as quickly as possible so that creditors may get paid as soon as possible."

The caseload in Greenbelt has doubled during White's tenure in office. The impression left on entering the bankruptcy trustee's office is one of constant motion, stacks of cases moving from office to office, and tense people waiting for their six minutes with the trustee that will hopefully launch them on a debt-repayment process and a better life.

"Give My Regards to Broadway": The Naturalization Ceremony

In addition to regular cases, the Greenbelt Court is periodically the site for naturalization and bar admission ceremonies. Judges Messitte, Williams, and Chasanow alternate the ceremonies between them every few months. What follows is a snapshot of one such ceremony.

July 13, 1998: Sixty-nine soon-to-be American citizens and their families filed into the Ceremonial Courtroom at noon. Yangla Tenpa came the furthest distance, from Tibet, one of twenty-six countries represented, including Argentina, Cameroon, Trinidad, and Vietnam. Mrs. Tenpa wore a green Tibetan costume with a multicolored apron of traditional design; others wore African dresses with yards of colorful cloth, Indian headpieces, or flowing Pakistani robes. A summer court clerk, sworn in as a citizen a few years ago in a mass ceremony at Camden Yards, home of the Baltimore Orioles, returned for today's event. A former citizen of Colombia, he is an economics major at Stanford University and on his way to a career in international law or finance. For many of the sixty-nine new citizens, career prospects are less heady. Mrs. Tenpa has a job with a local Giant supermarket selling flowers; someone else is a housekeeper (her sponsoring family brought flowers); another person is a restaurant cook.

Within a few minutes the large courtroom was filled, and a reverential hush fell over the gathering, except for a baby's cooing. The Leisure Time Granddads, a barbershop quartet, entered first from the jury room, looking like court security officers in new ties and blazers. Judge Peter Messitte told the assemblage, "Do not think for a moment that America is less than special because its streets may not be paved with gold or just because we still have our share of difficult social problems. The critical point is that this country cares about individual rights. If those rights are not respected, our courts are open to redress abuses. I have witnessed the courts providing these protections really and truly, day in and day out for many years as both a state and federal judge."

A representative of the Immigration and Naturalization Service petitioned the court for their naturalization, and the candidates took an oath of allegiance, after which the judge joined them in the well and presented each with a certificate, looking much like a large savings bond. The Daughters of the American Revolution, which arranges hundreds of such events in courtrooms throughout the country, gave each new citizen an American flag, and eleven-year-old Amelia Brose of the Children of the American Revolution led the Pledge of Allegiance. The Leisure Time Granddads sang "The Star-Spangled Banner" and a medley of patriotic songs, after which the group returned to the atrium for a brief punch-and-cookies reception, then headed quickly out the door to their jobs.

PART V

MAKING THE COURTHOUSE WORK

The U.S. Marshals Service

Each month, between 150 and 200 prisoners move through the Greenbelt Courthouse—murderers, embezzlers, white-collar criminals, large and small drug dealers. They are the responsibility of the United States Marshals Service, which transfers them from county jails and prisons all over Maryland for their arraignment in federal court. No prisoners are kept in the courthouse overnight, and while awaiting court appearances or sentencing, they are housed in several cells on the building's ground floor. Most are transported in unmarked vehicles, brought into the building through a closed sally port, and moved to courtrooms on special elevators with a locked cagelike door between them and the deputy marshals transporting them.

All prisoners wear arm and leg restraints attached with chains. Unless a judge orders a violent person to be restrained, the chains are removed in court, but a deputy marshal sits facing the prisoner, and another may be watching the prisoner's friends and families for any unusual movements, plus protecting the judge, jury, and witnesses. (Judges have panic buttons in their chambers and on the bench, and video cameras scan courtrooms as well.) No one has escaped from the Greenbelt Courthouse; no one has tried. And a computer tracing system prevents foul-ups of the sort that grab headlines in county papers—"Deputy Releases Wrong Prisoner by Accident."

In addition to the trim, hawk-eyed, muscular deputy U.S. marshals who carry out these tasks, there is a counterpart of contract security officers, most of them retired police officers. Drawn from county and local police and the Baltimore and Washington forces, they provide security in the courtrooms, protect judges and juries, and guard the building's entrance against possible terrorists. So far, no terrorists have come near Greenbelt; no prisoners have bolted for the door. The only disturbances have been flare-ups of defendants upset with their sentences who erupted verbally at judges.

The man who runs the whole show is United States Marshal George K. McKinney, who walks like a former paratrooper and exudes command presence. Even the retired police officers who spend their days monitoring TV cameras haul themselves to attention when he enters the room. Coming from a family of educators, pastors, and attorneys, he never doubted his ability. "If I knew the procedures, I could do the job," he said. After a promotion to the Security Staff of the Department of Justice, responsible for its numerous Washington buildings, he became United States Marshal for the District of Maryland in 1995, nominated for the position by Maryland Senator Paul Sarbanes and confirmed by the U.S. Senate.

McKinney (the name comes from Georgia, where one of the marshal's slave ancestors took the name of a kindly owner) flips the office radio on to the local classical music station, eases his muscular bulk into an executive chair, his weapon strapped to his belt. "The average citizen would find a quiet demeanor to this building," he says. "We pride ourselves on our professionalism. We try to treat all prisoners humanely. We talk to them, read the riot act to them, and let them know where they stand. Most have missed out on the opportunities of life. Their environment has played a role in where they are. With younger prisoners, there is hope. It can be a wake-up call for some."

His manner is cautious and reflective; his eyes searching the visitor and glancing out the window; but he is capable of occasional explosions of laughter. Outside, he is all business; inside he is a family man, grandfather, active in his church and the African American fraternities that did so much to advance blacks in the professions. A trained security management professional, in recent years he has conducted a "continuing investigation" into the family's genealogy, tracing it from Ghana to Georgia using 1870 census records and wills.

On McKinney's office wall is a courthouse artist's rendition of a watercolor sketch of three persons and the caption: "Egil 'Bud' Krogh, Jr., Special White House Counsel, with his attorney, surrenders to George K. McKinney, United States Marshal for the District of Columbia." McKinney grew up in Baltimore, was a psychology major at Morgan College (now Morgan State University), a Distinguished Military Student, and a paratrooper in Panama and Korea with the elite 82nd Airborne Division. He became a deputy U.S. marshal in 1966, one of a handful of African Americans to obtain such a job in Baltimore. A high achiever, McKinney was assigned to numerous special details, such as the Pentagon protests of the mid '60s and the summoning of Cassius Clay (now Muhammed Ali) for military induction in Houston. When Martin Luther King went to Memphis to lead the 1968 garbage workers strike, McKinney was part of the federal marshal's detail assigned to see that the march went as planned. After King's assassination, McKinney was shifted to Washington, D.C., then in flames. Following several years with the National Security Agency, some of it on spy cases, he became United States marshal for the District of Columbia.

Recalling the Pentagon protests, McKinney said, "We looked like the Katzenjammer Kids out there. Old blue suits, yellow armbands, and white helmets. The government didn't want its troops directly engaging citizens; we were in the middle. It was an exasperating time for Americans." I asked McKinney how he felt, an African American participating in the arrest of Cassius Clay, a leading African American figure of his time. "I've been in many multiracial situations. It didn't have any impact as such. I looked at the letter of the law. You put your trust in the government to do the right thing.

"In my deputy days in the '50s and '60s," he reflected, "bank robberies and thefts were the main crimes. Between cops and robbers there was a gentleman's agreement. Once the deputies picked someone up, there was no resistance. There are no rules of engagement any more. You've got some vicious shooters out there."

THE PRETRIAL SERVICES OFFICE

If the criminal justice system is somewhat like a board game, one of the first stops for criminal defendants after their arrest is the Pretrial Services Office, which decides whether they should be detained or released. The Pretrial Services officers must recommend the least restrictive conditions that reasonably assure the defendant's reappearance while assuring the safety of the community, for even though the defendant is charged with a criminal offense, he or she is presumed innocent until proven guilty. Approximately 35 percent of all defendants in the Maryland federal district are detained.

Maryland has almost 800 pretrial cases a year, split about 60–40 between Baltimore and Greenbelt. The Pretrial Services Office consists of nineteen persons, seven of them in Greenbelt. Each officer carries a caseload of approximately thirty-five defendants. Pretrial Services officers are skilled at gathering information in a short period of time on the defendant's family, employment, financial status, health, and criminal history for the judge before the defendant's appearance. If the defendant is convicted, the Pretrial Services Office's information assists the Probation Office in preparing a presentencing report.

Defendants are monitored in several ways. One of the most cost-effective is electronic monitoring. An electronic device is placed around a defendant's ankle and a transmitter is attached to the telephone. If the defendant leaves a predetermined range, a signal is sent by telephone to a central monitoring center in Colorado, and the Pretrial Services officer is contacted via pager. Recent developments in electronic monitoring technology will soon allow officers to monitor defendants using global positioning satellite technology. Compared to the cost of incarceration (approximately eighty dollars a day) and halfway-house placement (approximately fifty dollars a day), it is cost effective at only five dollars a day.

Some offenders can enter community service programs through a Pretrial Diversion Program. Not eligible are offenders with two or more felony convictions, addicts, corrupt public officials, individuals charged with offenses related to national security or foreign affairs, or persons charged with weapons offenses. If the U.S. attorney agrees to place the person in the program, a written agreement is prepared. After a year, if the person is clean and reports to the Pretrial Services Office regularly, charges are dismissed.

As with other federal courthouse jobs, there is tremendous competition for positions in the pretrial office. "It's the top of the game," William F. Henry, chief of the Pretrial Services Office, says, noting that a single opening in his office produced 139 applicants. Like the probation office, this is considered hazardous work, with mandatory retirement at age fifty-seven.

The Public Defender's Office

Entering the Federal Public Defender's Office in one of the buildings near the courthouse is like entering one of the mortgage companies or law offices on the same floor—slate-gray carpeting, framed art museum posters for an art show, copies of old issues of the *Reader's Digest* or *Travel & Leisure* on the waiting room table. In these offices eight public defenders, and fourteen more in Baltimore, represent what John Chamble, assistant federal public defender and Southern Division branch chief, calls "the best attorneys money cannot buy."

The public defenders, appointed by the court to aid criminal defendants who cannot afford counsel, are "a special breed," Chamble maintains. "We enjoy the challenge of being the gadfly, the underdog," he says. Chamble hails from Brooklyn by way of Fordham and Syracuse Universities, and spent several years in St. Croix, the Virgin Islands, and Washington, D.C., where he worked as a public defender as well. He holds a black belt in tae kwon do (Korean) martial arts and a brown belt in akido (Japanese) martial arts.

Federal public defenders, unlike their state counterparts, make the same salary as their rivals, the U.S. attorneys. Job openings are rare in the Public Defender Service, and there is little turnover. When an opening occurs, it would attract many applicants, many of them extremely well qualified by any standards.

Typically, each attorney has a caseload of about twenty felony or seventy-five misdemeanor cases. Between them, the two offices close more than 1,200 cases a year, less than 10 percent of which will go to trial. Public defenders spend little time in their offices—most of the clients incarcerated are in Baltimore City prisons or county prisons all over Maryland where the U.S. Marshals Service rents jail space. "There is a romantic call to what we do," Chamble said. "We're going against the might of the U.S. and all its resources; we are champions of the people, and we keep the prosecutors honest. When reason is abandoned by the prosecutors, we are called upon to rein them in, to put the possible in the impossible," a phrase he is fond of quoting, along with "putting the can in can't."

A romantic is "someone who is not overwhelmed by overwhelming odds, when you are fighting for someone's life and liberty. I see that as being a romantic.... There is an artistic, visionary aspect to criminal defense work. It is easy to be part of what is popular; it takes a special breed to defend the despised. Only romantics do that. I see us as warriors fighting for a cause." His face lights up as he talks, and he gestures like a schoolteacher explaining a favorite theory, sometimes pausing to stare out the windows of his corner office to the tree-filled landscape.

The continued rivalry between federal public defenders and U.S. attorneys is like the long-standing competition between two football teams, one small and scrappy, the other a confident winner with depth on the bench. If you are a prosecutor, Chamble says, "You have to leave your heart at the door. It is a legitimate function. I could not be one. A good prosecutor can be a good defense attorney, but a good defense attorney doesn't necessarily have the temperament to be a prosecutor." And while public defenders may go on to other legal endeavors, they rarely become prosecutors. It would be, according to Chamble, "a badge of dishonor for a public defender to go over to the other side." He continues, with a note of hyperbole, it would make the person "a Benedict Arnold." It is rare that, when a judicial vacancy is open, a public defender would be nominated to it, but many judges were formerly prosecutors. "Prosecutors think that judgeships are their birthrights," he observed, although a recent coveted opening on the Baltimore bench for a magistrate judge went to a former public defender.

Given such insurmountable odds, how many victories do the public defenders win? Not many. Chamble does not have the numbers but comments that "win and victory are redefined in federal court. I had a trial where the defendant was charged with rape, aggravated sexual assault, and attempted rape. The jury found him not guilty on the first two counts. Was that a victory or not? If you can get a mistrial, that is generally considered a win, or if you can tie the other side up with motions. Sometimes it is a victory in the sentencing process if you get a reduced sentence for your client. You have to be very creative in reading the Sentencing Guidelines." (The two-volume Sentencing Guidelines, as well-thumbed as a telephone directory, are in a prominent place on Chamble's desk.) "There is wiggle room, but very little. Sometimes prosecutors will wink, wink on a specific offense; sometimes a judge will give you a break. Those are the strictures no lawyers should have to operate under," brought about by the Sentencing Guidelines.

The Sentencing Guidelines, he says, "are the bane of any criminal defense attorney's existence." On a mechanical grid, much like a score card, they plot the person's previous criminal history, the gravity of the crime, the custody range, the supervised release range, and the range for upward or downward departures depending on cooperation, thus accumulating a number of points that lead to specific sentences. "They take away the judicial discretion that has always been the bedrock of our judicial system, to make the punishment fit the crime," he observed, calling the guidelines "horrific" because they do not consider mitigating circumstances in a person's life.

Chamble used the phrase "You've got to know when to fold 'em and when to hold 'em" in describing the negotiating process. He explained, "Any experienced trial attorney can look at a case and ask: Should we plead or go to trial? If you know the best you can do for your client is damage limiting, you don't want to go to trial. I've been around the block a couple of times. It isn't what your client says, it's what evidence the government has. Take a bank robbery case for example. If they have a picture that is so good your mother will want to have a copy after the trial, then it's time to talk with the other side. I tell clients there are two people you don't lie to, your doctor and your attorney. If they send me on a wild goose chase, that is valuable time lost I could have used to defend their case. You don't want your attorney to be the last person to know an injurious fact that the prosecution has been sitting on."

What percentage of the criminal defendants are African Americans? Chamble estimated about 70 percent, but less than 20 percent of the juries are, despite more than half the population of the four counties from which juries are selected being African American. "When I'm picking a jury, if I get three African Americans, I'm lucky," he observed, adding, "The jury panels I've seen in Greenbelt are seriously underrepresented in minority numbers."

So you don't have a race card to play? "The only card you can play is the moral card. You can appeal to a jury's sense of what is right and wrong."

Chamble's wife is an assistant vice president of an insurance company. They have two small children and juggle busy schedules with child rearing. He has thought of going into private practice but concluded that he would have to develop another specialty, such as personal injury liability law, acknowledging that many criminal defense attorneys do not make much money. An exception is the "snow lawyer," a lawyer whose bills are paid by cocaine money. "If a client with no visible means of support comes in and hands you $25,000, you have become a silent partner. That's not for me."

The Probation Office

As busy as the Pretrial Services and Public Defender Offices is the Probation Office, where each officer conducts five or six investigations each month and follows fifty to sixty cases as supervisors. Probation officers work mainly with the judges. After the trial they conduct background investigations and prepare reports judges use in sentencing offenders, discussing the offender's criminal history, family relations, employment, financial condition, and drug and alcohol use or mental health problems. (The reports, written for the judge, are also made available to the defendants, defense counsel, and U.S. attorney on request, but are otherwise sealed.) If the offense occurred after November 1, 1987, the date the Sentencing Guidelines kicked in, the presentence report contains information on the appropriate sentencing guidelines for the judge to consider.

The office's monitoring function begins when an offender is placed on probation or supervised release. This includes seeing that the offender remains crime free, works at a lawful occupation, pays the monetary fine levied, pays restitution to the victim, completes a period of community service, and participates in drug, alcohol, or mental health treatment programs. About 2,000 to 2,500 offenders are in the program, 800 of which have drug, alcohol, or mental health problems.

Cedric Easter is the Greenbelt Court's deputy probation officer. A trained social worker, he has been at this work for more than twenty-five years, ever since leaving the army. "We don't control the flow," he said of the fluctuating number of cases the office handles. "We take whatever the trends in prosecution produce." Approximately one-third of the district's 100 officers and thirty support staff are assigned to Greenbelt; the rest are in Baltimore, reflecting the one-third/two-thirds division of labor between the two offices.[89] Generally, there is not much turnover in the positions. People with a bent for social work like the job, even if it is hazardous duty with mandatory retirement at age fifty-seven. Officers have the option of carrying arms, and some do, considering they are going alone into homes and neighborhoods of known criminals. It costs the government almost $23,000 a year to keep someone in a federal prison, $14,235 for a year in a community corrections center, as a halfway house is called. A person under probation office supervision costs $2,606. Probation officers use the current technology in their work, including handheld substance-abuse testing kits, ignition devices to keep drunk drivers off the road, and electronic monitors; possibly seventy-five such devices are in use at any given time, usually with nonviolent white-collar criminals.

"It's a person's life you are dealing with," Easter remarked. "If you can help someone lead a stable and productive life, then it is worth all the effort. You can't explain the rewards of helping someone else. To see someone make it through that system and lead a productive life is a reward."

THE U.S. ATTORNEY'S OFFICE

The U.S. attorney is the federal government's lawyer for Maryland, one of ninety-three judicial districts throughout the country that are part of the U.S. Department of Justice. The sixty-five assistant U.S. attorneys (AUSAs) who work on criminal cases (eighteen of them are in Greenbelt) and another twelve around the state who work on civil cases are the crème de la crème of government lawyers. Although it used to be a high-turnover office, AUSAs rarely leave now; most acknowledge their work to be the most interesting in their profession, assembling and arguing complex, high-profile criminal and civil cases they would wait decades to try if they were working for a law firm.

Lynne A. Battaglia, the U.S. attorney, reflected, "Probably the most important change for us is that we prosecute more crimes of violence now than at any time in our history. Probably crimes of violence have gone up from 5 percent to over 20 percent of our caseload—that is in addition to our narcotics jurisdiction. That is a reflection of the administration and also the fact that we're called upon to engage more with the Baltimore City and Prince George's County police than before."

As society changes, types of crimes change to mirror society. "If there is an opportunity for crime, people will engage in it," Battaglia observed. Computer crime and credit card fraud are widespread, especially among minority groups such as Nigerians who have moved into surrounding communities in Prince George's

County. Improvements in color copying machines have been a boon to counterfeiters. Cybercrime is now a major issue. The Innocent Images program, a nationwide FBI effort aimed at detecting the sexual solicitation of minors and the transmission of child pornographic pictures on the Internet, is located in nearby Calverton. Not far away is the port of Baltimore and Baltimore-Washington International Airport, bringing technology export and drug import cases, mostly to the Baltimore Court, but some to Greenbelt. Health care fraud is a growth industry, and environmental crimes are widespread in a state with so much shoreline.

Historically, Maryland has produced its share of white-collar crime, including public corruption cases, and, as the suburbs expand, there is no lack of housing discrimination cases, a federal offense. There is also a steady stream of bread-and-butter cases, bank robberies, mail and wire fraud, tax fraud, firearms violations, and fraud against the government, including student loan fraud.

When Battaglia first joined the office as a career prosecutor in 1978, it consisted largely of attorneys from large firms. A new emphasis on drug cases meant more experienced state prosecutors were hired. At that time, the pay was low and the turnover high. "Now it's the highest and best opportunity for those who want to learn litigation," Battaglia noted. "The pay is at the top of the government scale for litigators. Even if it pays well, it doesn't pay as well as on the outside." The office would lose four skilled attorneys in 1999; one went to a private firm because he eventually wants to be a Maryland judge; the others had young families to raise and needed the added income private practice would bring.

The Greenbelt office represents an eclectic mix of lawyers. Many of them are young, culled from hundreds of applicants, including clerks to Supreme Court judges, lawyers from large and small firms, former Department of Justice staff attorneys, lawyers from the military judge advocates general, plus assistant state's attorneys. About half are women, some are minorities. There is no one profile of who joins the office.

LYNNE A. BATTAGLIA, U.S. ATTORNEY

Tall, attractive, and authoritative, Lynne A. Battaglia holds one of the most coveted positions in the pantheon of American lawyers, U.S. attorney, the government's head lawyer for Maryland. She grew up in western New York State, where her father was a town pharmacist. In Silver Creek, New York, in the 1960s, "a lawyer made a difference," she recalled. "From womb to tomb, every aspect of life was affected by law. Everyone talked about being a trial attorney; there is a mystique to it. It somewhat enveloped me." Her road out of the Buffalo, New York, region was via Washington, D.C., and American University, where she majored in international relations. After receiving an M.A. there, she moved to nearby Georgetown University for work on a doctorate in political science. But the law called, and she entered the University of Maryland Law School, receiving a Juris Doctor degree in 1974, graduating in the top 10 percent of her class. Articulate, boundlessly confident, and gregarious, she was active in student politics and honorary associations, ending up as a law review editor, a prestigious position for aspiring lawyers.

After four years with a major Baltimore firm doing estate and trust work, she became an AUSA in 1978, prosecuting bank robbery, mail fraud, drug violations, and tax evasion cases, the sort of work any young lawyer in their thirties could rarely dream of. This led to a promotion with the Department of Justice as a senior trial attorney trying complex tax shelter cases. In 1988 she became chief of the Criminal Investigations Division for the Attorney General of the State of Maryland, supervising lawyers prosecuting white-collar and environmental crimes. Interested in Democratic Party politics and good at management, she joined United States Senator Barbara A. Mikulski as chief of staff and ran the senator's busy Washington office and six state offices, also acting as the office's legal adviser. Battaglia's presidential appointment as chief federal government lawyer for Maryland came in 1993.

She also found time to marry, raise a son, divorce, and teach courses in Women and the Law, Counseling and Negotiation, and Advanced Criminal Procedure as a visiting professor of law at her alma mater, the University of Maryland Law School at Baltimore, which gave her its Distinguished Graduate Award in 1998. (She received an Honorary Juris Doctor degree from the University of Baltimore Law School in 2000.) Long active in women-and-the-law issues, she was chair of the Gender Equality Committee of the Maryland State Bar Association, has been appointed to the Howard County Commission for Women, is a member of Network 2000, and worked with the Citizens Against Spousal Assault, the Baltimore Women's Law Center, and the Howard County Sexual Assault Center. She is also a director of the Traditional Acupuncture Institute. Her interest in acupuncture is long-standing, reflecting a belief that "we need to explore all types of healing for individuals and society."

The office she heads does a brisk business. Forty percent of the Maryland federal district's criminal cases come to the Greenbelt Court, up from 25 percent a few years ago; and the numbers will probably stay that way for the next several years. (Ten percent of the criminals commit 90 percent of the crimes, and about 5 percent of all criminals are prosecuted in federal courts, the rest in state courts.) The number and type of federal cases depend on what investigators, including the FBI, the DEA, Customs, and other federal agencies, bring to the U.S. attorney, who then decides whether or not there is a case to take into court. U.S. attorneys take their cues from the Department of Justice's Prosecution Guidelines, which stress drugs and violent crime.

Reflecting on the Sentencing Guidelines, Battaglia said, "I was raised as an AUSA here before the Sentencing Guidelines. So the Sentencing Guidelines are more difficult for me than for a person who didn't know the other system. However, it brings greater certainty for people, whether they like it or not. It is a mathematical equation; it gives a greater consistency. People used to be unhappy that two defendants got different sentences for the same crime. I think we've seen so much harm to our communities from the drug culture, and the Sentencing Guidelines reflect the community's sentiment. In addition to our concern about the individual defendant, we need to be concerned about harm to the community."

BETH P. GESNER AND DEBORAH A. JOHNSTON, BRANCH CHIEFS

Heading the Greenbelt office were two talented women attorneys, Beth P. Gesner and Deborah A. Johnston. Johnston succeeded Gesner when the latter became a magistrate judge in Baltimore.

Gesner, an amateur golfer, exudes both authority and femininity. She is a product of Indiana University in Indiana, Pennsylvania, where an undergraduate major in criminology was followed by three years at Georgetown University Law School. She then took a clerkship with a federal judge and spent two and a half years with the leading firm of Hogan & Hartson before becoming a career prosecutor in 1987. She is also co-chair of a Federal Criminal Practice Working Group, composed of criminal defense attorneys and prosecutors to discuss policy issues before they become points of contention, as in the content of plea agreements. An outgrowth of then-Chief Judge Fred Motz's desire to keep civility in litigation, the working group put potential adversaries in the same room to talk about issues of mutual concern and to prevent differences over issues from disintegrating to personal invective.

How does a woman attorney maintain her authority in a world of macho weight-lifting FBI agents? "While historically there may have been individuals in law enforcement who fit that description, that is less true today. I've always had more success in trying to cooperate with people than in being confrontational. I have never found that alienating somebody or telling someone I'm the boss and I'm going to call the shots is helpful. I think it's best to just roll with the punches. If you prove yourself as an able prosecutor, you have more credibility—no matter whom you are or who you are dealing with."

What are the lessons learned in over a decade's work in the U.S. Attorney's Office? "I guess I have two responses. The most difficult aspect of what we do is sentencing, and for most judges, too...because even if you look at the most hopeless of defendants, they all have families and there is always someone in that family who is a decent, hardworking person, and you're not sure how things went bad. And you look at them and you say if they had different opportunities or approached things differently, they wouldn't be where they are. That is more true of the violence-and-drug kind of cases. In the white-collar cases it's sad because it's just greed for the most part, and those people are just like me or you, and you tend to relate to that. On the other hand, the best part of the job is the sense of public service in this work. The most important thing we can do is to be fair in how we do it. No matter who you are dealing with, a terrible criminal, a colleague, or an opposing counsel, you should treat them with dignity."

In the summer of 1999, Gesner was appointed a United States magistrate judge in Baltimore and was replaced as branch chief by a five-year veteran of the office, Deborah A. Johnston, an experienced prosecutor of large-scale violent crimes, especially drug crimes. A graduate of Catholic University and its law school, most of her career was spent in Prince George's County, where she clerked for a circuit court judge and worked as a public defender, an assistant state's attorney, and an attorney in private practice before joining the U.S. Attorney's Office in November 1996, just after the Greenbelt Courthouse opened.

In agreeing to take the supervisory position, Johnston said she wanted to continue as an active trial attorney. "That's what I enjoy; it is much more exciting than administrative work." Her hope is to keep office morale high. The office enjoys a good reputation with the bench and investigation agencies, and Johnston says that her "greatest fear is that, with the increase in workload, attorneys may not do as good a job with the individual cases as before, and may try to cut corners. One of my concerns is to prevent that from happening. I also want people to continue to have gratification from their jobs, which will be hard to do if the workload keeps going up. The number of indictments has doubled from 1996 to 1998, but our staff numbers haven't kept up with the expanded caseload."

The U.S. attorney's offices are crowded, with piles of legal documents everywhere. When children come to spend a day with parents, as they sometimes do during the summer, there is little extra room. One conference room I sat in had a basket of children's crayons, books, and videotapes piled next to the dog-eared posters from a long-decided, complex fraud case. Clearly, something will have to give soon in the Greenbelt Courthouse; some major unit will have to move to another building, which will work against the collegiality Messitte and his colleagues have striven for, but which is an inevitable result of an astronomically rising caseload.

The Clerk of Court

If an army travels on its stomach, a courthouse moves on its paper. Motions, depositions, orders, and opinions—the trickle of documents soon becomes a flood. Keeping track of them and being able to lay hands on them instantly for a judge who needed them five minutes ago falls to the staff of the Clerk of Court. Frank L. Monge in Baltimore, Richard J. Goodier, his deputy-in-charge in Greenbelt, and the Greenbelt staff of eighteen specialists call up a steady stream of grand and petit jurors, keep court documents flowing, collect filing fees, docket motions, field hundreds of public and lawyer's inquiries by phone or in person, and assign cases to judges. Three skilled court stenographers record many case proceedings; others are recorded by dual-deck tape recorders. (Transcripts and copies of tapes are prepared after requests by lawyers and the public.)

The grand jury selection process begins in Baltimore. Letters are sent to registered Maryland voters. Typically, sixty persons might be called and forty appear at the courthouse, from which twenty-three names are selected. Jurors are on call to serve for three months. Once the grand jury is empanelled, the U.S. attorney takes over. The only persons in the room with the grand jury are the U.S. attorney, a witness, and a court reporter. (A witness may consult his or her attorney outside the jury room.) Proceedings are usually brief; the U.S. attorney outlines the government's case, and a few witnesses may be questioned. The grand jury determines whether or not the evidence being presented justifies a criminal trial. If they agree, as they do in 95 percent of the cases, they return an indictment, or true bill, and the case is scheduled for trial.

Petit jurors are summoned for civil and criminal cases and call a Code-a-Phone daily to see if they are needed for trial. Ordinarily, twenty-four are called for a civil case, of whom six to eight will be picked; forty-two are called for a criminal case, of whom twelve will be picked. Each side is given four strikes, allowing them to dismiss potential jurors either preemptively or for cause. Not infrequently one or more alternate jurors are chosen in criminal cases. Although more than 90 percent of cases settle, the majority of the remaining cases are jury trials. Infrequently, a bench trial is held before the judge alone, when one of the parties believes they would have a better chance before a judge than a jury. The Sixth Amendment provides a trial by jury in all federal criminal cases; the Seventh Amendment allows for jury trials in all civil cases in which the value in dispute is over twenty dollars, a substantial sum in 1787.

How do the cases reach the judges? A computerized system of case assignments is used to distribute civil and criminal cases among Greenbelt's judges. Each case is entered for its type and complexity and then randomly distributed among the judges so that no one judge keeps being assigned the same type of case and lawyers cannot "shop for judges" whom they might regard as more sympathetic to their arguments. "It works like a deck of cards being shuffled," Monge explained. "Think of there being a card for each judge and a card for each type of case. All those cards are shuffled electronically, and whenever a case is assigned, a judge's name comes up. It also gives us the ability to look at reports each month to see if the system is operating effectively. Over time it evens out." When a civil case is filed at the counter, it is given a number by the clerk, who asks the computer to find the next available judge.

Incrementally, the Clerk's Office has installed a computer and data communications network that permits Greenbelt court employees to talk to counterparts in Baltimore and elsewhere in the judicial system. A new portable camera and screen system allows evidence to be presented visually in courtrooms through monitors, making it easier for lawyers to explain and jurors to see the evidence. Next will come an order-imaging system. Court orders will come from judges to the Clerk's Office and be scanned into a computer, which will docket them and then transmit them electronically to each attorney's fax machine and make them available to the public for electronic viewing.

Goodier, who holds both a law degree and an MBA, is proud of the young courthouse's esprit de corps and works hard to maintain it. "It is not often people get such a challenge to start an operation from scratch," he remarked. Present at the creation, he found himself literally carrying furniture and computers into the building for several months after it opened. The court also strives to keep ties to the community in which it is set. There are periodic meetings with the local, regional, and national bar associations, and each year several high school students earn academic credit for serving internships in the Clerk's Office.

"Clearly, we are called on to do more with less," Monge, a veteran court administrator from Chicago and Texas before coming to Greenbelt and Baltimore, remarked. "Each court has its own culture and climate, but with a little vision you can accomplish a lot of things." Court administrators talk about the virtual courthouse—the paperless courthouse—as a goal; but for Monge, who started low on the totem pole as a front-line employee in Chicago, the task is to look carefully at what technology is available and to gradually introduce it when budget and training opportunities allow. In this he is aided by the relatively recent decentralization of federal courts' budgets, allowing each district to determine the use of some of its funds and create programs or realign its staff in ways that are not carbon copies of what other districts are doing.

Space is at a premium. The U.S. Attorney's Office needs more space; so does the bankruptcy court. A magistrate judge's temporary chambers is nearing construction, and an additional bankruptcy judge position is on the horizon, which means finding room for another courtroom, plus chambers for the judge, clerk, and judicial assistant. Some occupants of the Greenbelt Courthouse will have to find quarters elsewhere. (Nearby office buildings already house the public defender, plus several law firms.) The building that wasn't needed is already overcrowded.

Openings and Closings

About 400 people came to the fifth-anniversary observance of the Greenbelt Courthouse on a cold, rainy Friday afternoon, October 1, 1999. Among them were a few I conjured up in my imagination, so that my experience of the day was a combination of the real and the fanciful, as depicted in the following account.

The usually near-empty parking lot was filled and cars parked out on the road. Important people came in big black cars with wire-thin antennae rising from several places in the car's trunks, flat as the decks of aircraft carriers. A county executive arrived in a huge recreational vehicle with massive shock absorbers and wide, bouncy spaces between wheels and fenders so it could tear around county roads with red, white, and blue lights flashing. A solid Packard town car of the 1930s somehow got in the mix. No one seemed to notice it, nor the large 1960s Buick with a bloated body and fenders, driven by a distinguished-looking white-haired man, a shade paler than most arriving guests. Outside, standing in the forest, were the original inhabitants of the courthouse space, a gathering of Iroquois in festive dress. Onondaga, the Iroquois chief, was carrying his metal-tipped hunting spears, and headed for the door with a shorter Indian, whom he later introduced as keeper of the five nations' Book of the Great Law. Joining the crowd converging on the courthouse entrance, they went through the magnetometer. I saw them, but the guards didn't. Red lights flashed when the spears came through, but the Indians passed by the guards, who then busily inspected the large shoulder bag of a surprised member of the Greenbelt City Council.

The pale, angular figure with the Buick and the one with the Packard were talking together, and now I remembered where I had seen them. Both were judges whose portraits appeared on the inner wall of the fourth-floor hallway and who had been leaders of the U.S. District Court for Maryland in Baltimore. I had known Judge Frank Kaufman for many years, and Judge William Calvin Chestnut had been on the bench from 1931 to 1961. Chestnut, who looked like a judge from a James Gould Couzzens novel, was of medium height and granite-like bearing, with rimless spectacles magnifying his observant eyes. The atrium was crowded by now, and they, Onondaga and his companion, and I gathered near one of the pillars, brushing against one of the local artist's paintings specially hung for the occasion. I talked with Judge Kaufman, whose lively face lit up, as it always did when I had visited him in his chambers in the old Baltimore courthouse. Just then the program began.

"Well, what do you think?" Judge Kaufman asked afterward. He was obviously pleased with the event, and lit up a cigar. The courthouse had a no-smoking policy, and people began shaking their hands like metronomes and moved away from us. The two judges spoke of how the federal judiciary in Maryland had changed from a small Baltimore-centered court to much larger courts in Baltimore and now in Greenbelt. I remembered it had been Kaufman, as chief judge in Baltimore, who had been a vocal opponent of the Greenbelt court. "Well, Frank, was it worth it?" I asked. Kaufman, who always spoke as much with facial expressions and gestures as with words, smiled broadly, shrugged his shoulders, and lifted his arms, palms up—a sporting gesture. "It's okay; it turned out well," he seemed to say. Judge Chestnut, whose time was before the courthouse controversy, said only, "When I was on the bench this part of the country was nothing but farms. My wife's brother had a summer place near here. We used to come down on Sundays. The roads had just been widened and the telephone poles were new. I remember when we had to call the operator if we wanted to talk to someone in Baltimore."

Onondaga and his companion asked for a tour of the courthouse, so we headed up the escalator, he holding his spear above the mechanism, Judge Kaufman pointing out people he knew. We saw the courtrooms, the judges' chambers, the holding cells, the prisoners' elevators, the judges' elevators, and the various offices with their computers. "The goal is a paperless courthouse," I said, repeating an often-used expression, and before I had finished the sentence, I realized Onondaga didn't know what paper was. The Book of the Great Law had been written on animal skins and bark. Onondaga's alert eyes darted about, instantly sizing up politicians and lawyers. He said little but listened intently when Kaufman and Chestnut talked. He and they conversed while I talked with Judge Messitte. Finally Onondaga asked Kaufman, "But do you have justice here?"

Kaufman thought a moment and answered, "Yes, as much as is humanly possible," adding, "Remember that laws are fallible, judges human, and the issues difficult."

"But the judges are honest and able," Judge Chestnut had joined us, "and they are pretty well protected so they can decide their cases without pressure. Even the architecture of the courthouse isolates them." We were standing in the Ceremonial Courtroom. "The high bench, the separate doors for judge, jury, and people, the separate entrances to the courthouse, even the physical space keeps them apart. I saw that happening in my time," the older judge reflected.

Kaufman gestured with what remained of his cigar. "You have to remember we have so many laws now, we even had them in my time. You need to know how to find a law, how to think fairly, and how to write quickly. A district judge is no great legal theorist; the caseload mitigates against it. They just apply the law."

Onondaga seemed puzzled, his colleague more so. "We spent much time under the palaver tree," he said, "or by the great rock. We had both the Book of the Great Law, like your laws, and also the wisdom of our elders. We talked and talked until we reached a decision."

"Do you know what makes a difference?" Judge Chestnut had thought of something else. "Somehow, from very early on, Americans developed a respect for the law. I think it was probably starting in your time. A great respect has grown up around the law—almost a mystery. People are cynical about politicians, and now the president and Congress, but not the judges. You sense it when you walk into a courthouse; it is almost like a church."

I would have liked to continue the conversation and ask the Indian leader about "then" and the two visitors from a more recent past about "now," but it was late and most of the crowd had left. The two judges departed together. Kaufman gave me a brisk wave, with a twinkle in his pale blue eyes. Chestnut, more reserved, smiled and tipped his homburg, one like Dean Acheson wore. Onondaga looked me straight in the eye and pressed a small amulet of red and white beads in my hand with a strength and a warmth I feel even today. Then he and his companion departed quickly, crossing through the glass wall. I watched them enter the forest, talk briefly with kinsmen who had waited for them, and disappear into the woods. By now the cars had formed a solid exit queue, the Packard and the Buick among them, the long line moving slowly toward the beltway, and wherever else it might be headed.

I stayed around, waiting for some telling insight with which to end this book, although I needed none, for, after two years of reading cases, watching trials, and talking with judges, the story was told. The Greenbelt Courthouse had easily survived its first five years and seemed to have settled in as a permanent part of southern Maryland's civic landscape. By now it was late, and the autumn darkness had set in, the wind and rain were strong. The courthouse was empty, the atrium filled with soft light. (Evening was the best time to see it.) I walked quickly toward the parking lot, past the metal sculpture with the laser light projecting the Iroquois Book of the Great Law on the courthouse wall. Flipping on the windshield wipers, I glanced leftward toward the forest. There in the distance, blending with the colors of the changing leaves, was Onondaga—or so I thought.

NOTES

1 Jim Sanborn, Jim Sanborn, Public Projects 1990–1997, 903 Girard Street, NE, Washington, D.C., 20019, 1998.
2 United States Courts, Courtroom Post Occupancy Evaluation, Greenbelt Maryland, Federal Courthouse, Administrative Office of the United States Courts, Space and Facilities Division, Washington, D.C., (Draft) N.D. , pp. 3–7.
3 Frank L. Monge, Clerk of Court, 1997 "Annual Report of the Clerk of the United States District of Maryland," Baltimore, Md., 1998, p. 2
4 Garry Wong, Yoshitatsu Sei, and Phil Skolnick, "Stable Expression of Type 1 Gamma–Aminobutyric Acid-a/ Benzodiazepine Receptors in a Transfected Cell Line," *Molecular Pharmacology*, The American Society for Pharmacology and Experimental Therapeutics, Vol. 42, 1992, pp. 966–1003.
5 Dr. Skolnick's title was Chief of the Laboratory of Neuroscience, National Institutes of Diabetes and Digestive and Kidney Diseases, Division of Intramural Research, Neurobiology Section.
6 *USA v Prince Kumar Arora*, Plaintiff's Brief, Civil No. PJM-93-1281, August 4, 1994.
7 *USA v Prince Kumar Arora*, Defendant's Proposed Post Trial Findings of Fact and Conclusions of Law, Civil No. PJM-93-1281, August 5, 1994.
8 *USA v Prince Kumar Arora*, Defendant's Trial Brief, Civil No. PJM-93-1281, August 5, 1994.
9 *USA v Prince Kumar Arora*, Plaintiff's Reply Brief, Civil No. PJM-93-1281, August 15, 1994.
10 *USA v Prince Kumar Arora*, Opinion, Civil No. PJM-93-1281, August 26, 1994.
11 William Cuddihy & B. Carmon Hardy, "A Man's House Was Not His Castle: Origins of the Fourth Amendment to the United States Constitution," p. 37 *William & Mary Quarterly*, 386 (1980)
12 Deposition of Charles H. Wilson Jr., PJM-94-1718, September 19, 1995.
13 Geraldine E. Wilson, Exhibit G. Wilson 3, 9-9-95.
14 42 USC Section 1983.

15 William Blackstone, *4 Commentaries on the Laws of England* p. 223 (1769).
16 "Arguments Before the Court," *The United States Law Week, Proceedings of the U.S. Supreme Court*, Vol. 67, No. 36, March 30, 1999.
17 Supreme Court of the United States, No. 98-83, *Charles H. Wilson v Harry Layne.*
18 Opinion of Stevens, J., Supreme Court of the United States, No. 98-83, *Charles H. Wilson v Harry Layne*, p. 2.
19 Joan Biskupic and Howard Kurtz, "Police Can Be Sued for Letting Media See Raids," *Washington Post*, May 25, 1999, p. A8.
20 As each case is docketed it is given a tag, civil or criminal, the year, the case number, and the judge's initials.
21 Jon Robert Lankford, FDA Investigator, Affidavit, May 4, 1994.
22 James M. Ritz and Nicholas Buhay, Interviewing Agents, to Christopher Meade, Assistant U.S. Attorney, Memorandum of Interview, Mutual Pharmaceuticals, Inc., September 1, 1993.
23 Melvin F. Szymanski and John Loh, Agents, Special Prosecution Staff, Interview of Sunil (Sony) Shah, September 1, 1993.
24 *United States of America v Suhas V. Sardesai et al.*, Indictment, Criminal No. PJM-94-0167.
25 *United States of America v Suhas V. Sardesai*, Affidavit of Robert E. Welsh Jr., in Support of Defendants' Motion for a Continuance of Trial and for a Speedy Trial Act Exclusion, June 2, 1994.
26 *United States of America v Suhas V. Sardesai*, Government's Consolidated Response to the Defendants' Motions for a New Trial, Criminal No. PJM-94-0167, September 29, 1995.
27 *United States of America v Suhas V. Sardesai*, Motion In Limine of Defendant Suhas Sardesai to Exclude Evidence of the Alleged Theft of "Trade Secret" Formulas," Criminal No. PJM-94-0167, February 14, 1995.
28 *United States of America v Sunil C. Shah*, Defendant Sunil Shah's Theory of Defense and Requested Jury Instructions, Criminal No. PJM-94-167, March 23, 1995.
29 Unpublished United States Court of Appeals for the Fourth Circuit, *United States of America v Suhas V. Sardesai*; Edmund J. Striefsky, No. PJM-96-4228, October 10, 1997.
30 *United States of America v Susas V. Sardesai*, Sentencing Memorandum of Defendant Suhas Sardesai, Criminal No. PJM-94-0167, January 22, 1999.
31 John J. Williams, "Fairness Hearing Re: Memorandum of Understanding Regarding *Vaughns v Board of Education for Prince George's County*," August 25, 1998, p.2.
32 Defendant Prince George's County Maryland's Pretrial Brief in the United States District Court for the District of Maryland, Southern Division, *Sylvester J. Vaughns Jr. et al., Plaintiffs, v Board of Education of Prince George's County, et al.*, Defendants, Civil No. PJM-72-325, November 11, 1997, p. 7.

33 Gary Orfield and Susan E. Eton, *Dismantling Desegregation, The Quiet Reversal of Brown v Board of Education*, (New York: The New Press, 1996), p. 280.
34 "Comments of Court-Appointed Panel at Fairness Hearing," August 25, 1998.
35 Peter J. Messitte, United States District Judge, United States District Court for the District of Maryland, *Sylvester J. Vaughns Jr. et al., v Board of Education of Prince George's County et al.* , Opinion, August 31, 1998, pp. 36–37.
36 Kevin Merida, "An Era Slowly Rolls to a Stop," *Washington Post*, September 2, 1998, p. D1–3.
37 *Alfonso M. Dyson v Denny's*, Plaintiff's Memorandum of Points and Authorities in Support of Motion for Leave to File First Amended Complaint, C.A. No. Y93-1503, In the United States District Court for the District of Maryland, May 24, 1993.
38 "Preliminary Report Concerning Events on April 1, 1993," contained in letter from Irwin Goldbloom, Latham & Watkins, to Brian F. Heffernan, Department of Justice, June 30, 1993.
39 Lynne Duke, "Secret Service Agents Allege Racial Bias at Denny's; Six Blacks to File Lawsuit Saying They Were Denied Service at Annapolis Restaurant," *Washington Post*, May 24, 1993, p. A4.
40 *Dyson v Denny's*, Civil Docket No. DKC-93-1503, Oral Opinion by the Court, August 1, 1994
41 *Dyson v Denny's*, Joint Stipulation and Order Concerning Transition of Monitoring Functions from the Office of Civil Rights Monitor to Advantica, C.A. No. DKC-93-1503, September 22, 1998.
42 The Associated Press, "Denny's to Televise Anti-racism Ads," January 13, 1999.
43 Faye Rice, "Denny's Changes Its Spots," *Fortune*, May 13, 1996.
44 *United States of America v Linwood Gray, et al*, "United States' Response to Defendant Linwood Gray's Motion for Modification in Conditions of Pretrial Release, Criminal No. DKC-94-0241, January 3, 1995.
45 Ron Shaffer, "Alleged Drug Kingpin Upsets Hearing; Alleged Heroin Kingpin Curses Court Officials, Curses Magistrate, Berates Marshal," *Washington Post*, January 27, 1979, p. B1.
46 Ron Shaffer and Lawrence Meyer, "Alleged Heroin King, 9 Others Arrested; The Amsterdam Connection," *Washington Post*, January 24, 1979, p. A1.
47 Paul W. Valentine, "Lawyer Says Ex-Client Threatened Him," *Washington Post*, December 29, 1984, p. E1.
48 *United States of America v Linwood Gray*, Jury Charge, Judge Deborah K. Chasanow, Criminal No. DKC-94-0241, ND.
49 *United States of America v Linwood Gray*, Transcript of Proceedings, DKC-94-0241, p. 4140.
50 Maury S. Epner, Assistant U.S. Attorney, to John Chamble, Assistant Federal Public Defender, United States. Robert English, Criminal No. DKC-98-0205, May 18, 1998.

51 Emily Bazelon, "College Park Head Teller Begins Trial in Robbery; Credit Union Heist Led to 4 Hour Seige," *Washington Post*, July 22, 1998, p. B8.
52 Emily Bazelon, "Teller Denies Involvement in Md. Bank Robbery," *Washington Post*, July 24, 1998, p. D4.
53 *United States of America v April Montague*, Closing Arguments, Criminal No. DKC-98-0205, July 24, 1998.
54 Emily Bazelon, "Head Teller Convicted in Robbery; $400,000 Stolen from Credit Union," *Washington Post*, July 28, 1998, p. B3.
55 In the United States District Court for the District of Maryland, *United States of America v April Montague*, Criminal No. DKC-98-0205, Baltimore, Maryland, July 24, 1998.
56 Ruben Castaneda, "Man Gets 11-½ Years for Credit Union Heist," *Washington Post*, August 11, 1998, p. B4.
57 *Judith L. McClosky and Shawn R. McClosky, Sr. v Prince George's County*, Civil Action No. S93-2369, August 13, 1993.
58 *Alonzo Jackson, et al. v Eddie Bauer, Inc.*, Civil Action No. AW-96-54, August 25, 1997.
59 DeNeen L. Brown and Margaret Webb Pressler, "A Problem That's Hard to Pin Down, Bauer Case Highlights Difficulty of Fingering Bias in Retail Security," *Washington Post*, October 11, 1997, p. C1.
60 Courtland Milloy, "Teen Stripped of More Than Just a Shirt," *Washington Post*, November 15, 1995, p. D1.
61 Jonathan Yardley, "Eddie Bauer's Unsportsmanlike Conduct," *Washington Post*, December 4, 1995, p. B2.
62 Steven A. Holmes, "Retail Incident Incenses Washington," *New York Times*, December 10, 1995, p. 36.
63 DeNeen L. Brown and Margaret Webb Pressler, "A Problem That's Hard to Pin Down, Bauer Case Highlights Difficulty of Fingering Bias in Retail Security," *Washington Post*, October 11, 1997, p. C1.
64 DeNeen L. Brown and Margaret Webb Pressler, "A Problem That's Hard to Pin Down," *Washington Post*, October 11, 1997, p. C1.
65 Ruben Castaneda, "Eddie Bauer Store Guard Contradicts Firm's Story," *Washington Post*, Friday, October 3, 1997, p. D3.
66 Ruben Castaneda and Philip P. Pan, "Eddie Bauer Denies Racism, Faults Guard," *Washington Post*, October 1, 1997, p. B1.
67 Ruben Castaneda and Philip P. Pan, "Eddie Bauer Should Pay, Jury Is Told, Clothier's Attorney Blames Store Guard," *Washington Post*, October 8, 1997, p. B1.
68 Ruben Castaneda and Jackie Spinner, "Teens Awarded $1 Million in Bauer Case," *Washington Post*, October 10, 1997, p. A1.
69 *USA v Charles C. Bosah*, Exhibit One, Statement of Facts, Criminal No. AW-96-0426, October 29, 1998.
70 *USA v Charles C. Bosah*, Transcript of Sentencing Before the Honorable Alexander Williams, Jr., United States District Judge, Criminal Case No. AW-96-0426, October 21, 1998.
71 Ruben Castaneda and Scott Wilson, "'Hit Man' Publisher Settles Suit," *Washington Post*, May 25, 1999, p. A1.

72 Declaration of Peder C. Lund, April 19, 1996.
73 Rod Smolla, *Deliberate Intent, A Lawyer Tells the True Story of Murder by the Book* (New York: Crown Publishers, 1999), p. 244.
74 Smolla, 1999, p. 141.
75 Ruben Castaneda, "Md. Journalist Pleads Guilty to Two Charges in Internet Porn Case," *Washington Post*, July 7, 1998, p. D4.
76 Castaneda, July 7, 1998, p. D4.
77 Craig Whitlock, "Reporter Gets 1-½ Years for Child Pornography; Newsman Said He Was Working on Story," *Washington Post,* March 9, 1999, p. B01.
78 *United States of America v Frank J. Cordaro, Ardeth Platte, Kathleen A. Boylan, Lawrence A. Morlan, and Carol Sue Gilbert,* Government's Second Response to Defendants' Motion to Dismiss Information, Criminal No. AW-98-237.
79 Interview with Senator Paul S. Sarbanes, Hart Senate Office Building, September 30, 1999.
80 Alexander Williams Jr., Office of the State's Attorney, *End of Term Report to the People of Prince George's County, 1987–1994* (Upper Marlboro, Maryland, 1994) 25 pages.
81 Liz Spayd, "ABA Rates P.G. Prosecutor 'Unqualified' for Bench," *Washington Post*, July 1, 1994, pp. A1, A11.
82 CeLillianne Green, "Unfair Hearing in Your Paper," *Washington Post*, July 9, 1994, p. A19.
83 Leroy W. Warren Jr., chair, NAACP Crime and Criminal Justice Committee, Letter to the Editor, *Washington Post*, July 8, 1994, p. A19.
84 Interview with Senator Paul S. Sarbanes, Hart Senate Office Building, September 30, 1999.
85 Neil A. Lewis, "An Appeals Court That Always Veers to the Right," *New York Times* on the Web, May 24, 1999, p. 1.
86 Lewis, May 24, 1999, p. 4.
87 "Supreme" was not always capitalized in the eighteenth century. There were no consistent rules for capitalization, and early drafts of the Constitution vary in capitalization and punctuaton. No ur-document exists, no original copy of the Constitution, as there is of the Declaration of Independence. The copy on display at the National Archives is a calligrapher's copy, but has no special legal status. Once I told Chief Justice Burger a copy of the Constitution we were translating into several foreign languages during the Bicentennial of the U.S. Constitution "would follow the original document" only to find out no such document exists.
88 "Overview of Bankruptcy Chapters," U.S. Department of Justice, Executive Office of United States Trustees, N.D.
89 Cedric Easter, Deputy Chief, U.S. Probation Office, Speech Notes, July 9, 1998.

Index